My Long Journey
Home

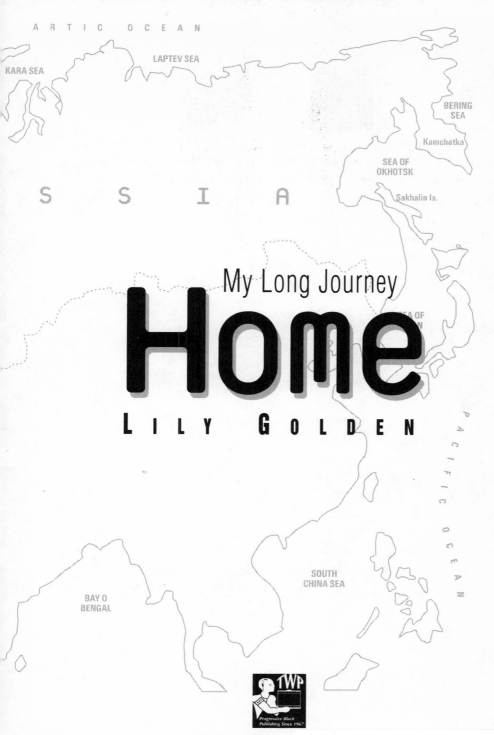

My Long Journey

Home

LILY GOLDEN

THIRD WOR~~LD~~
Chica~~go~~

Third World Press
Publishers since 1967
Chicago

First Edition
Printed in the United States of America

07 06 05 04 03 02 5 4 3 2 1
Cover design by Denise Borel

Library of Congress Cataloging-in-Publication Data

Golden, Lily, 1934
    My long journey home / Lily Golden.—1St ed.
        p.cm.
ISBN 0-88378-234-0 (cloth: alk. paper)—ISBN 0-88378-229-4 (pbk.: alk.
paper)
    1. Golden, Lily, 1934- 2. Scholars—United States—Biography. 3.
Scholars—Soviet Union—Biography. 4. United States—Relations—Soviet
Union. 5. Soviet Union-Relation—United States. 6. Afro-Americans—Soviet
Union—Biography. 7. Blacks—Soviet Union—Biography. I. Title.
    CT3990.G64 A3 2002
    947'.00496—dc21
    [B]   2002028719

To my daughter

Yelena

and granddaughter

Elizabeth

Table of Contents

Past and Present

Unlike the rest of this book, my first chapter deals with old times but from the perspective of the present. I only discovered much of the history of my family when I came to the United States ten years ago.

For me the story begins when my grandfather, Hilliard Golden, and his sister Viola were brought to Mississippi from North Carolina, where they were most likely bought in an auction of slaves just arrived from Africa. Like many other Black Americans, no hint remains of their origin on the African continent, or even of their names before America. Clearly, the name Golden did not come with them from across the Atlantic. But, judging from my knowledge of the history of serfdom in Russia, I could think of two possible origins of the name. Maybe it was the distortion of the name of their owner, who it is claimed was a Dutchman. Possibly, as I always preferred to believe, the name Golden was recognition of the skill in his hands—a common source of slave names in Russia.

Hilliard was brought to the United States when he was something like eight years old, probably in the 1840s or 1850s. Although American law did not allow the teaching of reading and writing to slaves, his owner must have noticed some sign of brightness in the boy, for he did teach him. When, in 1865, slavery was banned, few of the slaves really understood the meaning of their new freedom. But Hilliard, because he was literate and could read the newspapers, soon learned that ex-slaves could receive 40 acres of land and a mule. He applied for, and got, his share of the new property. In Yazoo County he built a big house—the biggest in Moorhead. He worked hard and quickly became a rich man. In Mississippi I was shown a list of the richest Black Americans and he was number one on that list. In the beginning, he bought a considerable acreage of land for the then pricey sum of $900 and in 1992 I was given the documentation of a bank account in his name at the Friedman's Bank. Every year he added more land to his farm.

Ten of his sons and daughters, and many of his grandchildren were born in Hilliard's "big house." The plantation became so big that he began to employ not only black but also white workers. This was a big mistake. His white neighbors and the ever-present Ku Klux Klan were incapable of understanding or accepting this state of affairs. His house was burned down. He built another, but this also was burned down, the flames consuming all his documents: thus he could no longer prove that the land belonged to him.

I still meet people who remembered Hillard and tell me that he was a good preacher and much respected in the neighborhood. He had two daughters by his first wife, but she soon died. His second wife, who was 15 years younger than him, possessed Indian blood. Her name was Katherine, but all the children called her "Sweet Mother." I hold in my hands an old, very early photograph. In the background stands a two-storey building, looking much like a hotel. In the foreground are standing my grandfather and grandmother. He is thin, very black, with a goatee beard. She is very tall, towering over her husband. The thinness of Hilliard's features serves to emphasize the generosity of Katherine's face. Members of the family remember my grandmother as being musical—she played many instruments—and a lover of nature who took every opportunity to go hunting and fishing. It seems to me that I resemble her. I have the same full features, height and broad shoulders. Now I think that my study and research of music seems to come from my love of music, which I inherited from her. The same with my love of nature. I love being in the forest, mountains or swimming in the river or sea.

Sweet Mother gave birth to eight children: Rebecca, Biddy, Marian, Mamie, Hilliard, Willy, Oliver and Viola. Of course there were many grandchildren and great grandchildren. After their second home was burned by the Ku Klux Klan, Hilliard and Katherine took the whole family to live in Memphis, Tennessee. In 1993, I was invited together with my daughter to that city. Each year Memphis celebrates history and culture of another country of Europe, Africa or South America. All the churches, universities, theaters have talks on a chosen city, and also musical programs, dances and singing. That year the choice was Russia and the two of us were invited to participate. My daughter and I were speaking in many places around the city about Russia, the history of Black Russians and about our life there.

During that visit with the help of the mayor we found the house that had been grandfather's. I experienced totally unexpected emotions. Walking through rooms that had been inhabited by my grandparents, I was keenly aware of their presence, though I had known next to nothing about them.

When they became old, Hilliard and Katherine moved to Omaha to live with their oldest daughter, Rebecca. He died in the 1920s. She lived until the 1930s. Viola, his sister, lived to be well over 90 years old before her death in 1939.

My father, Oliver John Golden, was born on November 18, 1887. I saw among family papers his soldier's identity book, which was in fact the only document relating to him or his family. I discovered that he was drafted into the U.S. Army at Clarksdale, Mississippi, at the age of 32. The ID described him as an "unmarried, Negro, with a full shock of black hair." He served from March 31, 1918 until July 14, 1919. I also learned that part of his service was in France. I am inclined to believe that it was there that he acquired his beliefs in "liberty, fraternity and equality."

His nieces referred to him as "Uncle Buck." When I asked why, they answered that he always seemed able to make money, was well dressed and often slipped dollar bills to his nieces and nephews. Before the army, Oliver studied at Tuskegee, which was a famous university devoted exclusively to Black students. One of his professors was the world famous scientist and researcher, Dr. George Washington Carver. His relationship with Carver continued even after my father went to Russia.

When Oliver Golden was demobilized from the army, he went to live in Chicago, where he married a beautiful young black woman, Jane Wilson. He worked as a waiter, barber and porter on the railroad. Much of what I know about these years of my father in Chicago and his studies in Moscow I learned from Harry Haywood's book, *Black Bolshevik*. Haywood relates that once my father met a friend on a Chicago street. Oliver observed the exotic dress of his friend (boots and kozak blouse), and struck up a conversation about this, among other things. The conversation detailing the strange and wonderful things that his friend had encountered in "the land of mystery" was the begining of my father's curiousity about Russia. The man invited him and his wife to study in the Communist University for Oriental Workers in Moscow.

I still have no idea whether my father ever joined the American Communist Party. Functionaries of the Communist Party in the United

States have told me that their archives contain no files or references about Oliver John Golden.

Harry Haywood was also among five Black Americans who came in 1924 to study in this university. He claims that my father was not an official member of the Party, and that he arrived there only because of his friendship with Lovett Fort Davis Whiteman, an activist in the United States branch of the Communist Party, who was executed in the 1930s in Russia.

Haywood begins the chapter "Blacks in Moscow" with a flattering, yet precarious description of my father. "Golden was very handsome with shiny black skin, a former student of Tuskegee Institute and a sleeping car porter." I got the impression that Haywood was not impressed with my father. As I read further, in the book it is revealed that Oliver was constantly mocking Haywood and making him and his brother Otto look foolish with his jokes. Haywood writes: "Golden had a very deep sense of humor, and was always playing practical jokes on us, and especially on my brother Otto. His southern accent was mixed with Russian, and we joked that he is the only person in the world who speaks Russian in a Mississippi dialect." I always found that my father's jokes held a deeper meaning, and indeed Haywood notes that Oliver did once draw Otto out. He was speaking of a person who had impressed Otto Haywood. "I saw the man's eyes, Otto, and you didn't. You drank too much vodka, Otto. Remember, be careful with vodka. You know that you can't drink. What did the slaves say when they revolted in Virginia? Beware of those who wear their master's old clothes! They can betray you!" Harry remembers that Otto got very angry and jumped on my father, but changed his mind because Oliver was much bigger. The person over whom they quarreled did indeed betray them later.

Haywood obviously was displeased because Oliver quickly had emerged as the leader, not only of their small group of Americans, but also of other students attending the university from different countries. Harry considered himself a Communist leader. In his orthodoxy and Communist conservatism, he saw Oliver's freedom of expression and keen sense of humor as dangerous and threatening to the Party. In fact, his conclusion that my father was not a Party member seems to derive from his feelings about my father's open speech and ways. The book gives plenty of evidence that Oliver Golden was able to laugh at the sacred cows of Communism.

In 1919, many Communist Parties from around the world formed the Communist International. The University for Oriental Workers that was created by this organization in 1921 existed for ten years. Students came from many countries of Asia and Africa, including China and India. There was perpetual controversy in the Communist movement over the Black Americans. They considered themselves African, but to the orthodox Communists they were representatives of the capitalist United States. For this reason, the number of Black Americans at the university was always small. The well-concealed purpose of the institution was to prepare leaders for the "world revolution." And, in fact, many of the graduates indeed became the leaders of their countries. Jomo Kenyatta became president of Kenya—his presence there still remains a closely kept secret—and Chiang Kai Shek assumed leadership of the Republic of China.

For many of the participating parties, however, racial problems were every bit as important as the class struggle that concerned their Soviet hosts. To the Moscow based institution, race was not part of the lexicon. But to its students, it was the problem. And so the Africans, including the African Americans, succeeded in creating the "International Trade Union of Negro Workers," which was headquartered in Hamburg, Germany. Its first president was James Ford, the leader of the American Communist Party, but George Padmore, who also edited the Union's paper, *The Negro Worker,* soon replaced him. The choice of venue was influenced by very strong support from Ernst Thallmann, the leader of the German Communist Party at the time. This Party was so strong in the late 1920s and early 1930s that it could offer physical protection to the Black communists against police brutality. The newspaper was distributed around the world with the help of German sailors out of Hamburg Port. *The Negro Worker* carried news items about people of African descent around the world, and reports and articles by personalities within Africa, the Caribbean and the United States, such as Jomo Kenyatta (Kenya) and Bill Patterson (USA).

The Union's first—and last—conference took place in Hamburg in 1929. During my research in the Russian State Archives, which were then still closed to the public, I found copies of the minutes of the conference. It made fascinating reading. The level of black consciousness was clearly evident. The conferees obviously sought to combine race and class issues, in clear contrast with orthodox Communist dogma. But still, supporting the main Communist idea that race struggle must become class struggle, they tainted the activity of Black leaders of the stature of Dr. William DuBois with bourgeois nationalism.

In 1933, Hitler came to power and Padmore had to flee the country. Twelve years later, when a Pan-African Congress convened in Manchester, England, George Padmore appeared as a staunch supporter of that concept. In 1948, he published a book entitled *Pan Africanism or Communism*, in which he criticized the Communist ideas as racist, and this time rejected DuBois as being too Communist. Many of the other African leaders had already left the Communist Party.

My father was outside all of this. He completed his studies in Moscow in 1927, and returned to the United States. He brought back with him a number of clear impressions. The Soviet Union possessed a failing economic system. Many of the country's own specialists had left after the Revolution or were imprisoned and killed. Conversely, the new social concepts propagated by the USSR had attracted foreigners. According to Paula Garb, in *They Came to Stay*, there were more than 2,000,000 Americans in the Soviet Union, among them people of Russian origin who had fled to the United States in Czarist times, and most specifically around the turn of the century. In 1918 alone, the U.S. State Department processed about a million requests from former Russians wishing to return. In parallel, the U.S. administration had deported upwards of a thousand Russians who were considered to be a subversive element.

But there were also plenty of white Americans. For example, in May 1921, more than 100 qualified mechanics from Ford Motors, led by an engineer named Adamson, went to help build the Moscow Automobile Assembly Plant. The Textile Workers Union purchased 170 sewing machines, which they sent together with other equipment and even food, to a garment makers' cooperative of 600 workers that they founded in Moscow. An American named Harold Ware formed a group that brought 21 tractors, two cars and other agricultural equipment to help Russian farmers. Yet another group went to Siberia, where they formed a colony under the slogan of "Let Us Make of Siberia a New Pennsylvania." People from Europe mirrored the flow from America.

My father had noticed all this movement. He also noted that all the migrants who had gone to the USSR to help were white. He felt that Blacks also had a role to play in the success of the socialist experiment. Oliver Golden was also persuaded that help needed to be given to the non-European peoples of the Soviet Union—the Uzbeks, Turkmen, Chukcha—who had been colonized and who in American terms were "colored." Nowadays, when I speak to American audiences about my father, I invariably get comments that he must have gone to Russia because of racism, economic depression and unemployment in the United States. I agree that all these played a role, but could just as easily have convinced him to go to France or some other European country to make easy money. He chose to go to Russia, like many other Americans, because he believed that Black people could help their own kind, and that there was no need to be perpetually dependent on others.

He came from Moscow to New York in 1928, where he opened a co-op restaurant. The food was good, and the place became a regular haunt of leaders of the Harlem Renaissance and other great African Americans such as Langston Hughes and Paul Robeson. He also opened an office, in cooperation with Amtorg, an organization that was hiring American specialists in industry and agriculture to do contract work in Russia. His first location was at 1800 7th Avenue, and then later at 136 West 28th Street.

Oliver Golden traveled around the United States, visiting colleges and universities, seeking qualified and willing blacks. Among the first, he approached his former professor, George Washington Carver. When I visited Tuskegee, some sixty years later, Daniel Williams, the director of the university archives, helped me to find correspondence between my father and his mentor. (See appendix.) It was a moving moment for me. For the first time I was holding in my hands some of my father's own writings, and was getting an insight into his views on the problems of Blacks in America and around the world. In the first letter, dated December 12 1930, Oliver writes that he needs Carver's help to get together a group of Black specialists with practical experience in creating a cotton industry. He would take to the USSR only the ones on the list approved by Carver. In several letters, he insisted that Carver should go personally to Russia for six months, to demonstrate his achievements in agriculture and advise on the creation of the cotton industry. Carver responded that he would be delighted to receive such proposals, and hopes to be able to help. However, he didn't believe that an absence of six months from Tuskegee was feasible.

In a letter dated April 18 1931, Oliver noted that he was receiving at his New York office more than one thousand applications every day. He had already interviewed 50 or more experts for possible work not only in cotton but also in poultry, rice and other agricultural branches. The monthly salary being mentioned was $200, which was a considerable amount in those times of depression. But, if Carver thought that any specific person was worth more than $200 a month, he would be willing to pay extra. Work conditions included a five-day week, free medical care and hospitalization, a paid leave of one month a year and free transportation to any vacation center. Oliver again raised the question of a visit by Carver, contending that it would both add to the prestige of Tuskegee outside the United States and enhance the stature of the American experts in Russia, including the Black men among them.

In May 1931, Oliver Golden visited George Washington Carver. From their continuing correspondence, it was clear that Carver was a very sick man, but my father was relentless in insisting that the distinguished scientist should visit the Soviet Union.

Carver, in his letters, offered advice on organizational matters. The flood of applicants included many that were unqualified but willing solely because they were unemployed. Among those that Carver insisted on was John Sutton who was extremely well qualified. He was an agricultural chemist with degrees from Tuskegee, the University of Iowa, Drake and Columbia. He was at that time 34 years old, and teaching in Jarvis College, where he had established a research department. Sutton became my father's best friend in Russia.

Another good friend was George Tynes, who had graduated from Wilberforce. Tynes specialized in breeding fowl, but had a reputation as a football star. Tynes later told me that he met my father on the streets of

Harlem, where he listened to Oliver speaking about the situation in the Soviet Union and its problems. On the spot he asked to join the group. That started a friendship that lasted as long as they lived. George was 25 years old when he left with my father for Russia.

In passing, many people have commented to me about my father's reputation as a powerful orator. One day on a Moscow street, I was approached by an elderly Black American who said that I resembled a man whom he had heard speak at a meeting in Harlem many years ago. He had never forgotten the man or his name—Oliver Golden. Hearing that I was Oliver's daughter, he asked to shake my hand, then said: "I heard your father speak but I was too shy to approach him. Since that moment I have dreamed of visiting the Soviet Union. Now that I have finally made it, I am very happy to meet you and to shake the hand of his daughter."

There was only one white among the 16 people who accompanied my father to Russia—my mother. She was an unusual woman. The daughter of a wealthy family, she was the fourth and youngest child—all the others were boys—of a man who had been a rabbi in Warsaw, Poland. The family immigrated to America after World War I. She graduated with a degree in economics from Rhodes in 1928. She was engaged to a wealthy businessman, but one of her brothers, who was very radical, involved her in revolutionary activities. She participated in demonstrations and marches—a widespread phenomenon in the late 1920s. She joined picket lines against strikebreakers. Bertha Bialik was arrested a number of times, and her family only learned that she was in prison from reading about her in the newspapers. Needless to say, they were very upset.

One day her fiancé left on a short business trip to Mexico. My mother was again in prison, where she met Oliver Golden, who had also been arrested for participating in a demonstration. The family legend has it that it was love at first sight —in a New York prison cell. By the time that her fiancé returned from Mexico, it was already too late. Her parents were horrified. Her brothers were furious. Her friends turned their backs. The parents might have forgiven their youngest only daughter great many things, but an attachment to a Black man in the 1920s was totally unthinkable. Bertha was compelled to move to my father's home in Harlem. Life with him was not easy for her. Whether in black areas or white, the response was one of rejection. They had to suffer all sorts of insults. They could not travel together on public transportation, or go together to public places.

She once told me that they had decided to see a play in which friends were appearing, in downtown Manhattan. When my father went to buy tickets, he was told crudely that there was no available space in the theater, even in the upper gallery. When my mother went to the box office, she was very politely sold seats in the front row of the stalls. On the evening of the performance, it was only with difficulty that they were allowed in, though they held perfectly good tickets. When they took their seats, all the surroundng patrons moved away. In New York, 65 years after the Civil War, they were not prepared to sit with a Black man. My mother laughed "We sat like royalty, and nobody could approach us." It is a good thing that she had a great sense of humor.

Nevertheless, it took time till she was ready to marry Oliver Golden. Even in the 1920s, marrying a Black man required from a white woman considerable courage. And she still wasn't aware just how brave she was. Bertha was approaching a nervous breakdown, and Oliver didn't know how to help. No white doctor would come to Harlem, and no Black doctor would risk lynching in order to touch a white woman. A doctor friend of hers told her that the solution was to make up her mind, then her nerves would calm. She decided to marry. From that day till her death, she never had a moment of sickness or regret.

Bertha supported Oliver's plans to go to Russia. She became a secretary in his office. All the letters that I found in the archives of Tuskegee had been typed by my mother, on the ancient machine that I still have. I gave it to my daughter as a family heirloom.

She understood very clearly that life in the Soviet Union was not going to be easy, but she was ready for all the difficulties. Oliver concealed nothing. She knew that there, in the Soviet Union were few creature comforts, that there was little food and widespread hunger. She told me that she left her furs and jewelry in the United States, for clearly she would not wear them in a country where people starved for lack of a crust of bread. Bertha's decision to go to the Soviet Union was the last straw for her family. Not only had she married a Black man, but also she was going to a god-forsaken country—and doing so with a group of Black people.

Before her departure, she invited several girlfriends to a dinner party in presence of my father. She recalled that they seemed scared, could not look directly at my father and were afraid to sit at the same table. Oliver was a charming man, and he soon changed the atmosphere. They were amazed to find that he was very well educated, knew foreign languages and had travelled abroad. He was always a brilliant storyteller, and by the end of the party, they couldn't take their eyes off him. Later, one of her friends told my mother: "I am beginning to understand you. If I had met a Black man like him, I might have married him. But to go with him to that country, where the bears walk on the streets... And especially with a bunch of Black men..." My mother considered the words of this woman racist. And still Bertha followed my father. She was 26 years old when they left the United States.

In October 1931, the *Amsterdam News* of New York published a story and photos of the group that was going to the USSR with my parents. The photos show a group of young blacks, among whom my father—at 44—was the oldest. My mother was 18 years younger than he was, and the others were between 25 and 35. Their faces radiated happiness and expectation, mingled with some uncertainty about the future. These were the faces of romantics and idealists, all of them looking so beautiful because their aim of helping others by their labor was so honorable.

I still have menus and brochures from the *SS Germany,* complete with glorified pictures of the port of Hamburg, with church spires climbing skyward and small boats on the Elbe where it poured out to the sea. I sometimes catch myself looking at the pictures and wondering just how it must have felt going to a new, so different country. These were still years when leaving the shores of a homeland to voyage into an unknown territory, as yet not projected across the world daily by radio and television, was a major adventure.

I was fascinated in particular by the items on the menu. Vegetables cooked in the German manner, bouillon, chicken in cream sauce, fried tongue, remolade sauce, potato salad, roast capons, pate in parsley, Californian apricot desserts, mixed lettuce salad, Bombe Supris, cookies and cakes, Swiss and Edam cheeses, fruits and coffee. That was only one day's selection. Food the like of which they would never see in Russia. The scarcity of diet in the Soviet Union never bothered my parents. They hadn't gone there in order to eat. In fact, I remember that my mother's only request to me was to find spinach—a vegetable seldom seen in the USSR.

After this beautiful dinner, they stepped ashore at Hamburg, where the boat docked overnight. Of course 1931 was not yet 1933 in Germany, when Hitler came to power. Fascism was just beginning and did not yet spread widely. But my mother told me later that she hadn't felt comfortable walking on Hamburg streets in the company of 15 Black men. German rowdies screaming insults and brandishing their fists followed them. However, this was the last racist incident that my parents would experience in their lives. They returned to the ship.

On November 7, 1931, the group disembarked at Leningrad, which was named like this after the death of Lenin in 1924. It was the 14th anniversary of the October Revolution. They were met at the port by delegations of workers from factories, representatives of the Communist Party and of the State. For a few days in Leningrad, they were in euphoria. They were shepherded to meetings, on visits to the museums and on tours of the city. Then they boarded a very comfortable special carriage, of the kind reserved for foreigners, for their train ride to Uzbekistan. After a ten-day journey across Russia, they finally reached Tashkent, the capital of Uzbekistan, one of the Soviet Republics in Central Asia. Here again they followed the same routine of meetings and receptions, until the time came to venture on into the Uzbek desert. Their destination was Yangi-Yul, which was a research station experimenting with different strains of cotton.

Everything that Oliver Golden had warned his friends about before they left the United States, came to pass. Creature comforts were totally lacking. Yangi-Yul in those days was a small *kishlak*—Uzbek village—consisting of yards fenced in by walls made of dried manure and mud. Inside the courtyards, the huts were made of the same materials. Everything was spotlessly clean since the yards were washed down with water at least twice a day because of the desert heat. The life style and accommodations were those of the dark-skinned Uzbek muslems. Many of the women were veiled and clothed in colorful silk dresses. The men wore long cotton gowns, tied with sashes. All sported *tubeteyka*—skullcaps—the men in black and white and the women's of gold and silver thread.

People in America were following with interest the exploits of this first group of black Americans in Uzbekistan. By early 1932, my father was already hosting visiting friends from the United States. The first among them was Langston Hughes, the famous Black American poet, who had been a frequent guest at my father's New York restaurant. He came to the Soviet Union at the head of a group of 22 Black actors, with the intention of making the first Soviet-American film about racism in the United States. The script, written by a Soviet author, was very naive and not particularly appropriate to American life. He had portrayed workers' struggle in which, according to the best Soviet propaganda precepts, Blacks and Whites linked arms and marched off into the sunset proclaiming universal solidarity in the class struggle. Langston could not accept the underlying naivete, refused to work for this film. While the rest of the group moved around Russia, he headed for Uzbekistan to visit Oliver Golden's group. One year later, he published a book entitled *An American Negro Looks at the Soviet Central Asia.* He found much that was common to Blacks in the southern United States and the peoples of Uzbekistan—but one major difference: in Uzbekistan there was no racism. The volume was published in the Soviet Union, and I have never been able to find it in libraries in the United States.

Twenty years later, in New York, he published his memoirs—*I Wonder As I Wander.* There, he noted his amazement at the hardships accepted by the group in Uzbekistan. Though the huts were livable, there was no means of heating, no indoor cooking stoves, no radios, no culture or entertainment. But, he had noticed that the group was not dejected or depressed, and did not seem to feel the deprivation. I believe that Langston Hughes was correct in this assumption. They were not unhappy. My father had prepared them for the material hardships. And, spiritually, they felt free and independent, warmed by the knowledge that they were helping others.

In 1997 I came to Philadelphia to visit my friends. They told me that one of the theaters in the city had a play about a Black Russian. I became interested and went to see this play. To my surprise, it was a story about my father. I was also in it, but as his son. My mother was a Russian spy and my father dies there not of his heart and kidney sickness in 1940, but of hunger and cold in Moscow in 1992. Okay, the author can say that it is fiction and the actors can do on the stage what they want. But the main idea was that Black Americans have nothing to do abroad and they cannot help anybody! That is why in one scene Langston Hughes is sitting there and hopelessly asking: What are you doing here? Why did you come here? And not one word about how the Uzbek people admired his work or a mention of his portrait on the walls of the National History museum in Tashkent.

It would be interesting to make a study of the differences between my father's group and others that came to the USSR with the sole intent of making money. For example, Bob Robinson, a black worker who came to Russia in 1928 and who became quite famous in the United States when he published his book, *Black on Red,* about his more than 40 years in Russia. Robinson admits that he came to the Soviet Union with the sole aim to make money, and I personally see nothing criminal in that. But my father's group was motivated by the plight of others, while Americans like Robinson were thinking, although legitimately, only of themselves. Robinson had even accepted Soviet citizenship in the belief that this would augment his salary. However, when he realized that citizenship offered no dividends, he sought a way to leave. But these were the years of Josef Stalin, and the idea of Soviet citizens leaving the country was unthinkable.

Robinson had been somewhat unique. He was the only Black among a large group of American workers who had come to build a large tractor plant on the Volga River. His white companions openly discriminated against him. He was beaten and driven from the communal dining room. This fact became known around the country, and Soviet workers across the country jumped to Robinson's defense. Following rallies and demonstrations, the racists in his group were arrested, taken to court, then kicked out of the Soviet Union. Bob remained angry and bitter. He considered the massive support from Russian workers to be a propaganda trick. When his comrades at work elected him to Moscow City Council, he again concluded that they were using him as a propaganda tool. It must be noted that the Soviets had shown their respect to other Blacks in similar fashion. George Padmore was also elected to Moscow City Council, and my father was made a member of the city council. But Robinson didn't see things in the same light.

My father's group had a two-year contract to work in Uzbekistan. However, despite the constant physical and material hardship, most of them renewed the contract at least three times. Some of them went to work in the Ukraine or Caucasus, some married Russian women. In the Tuskegee archives, I found a letter written to George Washington Carver by his beloved student John Sutton. John wrote that he had opened a technological laboratory in the Rice Institute. He was working on improved strains of rice, and noted that he was being offered work possibilities of a kind that were rarely extended to Blacks. He was doing his utmost to exploit the possibilities.

The political situation in the Soviet Union was worsening. The Soviet government was encouraging foreigners to leave. The alternative was to accept Soviet citizenship. At that point in time, in 1934, a number of elements of my parents' life converged. I was born on July 18th of that year. My parents were both offered work in Tashkent universities. Neither my father nor my mother was inclined to take their newly born child back to the racism and intolerance that they had experienced in the United States. The combination was enough to make Oliver and Bertha Golden accept Soviet citizenship and move out of the desert into the capital city of Uzbekistan.

CHAPTER TWO

Uzbekistan—My Homeland

Though Tashkent was the capital of Uzbekistan, the city was predominantly Russian. Throughout the Czarist regimes, it had been a place of exile from European Russia. Nicholas II even exiled his own uncle to Tashkent. The city became, and continued to be under the Soviet regime, a magnet for Russian intellectuals for whom life under the centralized power of the USSR in Moscow, Leningrad and Kiev was restrictive. It also became a center for Jews seeking to escape the anti-Semitism of European Russia and especially the Ukraine. Also, the city became the obvious refuge for political prisoners released from the concentration camps of Kazakhstan, the neighboring Republic, who were denied the possibility of returning to the European Republics of the USSR. As a result of all this, Tashkent was far more European than Asiatic.

In the 1930s, Tashkent was a city oasis of half a million inhabitants —a verdant city set in a desert. The climate was regulated by Tashkent's desert setting amid mountains. Days were hot and the nights were cool. But the city's streets were pleasant even in daytime because of the trees and water channels and canals alongside the pavements.

My parents' house was situated in the very heart of Tashkent on Proletarskaya Street. Just below the building was Revolution Square—a green flower garden with its statue of Karl Marx in the center. On one side of the square was the Central Asia State University, the largest institution of higher learning in Central Asia. Across the street from us was "Gorki Park of Culture"—a regular feature of every Soviet city. However, its culture consisted of crowds constantly moving from side to side, drinking vodka and smoking *papirosi*—cheap filtered cigarettes that were more paper than black tobacco. Poor, poor, misrepresented, great proletarian writer Gorki.

Our house was the only four-storey residential building in the city, and had become known as the "House of the Foreign Specialists," though my family were the only "foreigners" among tenants who were mostly high functionaries of the Communist Party, or famous writers, musicians and artists. My parents were allotted a beautiful three-room apartment on the second floor. We had a spacious veranda, protected from the sun's heat by climbing flowers. A wood-burning cooking range dominated the kitchen, which was quite an innovation in a city where most people cooked out of doors. The bathroom had the supreme luxury of a bath, though there was no running water as everywhere in the city.

My father was teaching in the Institute of Irrigation, and had been elected to Tashkent City Council. He was also a member of an organization devoted to the cause of civil rights around the world. That interest had taken him around Uzbekistan to explain incidents like the Scottsboro trial, in which a group of Black American youths stood falsely accused of the rape of a white girl. I still have a copy of a letter of protest sent by my parents to the Governor of Alabama—a letter that was published in many American and Russian newspapers.

His colleagues and students were frequent visitors to the house. My mother taught English in the Institute of Foreign Languages and the Central Asia State University. Her students adored her, and they too were always in our home. Between students, professors and our intellectual neighbors, the *samovar*—Russian traditional teapot—was always on the boil and my father was constantly cooking southern American delicacies for the guests.

We had three servants—all Russians. One woman came in every day to clean up after the constant flow of guests, and cooked for the family. A second woman came to sew clothes for my mother and her friends. From America, my mother brought with her three items rarely seen in Uzbekistan: a Singer sewing machine, an ice cream machine to satisfy my father's constant craving and a typewriter.

The third woman was my beloved "Auntie Nadya." My father, about whom Haywood had written that he was "the only person in the world to speak Russian with a strong Mississippi accent," wanted me to learn the language properly. To that end, he found Nadya, who was apparently a former actress, and brought her to work in our home. She was a constant companion for me. After a few months, I became fluent in Auntie Nadya's Slavic language. She spoke Ukrainian. So I learned to play the guitar and sing Ukrainian folk songs long before I knew Russian and Uzbek. The bond of affection between Nadya and I was so strong that she stayed on to live with us for more than thirty years.

She played a major role in my life, but I am very sorry, never discovered her history or family background. She never spoke of her relatives, and I do not know even if she was married. I spent my childhood soaking up artistic endeavors from Nadya, and my love of acting, singing, playing musical instruments and dancing has been a constant in my life since my earliest years with her.

Auntie Nadya became the "boss" in our home. She kept the housekeeping budget and managed the purchases, chose the menus and told my mother and father occasionally what they needed to do. In fact she relieved them of all the tediousness of day-to-day life of the Soviet people. She stood in the lines, hunted for food and arranged whatever needed to be arranged. Probably because of Auntie Nadya, my parents never really lived a normal Soviet life, with all its difficulties, problems and hardships.

My father's sole responsibility in the home was the cooking of Sunday dinner. Early in the morning, he would take a taxi to Alayski Bazaar, the most famous food market in all of Central Asia. Alayski was the true model of an oriental bazaar. Standing at one end of a lane of vendors' stands heaped with the delicacies of the East—watermelons, sweet melons, grapes, nuts—it was impossible to see the other end, somewhere off in the far distance. Each fruit came in every conceivable shape, size and color. My father would load his treasures into the waiting taxi, bring them home and, for lack of an ice box, would stack them in the ever dry bathtub. Then he would begin to prepare the meal in a solemn religious rite during which no one was allowed into the kitchen. When he was done, he would shout "Baby, the dinner is ready," and carry my mother in his arms to the table.

When I was three, I began to attend kindergarten. My parents were concerned that I should grow up in the company of other children. The kindergarten was located at the end of the yard of our house, so I had no distance to go. The director was a tiny woman, who taught me a lot, yet was too rigid and strict for my liking. Now I can understand that I was not exactly one of the better behaved girls. While the children were napping, she would take me to her office to sleep. Otherwise, my singing and storytelling would keep the others awake and laughing. The one-hour that I spent each time in her clean, white and sterile office was the most terrible experience of my young life. There always seemed to be just one fly that had sneaked in to drive me crazy. I could hear her clock as it ticked through each new minute. Ideas and thoughts would spin through my head, and I was unable to hook onto any one and hold it steady. By the time the hour was up, accumulated energy was bubbling through my veins, and I would burst out of the door to expend it on my friends.

I remember only isolated moments from my childhood before and during World War II...

I have a picture, taken in 1937, of my mother, father and myself sitting in a garden with Paul Robeson Jr. His parents, Paul and Eslanda Robeson, are standing on a balcony of the huge white-walled Kislovodsk sanatorium in North Caucasus. The famous Black singer, and civil rights fighter, and his charming wife, came in the years before the war to visit the Soviet Union almost every summer, and often returned to Moscow to give a New Year's concert. In this photograph, I look very sullen. I was 10 years younger than Paul Jr. and he didn't want to play with me. My father and Paul's father were busy all the time debating something of earthshaking importance.

Many years later, I discovered that Paul Robeson had come to the USSR that year, 1937, and found that many of his personal friends had disappeared—among them high officers, writers and musicians. I believe that the heated discussions with my father in Kislovodsk were about those purges, which neither of them was really ready to believe. Many years later my mother told me that Paul wrote a letter to Stalin about one of his Jewish friends, and received a reply that nothing had happened to the man. Back in Moscow, Paul invited his friend for dinner and was surprised to see him arrive with another unknown man. During the dinner his friend managed to tell him that the companion was a KGB agent, and he himself was brought to meet him directly from the prison. When Paul returned to America, he published *Here I Stand* without a word about the purges in the USSR.

Upon our return to Tashkent after a month in Kislovodsk with the Robesons, we were climbing the stairs to our apartment when I noticed that some of the doors were crisscrossed with tape. I asked my father what it meant and he replied that the tenants had been arrested. Later I found out that in that year when we were in Kislovodsk, the KGB had also come to arrest my father. My naive father took a gun that had been given to him by the KGB, for protection in his travels around an area where anti-revolutionary Basmachi Muslims were active, and went to KGB Headquarters. Handing in the gun, he said: "I understand that you came to arrest me. Here I am. If it is a crime to come to the USSR to help this country, and you consider me an enemy of the people, arrest me!" The answer was: "Comrade Golden, don't worry. We have fulfilled our quota of arrests from your neighborhood. Go home, continue working and forget about it."

Among the African Americans who had come to the USSR with my father, none were arrested in the purges of 1937. However, they were served notice that they had two options: either to leave the USSR or to accept Soviet citizenship. My parents and their friend George Tynes decided to stay. So great was their belief in socialism! Or it was love to the country without racism? Others chose to leave for different reasons, but with the intention of returning to Uzbekistan later. Those who left were eventually told later by Soviet officials that their Russian families were dead—victims of World War II. The families were told that their husbands and fathers had died in American prisons. The Soviet authorities were determined to close any avenue of contact with foreigners.

Many things changed in the life of my family. We lost friends, who no longer came to visit us as they had before. From fear of the KGB, people avoided us because we were of foreign origin, though we were Soviet citizens. Many of those arrested in the purges had been accused of contacts with "foreign spies," and of themselves becoming spies for other countries. Especially suspect were people of Jewish origin because of Stalin's obsession with "the worldwide Jewish conspiracy." This fear was cultivated among the Soviet people quite consciously. For example, application forms for the universities and for jobs contained a number of questions: "What is your nationality? Do you have relatives abroad? Where were your parents buried? Do you have contacts with foreigners?" Emigrants and Jews began to change their names into Russian names and conceal the fact that they had relatives elsewhere. And it is only recently, that they felt free to seek their families abroad.

Over the next two or three years, my father changed. He no longer told jokes or played games with people. He seemed to have lost the central purpose of his life. In 1940, at the age of 53, when I was six, he again suffered from heart failure and old kidney injury inflicted by a police nightstick in the hunger demonstrations of the 1920s in New York. This time, he did not have any resistance since, as I understand, he lacked the will to live.

The day of his death I remember very well...

That day was very hot. I was happily playing hide and seek with my girlfriends in the yard of my house. Suddenly, a woman who I didn't recognize came up and stroked my head, saying "poor, poor orphan girl." I didn't know the meaning of the word, but had a premonition that something bad had happened. I rushed home and was surprised to see how many people were packed into every room, all of them crying. I was told that my father had died. But, if the truth were told, I didn't yet grasp the meaning of death.

The death of my father did not change my life, except for the fact that Auntie Nadya took me to kindergarten each morning in my father's place.

The year was 1941. June 21st. Six in the morning. I'm going with the kids from kindergarten to a country house in Chimgan—a resort in the mountains of Tan Shan. As the car passed the front of my house, my mother opened the second floor window and shouted: "The war. The war has begun. Listen!" As she placed the radio on the windowsill, we could hear the voice of Soviet Foreign Minister Molotov, announcing that Germany had invaded the Soviet Union. I was too small to understand the meaning of these words. We continued our trip to Chimgan.

The year was 1942. September 1st. I am now eight years old. My dreams fulfilled, I said goodbye to my kindergarten and I am going to school. My mother wanted to take me to school, proudly holding my hand. For the first time in my life, I resisted. I won and am going to school alone. I was walking down Proletarskaya Street unescorted. I am grown up! I am very proud of myself, happy with the feeling that everyone must be looking at me going alone to school and thinking: Look at this grown up girl! She is going alone to school!

Life began to change at a more rapid rate. Not because I began my studies at school, but because of the difficult war years. Tashkent had become known in the USSR as the "Bread City." In days when people were dying of starvation in Leningrad, and western Russia was short of food, there was bread to eat in Tashkent. But still it was a very hungry time. We had to stand in long lines to trade our food coupons for small rations. One day, a major tragedy happened. I lost the bread coupons. Luckily they were the coupons for the last days of the month, and we could survive. My mother and Auntie Nadya never blamed me. They just did not talk about this. But I felt very unhappy—because of me they did not have food for several days.

The situation in the country was getting worse. Aunt Nadya had fired all the servants, but insisted that she would stay. She refused to contemplate the idea that my mother, a foreigner, could survive in the USSR without her. So she stayed and worked for no pay. She moved into our home and slept in the kitchen.

My mother very much wanted to do her part in the war effort. She gave up two of our three rooms. In one lived a Tartar composer, his dentist wife and their small child. The other housed a Ukrainian woman with two children. Her husband was in a concentration camp. We had to move all our furniture out of the two rooms and led a cramped existence amid all our possessions in the one remaining room. Mother also donated her last $700 that she brought from America to a fund to build tanks for the army. To support the three of us, she held three jobs. During the day, she taught at the University. She also translated articles into English for the local radio broadcast to India. In the evening she gave private English lessons at home. I often fell asleep listening to my mother's lessons. I never had a chance to study English, but I think that somehow I learned it during those wartime evenings, in keeping with the latest theories of educators that language can best be learned by hearing while you sleep.

We lived like all the Soviet people, with one exception. Care packages were coming from the United States with egg powder, condensed milk and cornflakes. But my mother's mother and brothers sent us nothing, and she was too proud to ask. As we later learned, her parents' estate was divided among the family and nothing was set aside for her.

Early in the war, I had been diagnosed as suffering from a heart condition. The doctors had told my mother that I must be fed high calorie foods.

To do it, she sold everything that she had brought from the United States, including the Singer sewing machine, her dresses and my father's prized ice cream machine. I remember that the sewing machine bought her 200 grams of butter. She gave me ten grams of butter every day for three weeks.

All that remained of her life in America was her typewriter, which was the means of our livelihood. This typewriter is now more than 70 years old. All this was happening at the time that she donated her last $700 and I still have a newspaper clipping about this donation.

Mother never complained and never asked anyone for help. Even now, I remember the nights that she and Auntie Nadya sat at the table, by candlelight during the frequent power cuts, counting our meager assets and trying to plan till the next pay packet. I had to prepare my homework by the same light. I tried to convince the two of them that I was ready to leave school and take a job in order to help the budget. But they insisted that I must continue my studies, while they would do everything to give me a good education.

When my father died, my mother was only 35 years old. There were quite a number of men who would have been only too happy to marry her. Among those I can remember were a general of the Soviet army, a professor at the University and an interpreter. They tried to win her heart through me, bringing gifts of candy and sometimes even slipping me money. She never did marry. She explained that none of them was as good as my father to become her husband, and she didn't want another father for me.

Looking back on it today, the war was not such a disaster for me personally. My mother and Auntie Nadya protected me from much of the hardship. I was too young to understand much of what was going on around me. And, in any case, we were living in Tashkent, which was quite far, almost four thousand miles, removed from the warfronts of the western Soviet Union.

On a broader level, life in Tashkent at war was exciting culturally and intellectually. Professors from Moscow, Leningrad and others of the western Soviet's best Universities and Conservatories were evacuated to Tashkent. The city became the home of symphony orchestras and musicians and also famous writers. The famous Count and writer Alexei Tolstoy was among the many that actually lived in our building.

I was, of course, too young to meet these people socially, but I was going a lot to concerts, plays and meetings with the brightest intellects of the USSR. Each Sunday, I went to symphony concerts and listened avidly to Beethoven's Egmont and his Ninth Symphony, the overture of Mozart to the *Barber of Seville* and other great music. To this day I remember note by note the scores of music that I heard as a child in wartime Tashkent. It was there that I heard recitals by Vertinskiy, the great singer just returned from emigration to China. Several times I saw the dances of the ensemble Igor Moiseev, and was stunned by the wealth of musical culture of the nations of the Soviet Union and the world. And I enjoyed the humor of Obraztcov's puppet theater.

My only onerous duties in those years were to stand in the long line every day from early morning for bread and the once-a-week solemn procession to the public baths. My task was to keep the place in line until our turn, then call my mother and Auntie Nadya to come to do the week's wash.

I did not have problems with my studies at school. I was considered a good student, though I was never the best, and could not become the best, because of mathematics.

Across the hallway from us lived Essie , a pianist who, like my mother, was widowed. Lala, Essie's daughter, was not interesting to me in those days. She was ten years older than me and already a grown woman. In the evenings she went with our mothers to the cinema. She had a boyfriend — a tall, very handsome young man who she was soon to marry. I was only two years younger than her brother Berlin, but at that age two years meant a lot.

Very often Lala and our mothers went to see a film. Berlin and I were put to sleep in the same room. As soon as the door closed behind them, we would jump out of bed and begin a frenzied pillow fight. For an hour and a half, he pounded me with feathers swirling around our heads. A few minutes before the moviegoers were due home, we would sweep the debris under the beds, climb back in and pretend to be asleep. Lala, who from my point of view was a nasty character, would head straight for the beds, look underneath, and announce with great relish to the two mothers: "They've been fighting again!" Invariably we were punished. I hated Lala.

Berlin soon began attending school, while I was still attending kindergarten. He very quickly became a snob. He was a student at school, while I was a child in kindergarten. I could not stand his scorn, and severed all relations with him. When I began my schooling, he was already finishing primary school and we had no common ground for conversation. Four years later, as I finished primary school, I needed to renew relations with Berlin, since I had to confess that I had no understanding whatsoever of mathematics. From then on, it was Berlin who saved me from disaster. In the beginning, he tried to explain to me elementary mathematics, but it was hopeless. For many years thereafter, he did my daily homework. Whenever we sat for a test, he would pass me notes. Since the classes were segregated, he even on one occasion disguised himself as a girl in order to bring me the notes with the math that I needed.

I was perfect in German. My command of the language was so good that, when our German teacher had to excuse herself from the classroom, she would leave me to teach the other children. Whenever we prepared for exams in German, girls would come home with me to study. Uzbek was equally easy and fast. My grasp of history was also good, mainly because we had an excellent teacher from Leningrad. Her name was Vera Alexeevna. She was quite deaf, but the girls sat through her classes almost without breathing, in rapt attention. I think that my own interest in history, which led me into research, originates with her teaching. My grades in Russian literature and geography were also more than adequate. I would not say that I was brilliant in chemistry and physics, but again my knowledge was adequate. But, algebra, geometry and trigonometry reduced me to dumb silence.

But Berlin played a more important role in my life than just the deliverer of mathematical first aid. He opened for me the world of foreign classic literature which the school was of course not teaching us. I read everything that he was reading as appropriate to his age. I was crazy about books. I read while I was eating or going to the bathroom and even while I was walking on the streets. Perhaps it was because I never read children's literature, but went straight into the world of Berlin' contemporaries that I became such an avid reader. Only later I understood that there was a gap in my education — that I had leapfrogged over a stage in normal development leaving behind me a serious deficiency. I had read no fairy stories , no detective stories, none of the adventures that capture the minds of children. I am conscious today that I lost a lot in childhood by not reading that literature. My time had been spent with Galsworthy's *Forsyte Saga,* Feuchtwanger, Balzac, Maupassant, Dumas and many others.

The Essies' family gave me something else. They opened the world of music to me. Our mothers decided that my mother would teach Berlin English, and Essie would teach me music. After two years of studying with her, she decided that I was prepared for more serious studies and must go to the Tashkent Conservatory music school. This is how my life was split between two schools—one for general education and one for music.

My music studies were extremely serious and I was lucky with my professors. At first I studied with Professor Kaminskaya, a very experienced teacher. Later, I studied with Professor Ginsburg, a famous pianist from Leningrad who had been evacuated to Tashkent during the war and stayed there for the rest of his life.

I had to study various subjects, such as the theory and harmony of music and musical literature and I majored in piano. I demonstrated good technique in Bach and Liszt and I could play very easily from any score without preparation. Everything I learned in music was absorbing and relatively easy, except harmony. To master harmony, I felt, one needs a command of mathematics, and here Berlin could not help me. I lacked the talents of an improviser and composer. As a result, I could never improvise jazz, and this has remained a sorrow throughout my life. I never considered myself a good musician since I did not develop that talent. Even when I won the 1948 Central Asian Piano Competition, I was not happy with my performance.

Luckily there was something else more fulfilling in my life—tennis. I do not remember how I first met my future friend Tanya Brodskaya. I was 13 years old and Tanya was 3 years older. It was a matter of pride that I had a friend several years older than me. I tried to emulate her in everything. One day I discovered that she played tennis. What she did, I must do. It was the winter of 1948. We caught a tram from near my house into the Old City, a long ride. It took time to get there, but finally we arrived at a sports installation of some institution and met a short man named Kaplan. He was a tennis coach. When he saw me, and heard that I wanted to play tennis, he fell down on the floor. At the time, I didn't know that he was playing a gymnastic trick. I really believed that he had fainted at this revelation from a 13 year old.

Before playing tennis, I had been crazy about basketball. But I stopped playing very quickly because I was taller than anyone around. It left me constantly afraid that I would do some harm to another smaller player. However, when I got kicked in the scramble to get a ball, I felt insulted and could feel the anger rise in me. Tennis seemed much more civilized. My contact was only with the ball and my adversary was at a distance across the net.

I became very obsessed with tennis and played every day. Only now I begin to understand that it was not a real indoctrination into the finer points of tennis. We just came and played as we wanted, without instructions from a coach. But by the spring of 1948, I was already playing at the downtown stadium almost professionally. At the end of that summer, Kaplan invited me to go to the All-Soviet Tennis Competition in Saratov, a city in the European part of the Soviet Union on the river Volga. I was ecstatic, not only because I was to participate in the competition, but also because it gave me the opportunity to travel around the Soviet Union, and, most importantly, to feel independent and adult. This was a time, not long after World War II, when people still didn't travel.

I had one problem. I was 13 and the competition rules specified a participant had to be 14. My coach, Kaplan had to send a telegram to the Ministry of Education asking permission for me to participate in the competition. The permission was given, and I went in August as a member of the Uzbek team to the ancient town of Saratov on the Volga River. Today it is impossible to understand the way that we traveled in those post-war days. We boarded a railway wagon that had no fittings except for bare boards—no seats, no mattresses, no pillows. We sat on the steps of the wagon, covered in coal dust from the engine, singing and happy to be traveling. It took us several days to reach the town of Gorki. In Gorki we boarded a river steamer. Again we slept on plain wooden shelves. Each time the ship stopped, we stayed on board to keep away from the hordes of hungry people on the quayside begging for a crust of bread. It was the first time that I saw conditions so different from what we had endured in Tashkent—and I felt guilty: We are enjoying life, playing tennis, and these people are hungry and many of them will be dead tomorrow. Many years later, I could still see the trembling hands and pitiful eyes of starving people.

That year, in Saratov, I played badly, and finished third from last in the competition. However, I was not worried by my performance. After all, I had only begun to play a few months before, and I was the youngest of all the competitors. I was euphoric. I had made many friends from Georgia, Estonia and the Ukraine. Everybody wanted to be photographed with me. Everyone was happy to meet an African—the first to participate in the competition. I made a great splash. All the newspapermen from all over the USSR wanted to interview and write about me. I was a phenomenon and the stories appeared even in the national press. People wanted my address, and some of the contacts have been maintained throughout my life.

We returned to Tashkent by the same route. The ship to Gorki and the train to Tashkent took thirteen days. We were tired. We were hungry. The food taken from Tashkent was long gone, and there was nothing to buy on the way. Some of the team were crying and begging to be taken home faster.

When I returned to Tashkent, I began to play more seriously. I spent more time on the courts, and I constantly sought games with players better than I. The results came quite quickly. I was seeded second in Uzbekistan. The next All-Soviet competition was in Kharkov in 1949, and there I was already in the middle of the list. Again I was meeting friends with whom I had corresponded during the year, and I was meeting new acquaintances. Among my new friends were the champion of Georgia, Mzia Bakradze, the Estonian champion Regina Oyavere, two girls from Lithuania and another two from Moscow. One of the Muscovites was Rita Yemelyanova who became champion of the Soviet Union that year. She still remains a friend.

Up to 1952, I took part in every annual All-Soviet Tennis Competition, each time in a different city or Republic. My results became better and better. I became champion of Tashkent, then of Uzbekistan, later of Central Asia and eventually achieved fourth place in doubles in the Soviet Union. But desire and even time spent on tennis courts is not enough. A good technique was also necessary, and there was no one to give us that in Uzbekistan. Although I understood that I would never become the champion of the Soviet Union in singles because the Muscovites had much more opportunity to acquire technique. Nevertheless I loved the sport. I enjoyed the atmosphere of friendship that brought sportsmen from different Republics together, speaking different languages and brought up in different cultures. I loved the parades that opened the competitions, with the audience applauding as I proudly led the Uzbek team.

I shall always retain the feeling of friendship, support, and protection I received from playing doubles on a tennis court, going together up to the net. Tennis brought me recognition and fame throughout the Soviet Union. My five years of competing nationally brought masses of letters that I was simply unable to answer personally. There were many offers of "hand and heart" from men wanting to marry me. I can still quote from one such letter from a soldier, written as a poem. He wrote that he would come to inspect me, and if he liked what he saw, he would marry me and make me a present of what was apparently his greatest possession—his Communist Party membership card.

Between music studies and tennis there was just enough time left for school life. In each year I was elected to various posts. I was president of my class, then later of the school. I participated in all the activities of the school.

During the war, the inhabitants of Tashkent worked on the cotton plantations every autumn in order to help the war effort. Our school participated in the project, but only the higher classes were allowed to work. My class, of which I was the president, was moved by a noble impulse. We approached the school administration for permission to help with picking the cotton, but were told that we were too young at the time. As the war continued, we reached the proper age eventually. At 11, at last we were permitted to go to a kishlak some 60 miles from Tashkent to pick up cotton.

Because of Uzbekistan's "continental" climate, we experienced extreme heat in daytime and bitter cold at night. There were no creature comforts at all. We slept in a cow barn. My preference was to sleep in the hay together with a cow, to enjoy her warmth. I suffered terribly from deep scratches, torn flesh around the nails and bleeding fingers. For a pianist, this was a terrible catastrophe.

Another problem was food. There was nothing to eat except what we could forage ourselves. Because I spoke Uzbek more fluently than any of my classmates, it became my responsibility to get bread for the kids. They would put me on a donkey cart and we would begin to drive around the Uzbek kishlaks-villages. There was no need to whip the donkey, for if he didn't want to move—he wouldn't. He chose the route for himself, and always brought me to a village where they happened to be making bread when I arrived. The Uzbeks have their own way of making bread. They slap flat dough onto the sides of a beehive-shaped oven, a hole in the earth. The result is exceptionally tasty. It was always the task of the women in the same way that only the men would make the rice and meat pilaf. If I was lucky, a crowd of hungry dogs would escort me for miles attracted by the smell of the fresh bread. The Uzbeks were especially kind and friendly to me. They seemed to enjoy my command of their language, and almost invariably produced other presents for the kids apart from the bread.

At each village, I would be invited to join the men at the *choyhana* —a big, very low platform covered with rugs, on which they squatted oriental fashion, sitting on crossed legs—to drink innumerable bowls of green tea. Women were not allowed to sit on the platform, but I was a guest and a child. The men were dressed in cotton quilt coats, tied with a sash. Twisted into the sash was usually a small lump of sugar, which they extracted with some difficulty, dipped in the tea, then sucked. Often, a man, instead of returning the lump of sugar to his sash after he had suck it himself, would hand it to me—in a gesture that said "this is all I have to give."

I am sorry to say that this employment of children in the cotton fields has continued up till now, though World War II is long over. Pupils are taken from the classrooms in autumn and put to work for three months. There are few cotton combines in Uzbekistan, and the ones that exist are very primitive.

In Tashkent, I had many friends from school, the music Conservatory and the tennis circle. I was quite tall for my age while the girls at my school were very short, presumably because of the bad wartime diet. Though the area produced a lot of fruit, the huge influx of refugees from western Russia meant that the diet was not balanced. But among my friends at school there was one other tall girl. Ina Dunaeva was red haired, extremely talented and outstanding in all her studies. Our mathematics teacher adored her. He would enter the classroom and announce: "Everyone, go for a walk. Dunaeva come up to the board." The two of them would begin to chalk up equations and calculations, beyond our understanding, in the raptures of their private euphoria. They were truly intoxicated by some refined mathematical happiness. But her talents were not limited to mathematics. Ina loved to write poetry. One day we were set a task to write an essay for geography. She produced her work in pure and brilliant verse.

But Ina Dunaeva had one shortcoming. Ina had no musical ear. At the same time she was crazy about music. She came to listen when I played, and would accompany me to concerts. Ina very much wanted to learn an instrument, but could not afford to buy one. Since she had no piano at home, she took a piece of wood and drew the keys on it. Using this substitute for her finger exercises, she taught herself how to play, then came to my home to play our piano. Exceptional as this sound, it was not unique. A youth named Koerer, was sent to Tashkent prison during the war just because he was German by origin. He taught himself the same way, and later went on to become later the Soviet Union's finest exponent of Bach and Beethoven on the piano. Had Ina been blessed with a musical ear, she could have become an excellent concert pianist.

All my ten years in that school were spent at the same desk as Ina. Together we went to Moscow to continue our studies. She chose, of course, mathematics. Ina visited me several times, then abruptly disappeared. It was only 40 years later that she told me that she had been afraid to maintain our friendship, because I had married a foreigner.

I did not date boys during my school years. Maybe this was because I was so obsessed by tennis and music. Maybe it was because the boys were always much shorter than me. Perhaps the reason was because friendship with Berlin was quite enough for me. I was very upset when Berlin finished school, fell deeply in love with someone named Anne and married her. In the past Berlin was thoughtful and spiritual. I believed that Anne was too earthy and matter-of-fact for him. I still retain that sadness because my intuitions proved correct. Throughout my childhood, Berlin was my spiritual inspiration. He became a very talented architect, and built many buildings around

Tashkent. He eventually ended up in a small village near Moscow where Anne put him to work growing potatoes and other vegetables in their garden. Given the situation in Russia, growing one's own vegetables to feed the family is of course admirable, but I had lost my spiritual mentor. Berlin and his entire family emigrated to the United States in the late 1990s.

Now I am able to comprehend that my studies in a Soviet school in the 1940s, and particularly in a province like Uzbekistan, did not contribute very much to the development of a young person. For example, since there was no time or resources to produce updated textbooks for history, we were required to black out the text and pictures that related to generals and revolutionary activists—like Trotsky, Bukharin, Tuchachevsky and Blucher—who had been purged in the 1930s. Our history books became no more than the story of the Communist Party as told to children. There were no alternatives. In biology, any response that we gave had to begin with a condemnation of bourgeois scientists whose findings were not consistent with Soviet Marxist biologists. We were required to constantly applaud the name of Lysenko, the scientist whose theories were so entrenched that anyone disputing them would find himself in prison.

The same problems obviously extended to Russian literature. We were not allowed to pronounce the names of Great Russian writers and poets who were not considered to be a part of socialist realism. Pasternak, a future Nobel Prize winner, was only publishable as the translator of Shakespeare. His own works were proscribed. Great poets like Marina Tzvetaeva (who killed herself because of hunger), Anna Ahmatova, (whose husband, famous Russian poet Gumilev, was shot), Ossip Mandelshtam (who died of hunger in a Gulag—a Soviet system of concentration camps) and many others, were not taught in school. Indeed, we were not supposed to even know or pronounce their names. We did have to know the names and works of poets and writers who conformed to the Communist Party concepts of socialist correctness. Among these were Demjan Bedniy (a "court" poet who even lived in the Kremlin), Count Alexei Tolstoy who returned from abroad to write historical literature that always managed to compliment Stalin, and Maxim Gorki who got lost in the compromises that he made with the regime. Gorki had also emigrated, but was enticed into returning by Stalin. Though he saw much that he did not like, he even wrote praise for the Gulag forced labor camps. Our required reading included a long list of writers who had written ecstatically about the Revolution and the role of Stalin.

For this reason, I was delighted to find myself included in the so-called "Thursday Parties." Every Thursday, the children interested in literature from each school in Tashkent would come to the Pioneers Palace in the home of the uncle of the last Czar who had been exiled by his nephew to Uzbekistan. I was brought there of course by Tania Brodskaya, my older friend from tennis, whom I followed everywhere. The chairperson of these meetings was a very beautiful young woman teacher from one of the Tashkent schools. I remember being shocked and enthused by the sense that a place existed where we could learn about the "other literature," and speak our minds openly. Today, I realize the risk that she was taking in allowing us free expression that was different from the conventional teachings of our textbooks and newspapers. I do not know how she was allowed to do such a thing, but she was obviously risking her freedom and perhaps her life.

To be truthful, in all the years that I attended those "Thursday Parties," I never spoke. Mostly, it was that I was very shy and afraid of opening my mouth publicly. But those Thursdays played a very big role in the development of my personality. They taught me that I could think alternatively, independently and critically. Now I can even admit to myself that I am too critical of some aspects. But I was beginning to understand that our formal teaching was no more than the required Communist Party brainwashing. The lesson of those Thursdays was an understanding of the process of brainwashing when I came to my studies in Moscow University.

I liked Tanya more and more as time went by. She constantly opened new doors to me, and the next one was to nature itself. One day I discovered that she was learning biology in a study group, and was going on a ten-day excursion to the Tan Shan Mountains. Though I was not crazy about biology, I wanted to follow all of Tanya's undertakings and adventures. I asked her to take me with the group. The leader of the group had to give permission, as did my mother. Luckily, I got both consents. It was the first time in my life that I was encountering real nature, and everything was beautiful and charming to my city-bred eyes. I loved the mountains and the colorful alpine flowers. I was entranced by the vastness of the skies that were studded with so many stars that there seemed to be no room for all of them. The narrow, fast-flowing and freezing cold rivers were enchanting. All of these memories have stayed with me throughout my life. This newfound love of nature enriched my life, and has left me with a permanent lust for travel and new sights.

However, the excursion was not easy. We had none of the wonders of modern day camping—no tents, no sleeping bags, and no walking shoes— but we were happy. In fact, we had no awareness that such comforts could exist.

We had to walk narrow paths occasionally, ending in nothing and requiring a leap over a gaping abyss. At one spot, I had to roll down a slope for there was no other way. There was constant danger from wild animals. During the nights, we could see green eyes watching us in the darkness and, indeed, we had to post our own sentries armed with a rifle. While we slept, jackals would steal bread from the sacks that we used in place of pillows. We learned to hang the sacks from trees, out of their reach. I still remember my turn at night guard duty, and the feeling of this vast sky and its stars pressing down on me while everyone else slept. In the gloom of night, I suddenly became aware of the flashes of green lights approaching our campsite. Closing my eyes, I aimed the rifle and fired. Suddenly the green flashes disappeared to be replaced by the howls of the departing animals. By the morning light, it was obvious that I had hit nothing.

As we went through all these difficulties and escapades, I constantly thought of my mother. Had she been aware of the hardships and dangers, there was no way that she would have given her consent for this trip.

Tanya had one somewhat strange characteristic. She would enthuse me into following her to do all these interesting things, but she never persisted herself. I would begin a new phase in my life and continue with it, while she vanished. Eventually, she vanished completely out of my life and I have no idea what became of her. The greatest happiness that she brought me at the time was tennis. Through that sport I found a sense of happiness, and friends in many different cities. I could not only play but also travel to different cities for championships—a virtually unknown luxury in those days, especially for those who lived in Central Asia. After the war, no one had the money to pay for tickets and the other incidental expenses of travel. Everything else was very far away. From Tashkent to Moscow is 3,750 miles. Leningrad is even farther off. Train travel consumed many days to get anywhere in the European Soviet Union. A normal journey to Moscow, in extreme discomfort, would take 10 to 15 days.

Commercial flights were almost an unknown. The only planes in the air were military. But I had a chance to fly in 1948. Among the numerous students who came to my mother for English lessons was the Minister of Foreign Affairs of the Republic of Uzbekistan. He decided to make us a present of a place in one of the Crimean government sanatoriums. My mother, who was always very brave, resolved to take a plane to the Crimea. The aircraft was a military cargo plane with no seats or prepared space for passengers. I suffered greatly throughout the flight. This was my first encounter with airsickness. I lay in agony on the floor of the plane for the many hours that this plane took to reach the Crimea.

The Crimea and the Black Sea were worth the effort. The sea, which I was seeing for the first time in my life, came as a shock. I sat for hours watching the waters as they changed through all weathers—the waves and the tides, the stillness, the difference between sunrise and sunset. I learned to swim, by my own efforts. I still retain the ability to swim long distances, but slowly.

I was taken by car, at night, to Aipetri Mountain to see my first sunrise. This was a major occurrence in the Crimea. The sky was so dark and vast, and there was no way to know east from any other direction. I was perched on a rock facing in the right direction and waiting, for what seemed an interminable amount of time, for the sun that I thought would never come —so dark was the night. Suddenly I saw a tiny red stripe on the horizon. It began to stretch longer and wider, becoming very bright—yet not looking like a sun. The brightness moved up into the clouds, changing through red and yellow to emerge as a recognizable sun. To me this was a process of rebirth, one which, upon our return to the sanatorium, I wrote up in my diary. I had never kept a diary before, but the sense of rebirth as a new person made me resolve to begin the rebirth of my new life by recording its events. Of course, nothing of that resolve came into being. I lost my diary. Several times in my life I tried to begin a new life and a diary after the effect of nature, or music, on my senses, but to my constant regret I always failed the constancy of keeping that record. The same goes for my new life, which I have tried to begin each new week, new month, new year, but have constantly failed.

The Crimean stay has also stuck in my memory, for it was here that I learned to dance. In my childhood, I had no chance to learn dancing. During the war, there was no place in which to dance. Our school was for girls only, and boys were not allowed to visit. In any case, in wartime the mood was not right for trivial pleasures. There was no dance hall or discotheque in the city of Tashkent. The first time that I saw people dancing was when the war ended, on the 9th of May 1945. Amid the fireworks, loudspeakers were broadcasting music from the thirties, mostly tango and foxtrot. I was 14 years old. I stood and watched enviously, not knowing how to dance. Now, in the Crimean sanatorium, there were dances every evening. My mother's friends would teach me the steps, though they insisted that I refer to the dances as "slow" or "quick." "Tango" or "foxtrot" belonged to the foreign bourgeois cultures. We were brainwashed by the Communist Party, which had begun a war against "cosmopolitism," which means the love to everything foreign, into believing that it is not corresponds with the love to socialism and we must resist all these alien influences.

I remember that, when we returned to Tashkent, I sat one day at the piano trying to play some kind of jazz. Suddenly my mother rushed into the room and began to close the windows. She explained that playing jazz could land me in prison. Later I found out that many jazz musicians had been arrested, including even complete orchestras like those of Lundstrem, Rozner and other famous Soviet jazz leaders. Apart from my lack of talent at improvisation, I believe that my inability to play jazz also stems from the fact that I didn't hear this music during my childhood. This is still a great sorrow to me.

The war on "cosmopolitism" was a campaign against Jews and those who had any contact with foreign culture. My mother was relatively lucky. She was not arrested, though she lost her job in the University and the

Institute of Foreign Languages. The ostensible reason was that her academic degree was from the United States and, therefore, unacceptable in the USSR. The real reason was undoubtedly that she was Jewish and a former foreigner. The factors that saved us from abject poverty and hunger were the private English lessons that she gave at home. In fact, the dentist wife of our Tartar tenant, whom my mother had taken in off the street, denounced her to the KGB in the hope that my mother would be arrested and our tenant would gain an extra room. Though she based her claim on the law that said private enterprise was not permitted in the Soviet Union, she was ignorant of another law that made an exception for widows of distinguish husbands. In addition to the lessons, mother also got a job as an announcer for the English-language broadcasts to India at the radio station where she had been doing occasional translations.

I am 16 and I must get my Soviet passport. I went to the police, who gave me a passport that recorded my nationality as "American." I told them that "American" was a term of citizenship, while I was "Soviet." The officer explained that "Soviet" did not mean nationality. After that complaint, they gave me another passport that stated that I was "Uzbek." Again I complained that I had no Uzbek blood in my veins. Then they wrote that I was "Russian." By this time, when I refused to take this passport, the policeman was impatient with me and asked: "What do you want me to write?" I answered: "I was born in the Soviet Union. So I should be Soviet, but you explained that there is no such nationality. I think you must write that I am a 'Negro,' which I am indeed..." At that time, Black people in the United States were fighting for the right to be called "Negro" with a capital "N"—and I was influenced by their struggle. Again, the policeman explained that there was no such nationality as "Negro." Negro was not a nationality, but rather a race. I insisted that, whether or not it was a race, I am "Negro."

The officer, attempting a reasoned argument, asked: "How will you prove that you are a Negro? One can come and say that he is a Negro. Others will come and say that they are something else. Must I believe everybody? Then anybody can come and say that he is a Negro. You think that, by stating you are a Negro, you will be able to leave the country?" I had to go home to search for a newspaper article from *Amsterdam news*, in which my father was mentioned as a Negro, and bring it back to the police. At last I could prove my point, and it was written, in black and white, that he was a Negro. Thus I became the only person in the world with a passport in which it was written that I was "Negro." The Uzbek policeman was a kind person.

CHAPTER THREE

Alma Mater—Moscow State University

I graduated from my high school in Tashkent in 1952. My scores were very good, but not brilliant—because of mathematics. I had also graduated from music school. Studying at school, at the Conservatory, playing tennis professionally, travelling around the country for sport meets—I never gave any thought to my future. Now, the problem towered over me. Where must I go to continue my studies?

This was where destiny brought me Wayland Rudd. He was an African American friend of my father who lived in Moscow. The first time that he came to the USSR was with Langston Hughes in 1932. Rudd had returned to the United States, but was unable to forget this country where he had encountered no racial discrimination. He became an actor, yet knew that he was condemned as a Black man to playing the role of fools or menial servants. His dream was to play the lead Shakespeare's *Othello*, but he realized that he would never have that opportunity in the United States. One day he went to swim at a public pool in New York City, and was physically ejected because of the color of his skin. This for him was the last straw. He decided to return to the Soviet Union.

In Moscow, he began studies at the famous Art Theater, under the direction of the great actor Meyerhold. While Stanislavsky had been the guiding light of the Art Theater, with his classic interpretations, Meyerhold was the pioneer of the innovative and modern. Becoming a professional in this new milieu, Rudd—just before World War II—achieved his dream, and became the first Black actor to play Othello in Russian language. During the war he formed his own theater company, to travel around the country. Eventually, after the war, this brought him to Tashkent, where he met the wife of his friend—my mother. After spending several hours talking to me, he announced to mother that I must go to the best University in the country, Moscow State University, to continue my education. My mother said 'no way'. She could never permit me to venture so far away from home and her care. Rudd argued that there was nothing to be afraid of, that he would be nearby, would help me and generally keep an eye on me. After long talks she at last agreed and my destiny was sealed. Though I could not have known it, this was the end of my happy childhood in which others bore all the responsibility for my life. I had no cause, until then, to worry my head about anything.

In July 1952, I came to Moscow. I called Wayland Rudd. He seemed happy to hear from me, but said that he was going for a concert appearance to another city, and would return in two weeks. I went to the country house of one of my mother's friends. For all of the two weeks, it was raining. I sat near the window, looking at pouring rain and thought about how to continue my education. To what institution should I go? If I would choose the Moscow Conservatory, I had no piano and no place where I could prepare for entrance examinations. That was out of the question. Next I explored the possibility of a grounding in economics, but remembered my doubtful talent for mathematics. That too was not a viable proposition. Next to be considered was history. I loved history and had a voracious appetite for new knowledge about the past of different nations and countries. I relished historical jokes and anecdotes. I wanted to see, beyond the pages of history books, the characters and personalities. So I decided to go to the History Department of Moscow State University.

I have always adored the stories of the famous Soviet writer Fazil Iskander, a Turk from the Autonomous Republic of Abhazia in Georgia. In one of his tales, he recounts how, in the same year that I came to Moscow, he arrived and tried to enter the Department of Philosophy at this University. Thinking that his membership of a rare nationality from a remote province would be attractive to his interviewer, he adopted the accents of his native home, and played on his uniqueness. His interlocutor asked indifferently: "Where's Abhazia? Is it Adjaria?" Fazil understood that his accent was not going to help. Discarding the accent, he politely explained in pure and faultless Russian that "Abhazia is Abhazia and Adjaria is Adjaria." The University official left the room, then returned bearing a heavy tome. After perusing its pages, he announced: "We have no quota for this nationality!"

My story was almost the same. The interviewer asked why I had written in my application that my mother was born in Poland, which had been a part of Russia in Czarist times and had gone to the United States. I said that she emigrated. He said: "Write to your mother, let her send us an explanation of why she emigrated from Russia." I said: "She was a small girl when her parents took her to the United States because of pogroms. What sort of explanation can she give you?" "O, she is a Jew?" My documents were returned to me with the terse announcement: "People like you are not accepted in this University!" What was I to do? Who could advise me? Obviously the answer was Wayland Rudd.

I phoned him and heard a woman's voice: "Who are you?" I replied that I was the daughter of a friend. "Yesterday, he died!" I was in such a state of shock that I dumbly replaced the receiver, not knowing what to say.

Here I was in this huge unknown city, alone and with nowhere to live. I didn't know whom to approach for advice. And my mother could no longer help me. In any case, she was very far away from me. Little by little, I came to my senses and called again to ask about the funeral. It would be the following day.

The funeral. Many unknown faces. Black and white. A big white man approached me. When he began talking to me I could sense that he spoke Russian with a heavy British accent. As it happened, he was English—a journalist named Ralph Parker who reported to several newspapers in Britain and America. He was surprised that I knew no one among the crowd. He told me that he had two adopted daughters, both Black, and he invited me to visit them. Parker introduced me to some of the Black people in the crowd. First I met George Tynes, who told me that he had come to the USSR together with my father, in 1931. Tynes introduced me to his daughter Amelia and his two sons, Slava and Ruben. Then Bob Ross approached me. He was black beyond anything that I had yet seen in my short life. Bob was thin and well built. When he talked, the whites of his eyes were constantly revolving. He said that he had also known my father, and promptly introduced me to his two daughters, Ella and Ina. Bob explained that Wayland Rudd had been the leader of the Black community in Moscow, but that position had now fallen to him. As such, he was ready to help me. I was invited to stay in his home.

Ross' life was difficult. He did not have a permanent job, but played small roles in films and traveled around the Soviet Union lecturing about the life of Black people in the United States. He had a huge appetite for life and was constantly euphoric. He never complained and would willingly give his last crust of bread to anyone in need, though he himself was quite often hungry.

Bob found out about my problems with the University and began to seek ways to help. One day he came home in high spirits. He had met somebody in a high position in the Central Committee of the Communist Party— then a very powerful body. Although the time for entrance examinations had already passed, this Party bigshot had ordered that I should be allowed to sit for the exams. I passed with good marks and was admitted. I had become the first ever Black student of Moscow State and the second Black to get an education in Russia: the first was a Great Russian poet of Ethiopian descent Alexander Pushkin, who had studied in the St. Petersburg Lyceum in the beginning of 19th century.

Ross helped me many times, as did many of my father's old friends in Moscow. Because of them, I was never allowed to feel that I was all alone in this great city, without family and friends.

I did not want to stay long in the Ross family apartment. He lived with his new wife and her daughter in a one-room studio. In those years, it was commonplace for many people to live in the same apartment, with several families in each room. Though he was being extremely generous in offering me a roof over my head, I felt that I could not take advantage. But, since I was a latecomer, there was no room for me in the Moscow State University hostels.

Of course it was again Bob Ross who fought the battle to get me a place in one of several student hostels, which was a one-hour train ride from the city. This was a wooden house in a village. Water had to be carried in buckets on a yoke from quite a distance. We washed outside in the yard, even in winter—which was especially difficult for me, after living in a hot climate.

Now I received help from a friend of my mother's, Lia Gavurina. Lia was also American, but she had come to the Soviet Union before my parents. She lived in the Hotel Lux on the main downtown Moscow Street named for Maxim Gorki. The hotel is now known as the Central. Before World War II, it had been a hotel for foreign Communist leaders employed by the Communist International. In 1937, the year of the most terrible purges, many of them had been arrested and executed. Some of those who were expecting to be arrested had preferred to take their own lives by jumping out of the hotel windows. Invariably, they opted for the inner courtyard windows, for they weren't willing to have passers by on the main street believe that something was amiss with the regime. I was told this repeatedly by the widows who still lived there.

Lia Gavurina rented a bed for me in the room of the widow of a prominent Dutch Communist and her mentally ill daughter.

This hotel was where I made my first Moscow friends outside the Black family that I had discovered. They were the sons of American, Polish and Bulgarian Communists, and all were students of mathematics at Moscow State. They cared about me. They helped me. They took me out and explained Moscow life. They tried to teach me to skate—an impossibility for someone brought up in the south. My friendship with them still endures.

The hotel was in walking distance of the University. It took me about 15 minutes. But, in my second year, I got space in the University hostel on Strominka Street where I shared a room with nine other students. All the facilities were in the corridor. The occupants of the room were very different from each other, but there were no quarrels. One of them was from Belorussia, a republic on the western border of the Soviet Union, who happened to have been in a German concentration camp and still had the telltale number tattooed on her arm. Another was a lively blonde girl from Novgorod who was always happy. She was a very big, beautiful girl a la Russe, with long, thick braids. Her life was one long chain of extraordinary occurrences, many of which concerned very famous, interesting and handsome men. Every evening, we would get together to listen to her stories of how she had met a cosmonaut, or an artist, or a famous musician. To this day I do not know whether the stories were true. Yet another occupant was a Polish girl who constantly amazed us with her trade and speculations. The corridor always contained motorbikes, ice boxes and other merchandise that she would buy in Russia to sell in Poland. From Poland she brought women's clothing to sell in Moscow. I bought my first slip and a red and white striped blouse from her.

I can still recall the names of two of my roommates. One was a girl from Berlin, Germany, named Sigrid, who constantly reminded me of my inferiority complex because of her strict self-discipline and work abilities. She was awake while we all slept to perform her morning gymnastics. Then, while we still slept, she did her homework. I would hesitantly open one eye, watch her, and suffer, because I could not do the same. I just could not get up so early. I hated her for this. By the time we got up, she was already running around the campus. Twenty years later, we met by accident and became close friends though we lived in different countries. She would come to Moscow twice a year to visit me, and I went a couple of times to Berlin, even though it was difficult to receive permission to travel abroad.

I also remember the name of another girl, Aisha, from Karakalpakia, an autonomous republic in Uzbekistan. We were always impatiently waiting for her to come back from tests which she only seemed able to pass on the second or third attempt. Aisha was small, thin, quiet and Mongolian in features. She had many Asian friends who all came to the room to celebrate every time she succeeded in tests. The celebration, complete with Asiatic cooking, took place even if she barely passed the exam.

As in any Soviet hostel, household duties were shared among us. These included cleaning the floors, preparing food and reading textbooks for a blind girl. She was never allowed to be upset by anything. We lived in a commune, within which each of us had our own lives. By the way, as I learned from his autobiography, Mikhail and Raissa Gorbachev were living on the same floor of my hostel during their studies in Moscow State. They were there at same time I was there. My last two years were spent in the University's skyscraper hostel on the Lenin Hills (now called Vorobyev Hills), where I had a separate room with all the services.

At the same time, I was living in the Black community of Moscow. There were only two survivors of the group that had come with my father in 1931: my mother and George Tynes. George lived in the suburbs, breeding Pekin ducks and catfish. From time to time, he would phone and would say, with equal difficulty in Russian or English because he did not learn Russian well and forgot English, "Let's get together." All the Moscow community would go out to his suburban home. He was the one who remembered, and kept alive, all the American holidays; Thanksgiving, Labor Day, Memorial Day and, of course, Christmas. We, in the younger generation, shared no recollections of these holidays. A rich table would be spread, and we were happy to be together as one family. George's son, Slava, was a journalist working in a news agency. Amelia, his daughter, was a tall beautiful mulatto who for many years taught chemistry at school. She married an African and went with him to Ghana. But that life did not work out and she returned to the USSR. Amelia had two daughters, one of whom graduated from Columbia University in New York. Ruben, the third child of George Tynes, was rarely seen.

Here I must mention that all the Black Soviet girls, including me, eventually married Africans. This was the end of the 1950s, the beginning of the 1960s. It was the dawning of a new epoch in Africa and we were in euphoria over the beginnings of self-determination. We felt that we must go to Africa and, having a good education, we must help the continent to build a new life. The only sure way, being in the Soviet Union, to go to Africa and help her was to marry an African. Marrying Africans presented no great difficulty. They appreciated the fact that we were educated, black-skinned, and of African origin, so they chased us. All of us married Africans, and every one of us went to live in Africa. All of those who went ended up returning to the Soviet Union. They could not adjust to a style of life that was so different. They could not compromise with polygamy and found that there was no possibility of employment, despite their education.

The same was true of Lena, one of Ralph Parker's two adopted daughters, a trained engineer. She had married an Indian but returned from India to Moscow. Lena, with her quick mind and great sense of humor, was very special to me, and I named my daughter after her. Her sister, Mardji, married a Russian ballet dancer. She studied in the ballet school and became a leading ballerina of the famous Bolshoi theater. She now works as a choreographer and has staged Russian ballets in Finland, India, Turkey and other countries.

The Moscow Black community consisted of the second generation of those who had come with Langston Hughes in 1932. Rudd's son and daughter became singers. Lloyd Patterson, an original member of Hughes' delegation, became a radio reporter, but was killed during a German air raid on Moscow. He left behind his wife, a famous Russian artist, and three children, one of whom—Junny—was killed in a car accident. Another son, Tom Patterson, became an extremely skillful cameraman for Moscow television.

The third son, Jimmy, is a very famous Soviet poet. He graduated from the Naval Academy and became an officer in the Red Fleet. Later, he studied in an institute of literature, where he honed his talents as a poet. But his fame was first acquired in 1934, when as a two year old he played in a film, *Circus*. The lead was Vera Orlova, the first American-style Soviet film star. The movie was the first Soviet attempt at making a Hollywood-style musical. The scenario, in the best traditions of propaganda, was about a white American woman who had conceived a Black son. Fleeing from Ku Klux Klan persecution, she was taken to Russia by a German artist. Rejected by her, the German sought to destroy her by revealing to her colleagues at the Soviet circus where she was employed that she had a Black child (played by Jimmy). In true Soviet fashion, the revelation was the cause of great joy and the boy was promptly adopted by all. Jimmy, by now, has published several books of poetry.

Of those African-Americans that came to the Soviet Union in the 1920s and 1930s, none are still alive. In the next generation of their children, Jim Patterson, Margie Scott and I are the oldest. Our children, the third generation, already have offspring of their own, who have become the fourth generation living in what was not long ago the Soviet Union. Generally, people of African origin were easily absorbed into Soviet life. All have married Russians, including those young Black women who initially wed Africans then returned from Africa. Some became members of the Communist Party, which helped them get good jobs and travel abroad.

I had other friends, outside the Black community and beyond the walls of the hostel. On my first day in Moscow State University, I sat in class next to a tall, well-proportioned girl with big eyes and long lashes. This was Olya and we were to sit together for the next five years of my life in the University. I majored in the history of the United States. Her major was the history of Sweden. That was the only thing that separated us. Not only did we study together, but we spent our free time together, went to the theater and concerts and traveled together. I introduced Olya to her future husband, Kolya, and persuaded her to marry him. Kolya was a tall, blue-eyed blond though, as we later discovered, he was Armenian—traditionally a dark race.

Gans from Germany, who also studied with me, was blessed with total recall of everything that he saw or heard. We decided to make a test and gave him a thick textbook of ancient history. He quickly turned the pages. Then we began to examine him on the contents. He had all the facts and all the dates. Gans knew the length of the underground railways in every city of the world, he could list all the relatives of reigning monarchs. During his five years in Moscow State University, he learned 25 languages, all of which he spoke fluently with no trace of accent. His family had run away from the Nazis in 1933. Like my family, they had come to live in Tashkent, though I never met him while I was there. Gans' father was a professor at Tashkent Conservatory. Everybody in the class loved Gans. When he graduated from University, he returned to Germany, where I visited him twice.

Apart from Olya and Gans, I had two other close girl friends, Vera and Galya. Galya was short and brunette, endowed with good humor and also with an extraordinary memory. She was very modest. Vera was blonde, sharp to react and easily amused. We spent a lot of time together and laughed a lot, but there was something else that cemented the relationship. All three of us were repelled by a group of students whom Vera nicknamed "the good-ness clique": all were hidebound orthodox *Komsomol*—Soviet youth move-ment of the Communist Party. They all came from the suburbs, which in Moscow parlance meant that they were peasants coming from an intellectu-al wilderness. In intervals between lectures, they would gather in the yard and, linked arm in arm would sing militant songs. The two most repeated of which declared: "Our armored train stands ready to fight" and "Rifle, my rifle..." These girls were always the first to criticize other students for defi-ciency of Marxist ideology. In modern terms, they were always politically correct.

I was still occupied with my music and tennis. Therefore, I was not that involved in student life. But Vera and Galya would always keep me informed of the most recent heroic *Komsomol* deeds of the goodness clique. One day the two of them approached me on behalf of other students who felt the same as us, with a proposition that they would elect me a *Komsomol* leader of our class. I told them: "Are you crazy? What do I need it for!" Their response was: "Don't worry! We need to take the power away from them. We have enough votes to do it. You will not need to do anything. We will do all the work. But we need you and your name because students trust you. They know that you will never report on them to the KGB. If one of our goodness gets the post, as part of their *Komsomol* career, they will denounce us constantly to the KGB." After much discussion, I agreed. As they put it, if I shall not do this, I stood to be one of the first victims because of my foreign origin. So the election was in my best interests. Though I have no idea how Vera and Galya engineered it, I was elected by a majority vote—and remained *Komsomol* class leader for five years.

At the same time, through all these years, Vera was our elected trade union leader and Galya was a chairman of the class. Such distribution of power in the class was the salvation of our entire group. These were dangerous years in Moscow State University. It was a time of widespread denunciations of "traitors" and of betrayals, even by supposedly close friends. The self-righteous *Komsomol* led the pack. Several of the students—the most talented and the most capable of critical thought in our history department— were arrested. They were reported for discussing the works of Lenin and trying to understand why his ideas were not working in the Soviet Union. Their own friends reported them and they spent many years in Soviet prisons. It was sheer chance that I was not among them. Having heard about this group of talented students, I would have liked to attend their sessions. But, as I told Vera and Galya: "Let's pass the exams first. Afterwards we will have the time..."

One of my friends, Volodya Kryilov, an extremely talented young historian, participated in one of the sessions. He did not agree with the ideas being expressed there, and left, slamming the door behind him. Volodya did not denounce the group, even though he was a *Komsomol* leader. For that omission, he was expelled from Moscow State University, prohibited from any intellectual activity, and sent to work in a factory where he very quickly became a drunkard. I will never forget the *Komsomol* meeting at which his wife, a very beautiful and very smart Tartar girl, condemned Volodya to a stunned audience of fellow students, while the goodness clique jumped for joy. After several years, which Volodya spent in the factory, he died.

During my first year at Moscow State, the party leader of the history department fell in love with me. He chased me incessantly, always trying to sit by me in class, following me to the hostel, waiting for me at my door. Olya and I were not going to allow anyone to sit beside us, or to be near us, or divide us. My suitor lived at the same hostel, but I noticed that he would frequently disappear for days at a time. This was a phenomenon that I used to my advantage, telling him that he was obviously chasing other girls. I told him that there was no way that I could spend my time with such a man! And so on and so on.

Trying to disprove my thesis, he would very frankly disclose what he was up to. To establish that he was not spending time in brothels, he would tell me about his "heroic deeds": "I have just come from Leningrad to kneel at your feet. I was participating in the arrest of counter-revolutionaries. Can you imagine, I entered the office of a factory manager who screamed 'I was a friend of Lenin,' and I arrested him. Everybody says that Leningrad is the cradle of the revolution, but it is indeed the cradle of counter revolution..." To persuade me to marry him, he proposed: "We will work together for the KGB. I hate the intelligentsia. I will work with the workers and farmers. You will deal with the intelligentsia." By the way, it was not the only such proposal.

One day I could stand it no more, and I told him to his face what I really thought of him. The Next day, there was a *Komsomol* meeting at which I was reprimanded for being a bad leader of the class on the pretence that my students had not attended a New Year's party. Luckily for me, Stalin had died and the atmosphere in the Soviet Union was changing. In other years, my fate would have been very unpleasant.

I knew nothing of Stalin and Stalinism. Nobody among my Black friends had been oppressed except one who was arrested for polygamy. Like many other Soviet people, I had known nothing of concentration and forced labor camps full of innocent people. Stalin was very far from me apart from the portraits in every office, on every wall, and on every street. But he was a being in another world, and I could not imagine what kind of a person he was. When I found out that he had children, I was very surprised. It was hard even to imagine Stalin sleeping with a woman.

At the end of my first year in University, Stalin died. Everyone around me was crying hysterically. I was trying to muster a sad face and squeeze out some tears. I felt ashamed at my inability to suppress my cheerfulness. Nothing helped and my tears wouldn't flow. I remember one of the days following his death, I was standing with Lia Gavurina on the platform of the Metro waiting for a train, while all our neighbors were weeping and tearing their garments. Suddenly Lia turned to me and whispered, in English: "All this will finish very quickly, and no one will cry over him." "Why?" I asked. She did not answer, but began to look around for fear that we were being overheard. Now I can understand that she knew about Stalin's deeds, but was afraid even after his death to speak of it.

The years when I studied in Moscow State University, 1952–57, were not the best in its history. The waves of the Communist Party struggle against "cosmopolitism" were still pounding on the shores. There were people who remembered the names of famous scholars, with worldwide reputations, who had been ejected from the University, thrown into prison and even shot. Those professors who were teaching us had, for some reason, survived. But they were very careful and scared of everything.

The Dean of History was a world-famous archaeologist, Artzihovsky. For many years he had been pressured to join the Communist Party, because of a rule that said the dean had to be a Communist Party member. As an old man, he could no longer resist. Artzihovsky taught archaeology, but for some reason he did not like girls. When he lectured us, or when we sat close to him for exams, he would not look at us, girls. In tests, he quickly gave marks that were not of the highest, and dismissed us from the class. But I was successful with him because of my medals from tennis, which he respected.

Sergei Tokarev, a world-renowned ethnographer, had by some miracle retained his freedom and his life. His books were published everywhere and he lectured in France, Germany and other countries. However, he never attained the rank of academician or even associate, the highest accolades that a Soviet scientist could achieve. The reason was that he never was a member of the Communist Party, and in his youth, he had briefly been a Menshevik or socialist revolutionary.

Our group tutor was Karolina Miziano. She was Italian, and it was a matter of constant surprise that she had survived the years of the great purges of foreigners. Everybody loved this short, quite ugly but very charming woman. For students who lived with poverty, it was a revelation to see a woman who was always well dressed, her fingers covered with rings and her arms ever waving in Latin gestures. We adored her and with immense pleasure studied her course in world history.

We were still living in the conditions of World War II. Though peace had come seven or eight years before, many of us were still hungry. We dressed modestly and in poor taste. Through all my five years at the University, I only owned one dress and that was red in color. Our stockings were, of course, lisle. Not one of us had a fur coat, a basic requirement for Moscow winters. I wore an old coat, with a collar of scrubbed cat. Boots did not yet exist as far as we were concerned. I froze throughout the winter in a pair of summer shoes. My scholarship was meager 28 rubles. This sum cannot be compared with dollars, but cents. The fare by tram and Metro from the hostel to the University was a total of eight kopeks, but I had to economize and used to walk all the way.

I now find it strange that I didn't suffer from this poverty. I had no debts, and life was full of hope, enthusiasm and happiness. With great joy, I danced to the new and controversial rock and roll, despite the efforts of the *Komsomol* activists to persuade us to abandon bourgeois pursuits. Girls in high heels, or boys in the stovepipe fashions of those days were likely to find their clothes cut, their hair shorn and themselves held up to ridicule in *Komsomol* meetings. Ultimately, the student might face expulsion from the youth movement and the University.

But not all the members of *Komsomol* were so militant. There were among them decent people. I will never forget Yura Afanasiev, the secretary of the Communist Party organization of our course in the History Department of Moscow State University. In those years I never thought to see him standing at the Congress of Deputies together with Andrei Sacharov, a famous scientist, father of the Soviet atomic bomb and a distinguished dissident. Yura was a village boy from Siberia, but it seems that he came to us directly from the army, for he was always dressed in uniform, without insignia, and army boots. He appeared that way throughout five years of study in the University. Tall, black-haired and handsome with rosy cheeks set in a tanned face, Yura was both modest and a brilliant student. As the Communist Party leader, he would never arrange the inquisitions at which people were denounced for the offences that could land them in KGB hands. However, he must have been sufficiently orthodox, for the all consuming killing machine did not swallow him.

After the University, he took up a high Communist Party post in Siberia. I lost sight of him for a long time in Taiga, the Siberian forest. In the 1970s, I came to Siberia to lecture. The wealth, modernity and comfort at Krasnoyarsk Electric Station, amazed me. As I was guided around the city, my hosts constantly repeated "thanks to Afanasiev, we have this..." or "he got us that..." At last I asked: "Who is this Afanasiev? Where did he come from?" They were surprised at my ignorance. Lovingly they explained that he had come to them from Moscow University, and that he looked like Alain Delon, though he was of course more handsome than this French actor. He had countless medals for his selfless work, there are songs about him and the best Soviet poets had praised him in their poetry in the newspapers. Out of all the legends told me about this unknown paragon, I remembered one about the period when they were building the power station. There had been more men than women, and Afanasiev was sent to Leningrad to solve the problem. He spoke at many factories, inviting young women to come to Siberia, promising them that they will marry there. When he returned, he was followed by several trainloads of women. The statistics of how many women followed him differed, but the story always remained the same. Listening to all the legends, I could not imagine that they were speaking about our Yura.

When I returned to Moscow, Yura invited me to spend New Year's Eve with his family. Sitting at the dinner table, I heard him say something about Siberia. I asked whether he had been at Krasnoyarsk. He admitted that it was indeed so, and I was happy to learn that it was my friend who had such a glorious reputation in Siberia. But he had not yet lost his orthodoxy and dogmatism, because he was then serving as president of the highest *Komsomol* school. Later he went to France, where he wrote his Ph.D. He defended his doctoral thesis outstandingly, and went on to become the head of the UNESCO Department in the World History Institute of the Academy of Science—and head of the History Department at the *Communist* magazine, published by the Central Committee of the Communist Party.

This was where something began to happen to him. *Perestroika—*

Mikhail Gorbachev's reform—was not yet happening, but Yura published an article on "The Past and Us." In this article, it is still possible to find the class approach to the study of history, and orthodox ideas. At the same time, there were new ideas that were too brave even for those years. The critics did not like his assertion that the past was necessarily exclusively beautiful and to be admired. Yura had written that there were in the past of Russia things to be proud of, but there were also things of which Russians should be ashamed.

There were flag-waving "patriots" who had set themselves up as guardians of the past, with its symbols and monuments. These were the people who later became members of the *Pamyat* (Memory) organization, which moved toward fascism, with its uniforms, marches and slogans, and spread its efforts out into anti-Semitism and racial discrimination. They fell on Yura with great fervor. He lost all his posts, but Perestroika was soon to begin, and Yura was appointed head of the Historical Archive Institute. He continued to move to the left at a speed beyond the public's ability to keep up with him. He was always several steps ahead of Perestroika. Yura was elected to the Congress of Deputies, becoming a major parliamentary figure. There, he floored everybody by announcing that the entire Congress consisted of "Stalinist-Brezhnev silent conformists in an aggressive majority." Now we know that he was right, but at that time it sounded like an attack on our euphoria over the achievement of democracy.

The history department in Moscow State was split into groups studying the history of the Communist Party, of the Soviet Union, of Slavic Peoples, of Asia, of both Americas, and so on. But none of these attracted my attention. While I lived in Tashkent, I had never thought of myself as different from others. The color of my skin was totally without relevance. But, in Moscow, I began to think about this and developed an interest in the history of peoples of African origin. It happened because I was the only black-skinned student in a University population of 12,000. Many people, and especially those from remote provinces, would approach me with questions about Black people in the United States or in Africa—but I had no answers. And so I developed the interest, the desire, to study Black history. The department of history listed no such courses in the curriculum. I had to go to the administration to explain my historical interests. They invited a professor from the Institute of World History in the Academy of Science, to teach me Black history. This Professor was Igor Dementiev. I spent all my five years studying with him, and I eventually wrote my thesis: "The Struggle of Radical Republicans in the American Congress against Slavery."

My research for the thesis led me to read volume after volume of American history, and to study documents of the U.S. Congress with the dictionary. All this helped me to develop an understanding of the English language, which I had never studied. My school years had been devoted to the study of German, ancient Slavic and Latin. My mother, of course, had spoken English to me, but I always answered in Russian.

When I completed my thesis, I could not submit it. All papers then written, though it was four years after Stalin's death, had to quote from his works. I had to rack my brains to find a way out of the dilemma for the great Soviet leader had never written about slavery in the United States. Here I must offer thanks to my friends who taught me the way all Soviet historians construct their papers and articles: how to slip quotes from Stalin into my work. Quite cynically they explained to me that I must take some of his quotes and give text according to them even if all this has nothing to do with my work. It is important, they said, that you are to use his words, even if it is not important for your work. Doing like this eventually enabled me to defend the thesis and get my degree. Sometimes I wonder why we attack prostitutes. All of us are prostitutes, only some of us sell our bodies and others our brains. I had to do this many times in my life as a scholar.

Throughout my studies, I continued to play tennis, but not with the same professional intensity as in Tashkent. Firstly, the climate in Moscow was different from hot Uzbekistan. In those days in Moscow were only a few covered tennis courts. Then, of course, I had little time to spare. I was trying to keep up my music lessons. In the next door building to the History Department was the University Club. There, I found a music class, taught by Undina Mikhailovna. She was strikingly blonde, covered in black beauty spots and always perfectly dressed. The Muscovites who had pianos at home were doing very well in her class. They even were giving concerts in Bolshoi theater. Living in the hostel, I had no piano and could not work at my music lessons. So I was not a great success with Undina Mikhailovna.

In the next room was a group of students who were trying to play jazz. There had been a tradition of condemnation of jazz, which had begun with the return of the famous writer Maxim Gorki from a visit to the United States in the 1920s. He had written that it was the music of the fat bourgeois, and it reminded him of the slamming of a lavatory seat and the flush of the toilet bowl. Since Gorki derived his literary authority from the backing of Josef Stalin and became a Communist icon for the Soviet people, the rest was inevitable. During this time, it was no longer an offence that could bring immediate arrest by the KGB, but jazz was still not widespread. The ideological leaders of the club would faint every time I mentioned such words as "blues," or "gospel," or "spirituals." To get permission to sing "When the Saints go marching in," I needed to deliver a lecture on the history of Black music. Jazz and spirituals had been considered "bourgeois" music. When I wanted to sing an aria from *Porgy and Bess,* the club director categorically banned my performance. I begged him. I tried to tell him that Gershwin had come to the United States from Russia, had studied Black music and used it for his opera. Nothing helped. I produced my last argument: "Not long ago, a group came from Harlem to Moscow to sing this opera. It was even broadcast on Moscow Radio." His answer was: "Yes. It was broadcast... but only on the second wavelength—not on the first", which was official, for government programs. The response demolished me. I had no ammunition left with which to persuade him.

I was, in fact, the first person to sing jazz and spirituals publicly in the Soviet Union at the gatherings of this jazz club. I was perhaps helped by the recognition that I was Black with American origins. It was, as I protested, "my music, the music of my people."

Our group was invited to give a concert in the Udarnik Cinema, the biggest in Moscow. I was delighted to see several hundred people clapping and enjoying the music to which I was singing. After the concert, I was approached by a man who said: "Are you aware that, in Leningrad, there lives a man who looks like you and has your name?" I remembered vaguely that, when I was a small child, my mother had shown me a picture of a colored boy with Mongolian eyes. She had told me that my father had a son, during an earlier visit to the Soviet Union in 1924. When my parents came to the USSR in 1931, they had brought presents for the boy; though they looked for him, he was lost without trace. The man, whose name regrettably I never knew, now gave me an address of my half-brother. I wrote a letter to Leningrad and, within a few days, Ollava Golden came to see me in Moscow. He was a thin man, dark with curly hair and the Mongolian eyes that I remembered from the photo. Several days later, he was followed by Anna, his mother.

Anna was a tall woman with pronounced Asiatic features. She was the first Udmurd woman to have received an education. She had come to Moscow, on foot, in 1924 from Udmurdia, to study at the Communist University for Oriental Workers. When the first group of Black Americans came to the University, she was astounded. She had never before seen Black people. She was particularly shocked to see my father, who was the biggest and the blackest man in the group, and always very prominent and outspoken. But he was married. The wife who came with him from Chicago was soon to die. In his unhappiness, she was a source of consolation. Anna looked after him. Three years later, Ollava was born. I believe that my father had chosen the name in order to demonstrate his love: all love—Ollava.

I very much liked my newfound relatives, as did my mother when, in 1954, she came from Tashkent especially to meet them both. I called Anna "Mamanya"—a combination of "mother" and "Anna." She called me "my dear daughter." My mother called Anna "dear sister." Mamanya was often to live in my home, particularly when my daughter was born. She taught me to cook very tasty dishes and how to sew. She looked after the home, doing the cleaning and laundry. Ollava was unusually charming. He was a dancing teacher, ballet was such an obsession that he would think about it all the time. He had another obsession. He loved animals of all kinds. In Vladimir, the city where he now lives, he moved from a good apartment with modern facilities to a dilapidated house, solely because it had space. The place had been a garbage dump, but the city allowed him to create a garden with fountains, a lake and waterfalls. This was where he kept his animals—dogs, cats, rabbits, hedgehogs. Once, when I stayed with him and was looking for sheets for my bed I discovered a hibernating snake in the linen cupboard, which prepared to spend winter there. I must confess that the discovery of my half-brother brought new warmth to my life.

Mamanya would tell me the story of her relations with my father. She said that he left the Soviet Union after completing the University, promising to return soon from the United States. She lost track of him, and asked all sorts of organizations to help trace him. The official response was that he had been killed in an American prison. My mother had told me that my father told her about this relationship before they got married. He was trying to find them, but he also received official answers from Moscow that Anna had died. During World War II, Anna had served in the Red Army, getting as far as Vienna.

After the 20th Congress of the Communist Party, in 1956, revealed a lot of secrets of the deeds of Stalin, there was a sense of renewal. Within society, people felt a slight thaw in the ice of rigid conformity. Khruschev came into power, openly condemned Stalin and spoke of the existence of concentration camps in the Soviet Union, which shocked the millions of Soviet people who had no idea of the depths of repression. It would later be clear that he was fighting his own campaign for power and it was for this reason he had revealed the secret existence of the concentration camps. The immediate effect was a sense of dramatic change. Students in the University began to speak out at meetings criticizing the KGB informers, and the infiltration by the Communist Party and KGB into every aspect of student life. But the fresh wind did not blow for long. Several incidents combined to indicate that the old regime was returning. The atmosphere again became heavy and oppressive.

The dining room at our hostel became a scene of confrontation between the conflicting winds. The food served there was so terrible that many students were afflicted with dysentery, and some were even hospitalized for stomach ulcers and food poisoning. For the first time in the history of Moscow State University, under the influence of what appeared to be the new freedom of speech, the residents of the hostel declared a boycott. We formed a delegation, and demanded to meet the Minister of Education. But the Communist Party and KGB machine of the University considered our action to be political and anti-Soviet. One by one, the students participating in the boycott were summoned to the Party and KGB headquarters to be interrogated. The interviewers demanded to know who the ring leaders were, and who had said what. Not all of the students were capable of standing up to these pressures. Some did inform on their friends.

And, of course, our old friends in the *Komsomol* group were delighted to proclaim that we were all anti-Communist and anti-Soviet counter revolutionaries. They demonstrated, screaming like monkeys and waving their flags in glee at the opportunity to show that they were the true pillars of Soviet society. Party leaders flocked to harangue us on the evils of our ways. However, for all that the response was retrogressive. None of us was arrested. All that happened was the insertion of bad marks in our records of study of Marxist disciplines.

I remember my last year of study in the University for many reasons. First of all, I lost many of my friends. Some of them committed suicide, others went insane—all because of the pressures to which we were subjected in the University. In our class there were several students who we called "the war children." They were so named because, during World War II, grenades with which they had been playing had injured them. Some became blind, others had lost fingers or entire hands. My friend Vasya had neither hands nor sight. Nevertheless, he was a brilliant student. Throughout his years at Moscow State, his girlfriend, Galya, guided him everywhere and helped him with his studies. One afternoon, I was standing by the 12th floor window of the 32-storey University building on the Lenin Hills, when suddenly I saw a heavy object dropping past the window and heard a scream of horror from below. On the day of his graduation, after receiving his diploma, Vasya had jumped to his death.

One of Khruschev's innovations was the development of the "Virgin Lands" in Kazakhstan. Many students, and especially *Komsomol* members, went out to work the land. Now we know that it was one of the biggest mistakes of the Communist Party. The Kazakh people had traditionally never touched this land because they knew it to be unfarmable. The Party sent thousands of people there. The do-gooders ploughed and sowed, then watched the topsoil blow away in the wind. One bus carrying students from our University overturned in a nasty accident. Some died, some were injured, and some lost their minds. One girl from our hostel returned full of frenzy, and retained a healthy passion for social activity.

This was a period when the USSR was preparing for the "World Festival of Youth," the first international event in the history of the Soviet Union. The effect on this girl was dramatic. First, she scoured the city to buy flour and bake cakes, possibly in the belief that she was going to feed thousands of visitors from abroad. Then she went to the Moscow Botanical Garden and purchased every available potted cactus. She proceeded to place them in every room of the University, and even in dark corridors. One day she invited a group of Chinese students to a tea party in the hostel. The guests sat in our visitors' room, facing a row of Soviet students, watching everything with great interest. There was no communication whatsoever. They spoke no Russian and we spoke no Chinese. They sat, politely and quietly, for an hour or more, then left. Maybe the idea had been good, but we were still unused to participating in events that had not been directly sanctioned by the Communist Party or the KGB. I imagine the same was true for the Chinese students.

We thought we were beginning to understand this girl when, one day, I was called urgently to our common kitchen. She was frying in vegetable oil all her lecture notes from classes in Marxism. We had to take her to a mental health hospital. In Moscow, that is a difficult thing to do, since there is so little space in such institutions. So we had to enlist help from our tutor, Carolina Miziano, who was not without influence. By sheer coincidence, my German friend, Sigrid, told me that the same thing had happened with an acquaintance of hers in Berlin, who had also fried her Marxism notes in vegetable oil. To this day I have not grasped why Marxism evokes a desire to fry class notes in vegetable oil, for me Marxism was simply a subject.

The last year in University was very critical. A graduate's ability to find employment in the future was dependent not only on his or her final grades, but also on activities in social life in the University. The implication was clear. The student had to be on record as having participated positively in *Komsomol* or Communist Party activities. It happened that a student in my group, Sveta, whose father was a high ranking KGB officer, decided that she must have my post as *Komsomol* leader in order to assure her own future career. At the annual meeting, convened to elect the leader for the final year, Sveta spoke heatedly about my inactivity and incompetence in the job. The gist of her argument was true, and I had no particular interest in retaining the post since, given my foreign origins, it would make no difference to my future. I was ready to step aside, but all my classmates came to me in a panic: "You are proposing to abandon us at the hardest moment of our University life. Now is the time that we cannot afford to have *Komsomol* or Party activists writing bad references in our files. We know that you will not permit them to do so." I finally replied, "Do what you want, but do not involve me in political intrigues."

The election proceedings were repeated four or five times. Each time Sveta criticized me vehemently, and each time I sat silently. A vote would be taken, and more than 90 percent would vote for me. She protested that I had somehow falsified the results, and a fresh election would be held. Finally, she brought along representatives of the Communist Party and the KGB to serve as impartial witnesses. The result was the same. Without lifting a finger, I was reelected. Of course, I understood that I was gaining this immense support not because of my beautiful eyes, or because the students loved me so much, but because this was their fashion of protesting against Party and KGB involvement in our student affairs. Sveta eventually grasped that my post was not up for grabs. She went elsewhere, found herself a high *Komsomol* position, and graduated brilliantly with all the required references. She became a senior official of the Foreign Ministry of the USSR. I would never be able to get such a post even if I were Russian and a member of the Communist Party.

While still in the University, I began to think about what it had given me and what it had not. Even then, I could understand that it did not give me very much, but in those years there was no better alternative. With horror I contemplated other Universities throughout the Soviet Union. I thought, if this was what Moscow State could provide, how bad the situation must be in other cities. For example, we studied the thinking of Marxist theorists only through books written about them for fear that the original thinkers might have made ideological mistakes according to Stalin. For example, Marx's own paper on oil in Rumania and many works of Lenin were not published in the Soviet Union. We were not given the opportunity to read Hegel and Kant. These other books and works were kept in special depositories where students or researchers could enter only with the express permission of the

KGB. The function of the University was to prepare dogmatists. Graduates who were well read in the narrow confines of current Communist scriptures.

Many years later, I saw an American textbook of the history of the Soviet Union. I found mention of historical facts, followed by questions: "What is the point of view on this or that of Mensheviks, Troskyites, social revolutionaries and yourselves?" Such pluralism of opinion was impossible in our years at a Soviet institution of higher learning. The very mention of the words "Menshevik" or "Trotskyite," even objectively and without denouncing them, could result in expulsion from the University. All the answers that we sought were to be found, exclusively, in the *Short History of the Communist Party,* edited personally by Josef Stalin. Nobody was allowed any opinion other than those expressed in this book. Thus, we were taught how not to think.

We were carefully instructed to respect the predominance of Russia in everything. When we sat for tests on Russian history, the last question would always relate to the national primacy in the invention of electric light, radio, ball bearings and so on. One very serious doctoral dissertation discussed "Russia, the Homeland of the Elephant". This is no joke.

At the same time, we did not study the "Silver Epoch" of the 1920s, with its poetry by Akhmatova, Gumilev, Mandelshtam and others that had been persecuted by the Soviet regime. We were not even allowed to pronounce their names. From the history of Africa, we were only permitted to learn about Ancient Egypt and the much more recent Boer War. Nowadays, things are very different, but I had no choice other than to educate myself. Fortunately, I always had friends who knew more than I did from whom I could learn a lot. They gave me books that had been banned in the Soviet Union. They helped me to meet interesting people, many of whom were persecuted for their thoughts. Few people in Moscow had my opportunities.

During my last year in Moscow State, there was a major historic event. Khruschev decided to open a window to the outside world, and so we had the "World Festival of Youth." Not long before the festival, our first three Africans visitors came to Moscow State—two from the Sudan and one from Libya. My friends and I were happy to help them buy warm clothes, find their way around the University buildings and so on. This was the first time that I had seen Africans.

I had been invited to sit on the organizing committee for the festival and was nominated to be responsible for all the delegates from African countries. At last the Festival began, and there were several thousand Africans with thousand of problems. Fortunately, I had several Russian friends who volunteered to help me. We had to do everything, including taking care of plane tickets, finding books on Russian art, arranging trips around Moscow and organizing meetings between Black Americans and Africans. For me, the most important and interesting events were the musical encounters in which Africans participated. I was particularly enthralled by the African ritual dances. I can still remember one pair. She was from the Congo, a short, light-skinned mulatto named Anita. He was Diop, from Guinea, tall, well built and black as ebony. I followed them everywhere, to all their concerts. They danced a ritual, which always ended in Anita collapsing on the floor, quivering and unconscious. Diop carried her behind the scenes and laid her on the floor. Each time it scared me, and I tried to calm her. Anita's trance affected everyone in the hall. Some jumped up to dance, some fainted.

One day Anita confessed that she would like to study classic dance at the Bolshoi Ballet School. I found it difficult to believe. She danced in a way that no Bolshoi ballerina could hope to match.

The participants in the Festival were invited to a reception in the Kremlin. It was the first time that I had set foot within the ancient walls. I was impressed with a tangible sense of history, from ancient times through to the present day. Buildings from the fourteenth century alongside modern twentieth-century structures produced feelings of enchantment within me. Walking across the wide plazas, I was aware of the footsteps of Ivan the Terrible, Peter the Great, Lenin and Stalin. All the squares had become a gigantic dance hall in which the foreign guests danced to the music of jazz orchestras.

Diop asked me to dance. For the first time in my life, I understood the joy of dancing with someone who could so deeply feel the music and respond to your every movement. It was such a moving experience that I broke away, leaving Diop not understanding what had happened, and fled to my Lenin Hills home weeping all the way. I could not explain my two conflicting emotions: the joy of the dance and the terrible understanding that the Africans would all leave and I would never again have such an experience. Obviously I would never travel abroad and, equally obviously, Africans do not come to Russia. The normalcy of Soviet life was such that contact with outsiders was unthinkable.

Many Soviet people were in cultural shock at meeting Africans. The majority of Muscovites, and especially those who had come from the distant provinces for the festival, had never seen Africans before. Some had never seen foreigners, because of the "Iron Curtain." Everything was of interest. What do they eat? How do they dress and behave?

The guests from Africa had never encountered such success. They told me that no other country had ever offered them such admiration and attention. I remember walking in the streets with Diop as young women sidled by and pushed notes with phone numbers into his pockets or followed him for miles. A prevalent Soviet joke claimed that the next festival would only include our own people, for by then, we would have enough locally born Africans. Joking apart, the numbers of people of African descent in the Soviet Union began to grow from that time. There were, of course, growing numbers of African students coming to study, a trend maintained through the last thirty years.

As for my private life, I fell in love on the first day that I came to Moscow State.

From childhood I knew with whom I would fall in love. He would be at least two heads taller than me. I was already tired of looking down on the tops of the heads of boys. He must play tennis, and be able to beat me. How could I respect a man whom I could vanquish? He must be able to dance to rock and roll and play with me four-handed piano. He must be able to read books together with me and discuss them frankly and openly. Then each of us would repair to our own homes. For some reason my fantasies did not go farther. There was no sex in this scheme. I visualized my future life as beginning with an encounter in the library, or on the tennis courts, and continuing with the fulfillment of the entire program of activity.

Valya was different from the man of my dreams. He came to the University from Taganrog, a provincial city in the south of the Soviet Union.

He was majoring in theoretical physics. Valya was really the antithesis of my childhood dream. When I told him about my dreams, he was amazed and announced that he would collect all the books that I had read and throw them on the fire. For me it didn't matter that he didn't conform to all my requirements. He wasn't tall. He didn't play tennis. He couldn't dance or play the piano. He had never read the same books I had—in fact, he didn't read books at all. But he had a beautiful muscular neck from his one sport: wrestling. He was always surprised by my ideas, and really did not know what to do with me. Nevertheless, we met almost every weekend. I was trying my best to understand his problems. I even went with him to see a soccer game—once. There, despite the shouting of the fans, I fell asleep. Several times I drank beer with him, though I never normally touched alcohol. I must admit that he was very careful with me, a young woman who heard about love only from books and never about sex. During those years in the Soviet Union there were no books about sex yet. The first time we heard this word was when Donahue came to Russia from the United States. He made a television program between American and Russian women. American women were speaking featuring mostly about how they like to shop. Russian women's dialogue never uses this word. Instead of the word "shopping" they were using the word "to get." It is not such fun and demands a lot of effort to find what you are looking for, then to stand in the long line and so on. Russian women were mostly speaking about their jobs. One American woman who thought they must speak about something feminist, asked: "What about sex? Do you have sex?" One Russian woman suddenly jumped from her seat and doing energetic denying jests with her hands above her head shouted: "We don't have sex! We don't have sex!" Today it sounds as an anecdote but it happened in reality and was not far from the truth. The next time Russians heard the word "sex," it was from my daughter when she began a talk show on Moscow independent TV—*Love and Sex*. Of course, the show caused a big scandal. A crowd of former communists marched on the Red Square with slogans: "How long shall we permit this mulatto to seduce our husbands and sons?" Many of my friends told me that they do not want to watch this program. They, as it was explained to me, are not interested in sex and do not want to hear about it. Usually, after this they will ask: 'Why does your daughter's talk show begin so late at 12:30 in the morning?' I am from that generation.

After three years of our meetings, Valya moved from Strominka Hostel to the Lenin Hills where he got an apartment of his own. Whenever I came to visit, a thin blonde girl also called Lily would get up and leave. In 1955, Valya informed me that he wanted to marry Lily. Remarkable as it may seem in the context of the 1990s, there was no room in my theories about married life for sex. And so, my relationship with Valya had remained platonic throughout. That was at the root of the relationship that he began with Lily. I think she knew about sex. It came as a terrible blow to me. I felt that I could no longer stay in Moscow, and I went home to my mother in Tashkent.

But this time, I felt no joy in returning to the city that I had loved so much. In my sadness I was even thinking of how to kill myself. At the same time, I realized that if people could endure such suffering, there must be a way to recover. All I needed to do was find that way. A process of self-persuasion began as I reasoned that Valya had not corresponded to any of my early conceptions. Therefore, it was not possible that I had been in love. Consequently, so I thought, it had to be a sickness; and every sickness had its cure. But all these theoretical constructions did not help me.

I returned to Moscow that fall. My emotional sickness did not go away, but at the same time I contracted a real disease. I was crying all day. One day, I sat in the library, reading textbooks, when I suddenly began to weep and felt a lump in my throat. World-famous endocrinologist Sherashevsky diagnosed an affliction of the thyroid gland, and prescribed a drug that had bean named for him. I took the drug for years, but to no avail. Eventually Sherashevsky said that he would operate. However, when my daughter was born in 1962, the condition vanished as mysteriously as it had come without need for the scalpel. Now I believe that all sicknesses come from our mind. But I came to that realization much later.

In the winter of 1956, I went to the Moscow State University's rest house, where we skied on the fields of Borodino, where Napoleon had been defeated in 1812. There I met four girls—harp players and a pianist, all students of the Moscow Conservatory. The harpists were good friends, yet each was totally different. Two were very tall, one a brunette and the other a blonde. The third was medium in height and the fourth was a short, black-haired and dark complexioned Greek. Their friend, the pianist Yura Makarochkin, was taller than I was, with narrow features and striking blond hair. I liked all of them very much. I was impressed by the fact that they were professional musicians which I had wanted to be. All played table tennis very well, especially Yura. He won all the time, and though I do not know why, I didn't like it.

They all read books the likes of which, in my provincial Tashkent upbringing, I had never thought could exist. For example, Yura could quote by heart from the works *Twelve Chairs* or *Golden Calf,* of Ilf and Petrov, who had been banned in the 1930s. He played for me the music of Rachmaninoff and Gershwin, both of whom were also proscribed in the Soviet Union. Yura was exceptionally talented and possessed absolute hearing, an asset to any good musician. His piano teacher was Sofronitsky, a relative of the composer Skryabin, and a fantastic pianist. Though no effort was expended in courtship, I married him several months later. He did conform to my original conceptions, except that he didn't dance.

Shortly before the marriage, Valya appeared and begged me not to marry Yura. He had made a mistake, so he said, when he decided to marry Lily. All he really wanted in life was to marry me. He was ready to try to understand my ideas. He would give up soccer and beer and begin to read the books I read. He was ready to devote his entire life to me... I wasn't interested. My only thought was: how could I have been so stupid. My God, I had been ready to kill myself for him. There was nothing to say. Valya became an expended material for me.

I saw my future only with Yura, and was sure I would be happy with him all my life and would never part from him. I couldn't imagine that, very soon, I would lose him.

We were together all the time. The history department of Moscow State University was adjacent to the Conservatory. We met all the time, between lectures, after classes. We played table tennis, went to concerts, discussed interesting books and played the piano.

Yura had absolute hearing, but could not sing. This surprised me and I asked him how he coped in musical theory class and harmony, where you needed to sing. He responded that he whistled instead. This in fact was how I heard Gershwin's music for the first time. Yura whistled his songs for me. I will never forget how we went to hear Gershwin's *Rhapsody in Blue* when it was performed for the first time in the Soviet Union in 1956.

The big hall of Moscow Conservatory was jam-packed. The conductor was Robert Rojdestvensky, a world famous maestro. Rojdestvensky's mother, an equally famous singer sang Gershwin's songs. The audience waited with bated breath till the end of each song, then applauded wildly. We were standing in the last row of the upper balcony, in the place reserved for students. I wondered why we were not allowed before to hear Gershwin and other beautiful foreign composers. Why couldn't we permit ourselves this joy of listening to good music? I loved Tchaikovsky, but you can't listen exclusively to him several hours every day of your life. We were being spiritually deprived of world culture.

When we wed, there was a problem of where to live. Though I had a separate apartment in the University's hostel, husbands or wives were not allowed to stay overnight. The hostel administration and Communist Party functionaries held nightly searches looking even under the beds and in cupboards. On the other hand, I couldn't move in with Yura because his parents and brother were all living with him in their tiny two-room apartment.

Yura's family accepted me quite nicely, though without much excitement. The father was very favorably disposed to me. He was a very tall, silent man, who occupied some high position in the government. Quietly, he always took my side. Yura's mother looked ascetic, and behaved accordingly. She was always dressed in the same red wool suit. She held several University degrees from the Conservatory, the Institute of Foreign Languages and some technical institution, where she acquired education especially to be of help to her husband. She spoke several European languages and played the piano. Yura's brother also studied at the Conservatory.

The most interesting member of the family was Yura's grandmother. She was extremely erudite and enjoyed fame as a bibliographer. Although she was very old when I joined the family, nobody would dream of calling her old. In any company, she was always at the center of attention. With a command over several languages, she was always perfectly dressed and coiffured.

She never concealed her friendly attitude to me.

Yura's mother was the only one who harbored some reservations about me, and I could understand her viewpoint. This was a time of considerable housing problems in Moscow. Many girls from the provinces were marrying Muscovites in order to register as eligible for housing. There were frequent cases where these girls laid claim to a share of a family apartment. Marrying a Muscovite also would give me an official permission to reside and seek employment in the city. She was scared that I could to claim for a part of their apartment and that was why I had married Yura. I was a threat to their ownership and she felt that we had been too hasty in registering our marriage. Her own marriage, she told me, had only taken place after she and her husband had courted for three years. I was openly given to understand that, if I had a child, I could expect no help from her. Because of the problems of my registration in Moscow, the fact that we had nowhere to live and no money—for his scholarship was even smaller than mine was—I was not contemplating any idea of having a child.

Everything was happening exactly as I had dreamed as a young girl. We met in the daytime, did together all the beautiful things that I had foreseen, had a wonderful time—and then each returned to his or her own home. The only place where we were meeting every day was the radio station of Moscow State University. The head of the station was a silent, colorless man named Vilenin—after Vladimir Ilitch Lenin. He disappeared early in the morning from his office. As we discovered later, his destination was somewhere where he could get a drink. Yura would arrive there with great pleasure. There were several carpeted rooms, each with grand pianos. He played for us without interruption. My girlfriends, Tanya and Luba, and I listened to him with great pleasure. Luba was a small hunchback, who walked with the aid of crutches. She was very favorably disposed to the whole world. She loved everybody and radiated human kindness. Her huge eyes looked out happily through long lashes at everyone who came to her room. And come they did, to take some of the love and happiness that this sick girl was ready to give. Luba was an editor at the radio station.

Tatyana was also an editor. A thin young woman, with blue eyes, she always seemed to be asking: "How can I help you?" Both these girlfriends were unhappy in their private lives. Their salaries were miserably small, but neither ever spoke about their adversities and misfortunes. Never complaining, they were both always smiling and helpful. Yura and I felt that we had a family at the radio station.

A very famous writer, Alexander Beck, who happened to be Yura's uncle, published a very successful book about World War II. He made a lot of money and bought a car as a wedding present for us—and in it my husband was killed in a crash. I was widowed, for the first time, at age 23.

CHAPTER FOUR

To Choose A Life

The next distinguishable period of my life was very short—from 1957 to 1960—but decisive. I was influenced by the people whom I met, and it was they who gave me the initial push along the right road. From them I got both definition and determination. The choices that I made then have stayed with me through all my life.

I had little time to think about the future amid all the happenings of my years at Moscow State. But here I stood, diploma in hand, confronting an administration that, according to the law governing Universities, had to find me employment. In return, by the same law, I must stick with my first job for a minimum three years before I would be free to make choices of my own.

The University administration ordered me to report to a primary school in a village near the city of Saratov, on the Volga River, where I was to teach German language. I asked myself why I had studied five years in this University, and majored in Black history, if I was to end up teaching German in the provinces. But, if I refused the job, my diploma would be taken back and I would be denied any other employment in the Soviet Union. At the same time, I could not hope to find work in Moscow, since I lacked the necessary registration. And my years in Moscow had invalidated my right to registration back in Tashkent. Without registration, there could be no job. Without a job, there could be no registration. Finished. The closing of a Soviet circle!

The only place I could turn for advice was to the friends of my parents. Lia Gavurina, my mother's friend, was again the one to give good counsel. She sent me to the *Komsomol* Central Committee to ask their help. That same day, I went to the monumental building adjacent to KGB Headquarters, quivering with fright. I had never in my life approached such imposing places. Trembling, I opened the great door of the *Komsomol* building, walked in and searched for the room to which Lia had sent me. To my surprise, the occupants of the room listened to me attentively and politely. It later occurred to me that Lia must have known to send me to friends of hers, whom she had primed to expect me. In my nervousness, I gave a garbled explanation about wanting to receive a "free diploma," which would allow me to look for my own employment. I told that I was interested in Black history. There was source material in the Moscow libraries and archives, but no hope of continuing that interest in the village near Saratov.

To my immense astonishment, and without undue bureaucracy, I was given the prized permission to receive the "free diploma." At last I had the paper in my hands. But now what was I to do to unlock the registration-job-registration riddle. I rushed to Robert Ross. As always, he was in high spirits, his usual cheerfully uncomplaining self. He told me not to worry, but to allow him some time. After several days, he came, took me by the hand and led me to the Oriental Institute of the Academy of Science to meet the head of the African Department, Ivan Potekhin. Robert told this famous specialist on Africa about my background and story, ending with the plea: "Only you can help her! Lily's father made a big contribution to the development of the cotton industry in the USSR. She dreams of studying African history, but she does not have Moscow registration. If she has to leave the city, she will have to abandon her life's calling."

Potekhin, a short somewhat dry man with a deeply wrinkled face, was very reserved and laconic. Taking my papers, he studied them in absolute and prolonged silence. I was beginning to worry. And then, without removing his pipe from his mouth, he scribbled something on the papers and said: "To the police!" I grabbed the paper. He had written "...Agree to give her a job." I was wordless with joy. The circle had been broken.

Robert and I rushed to Police Headquarters. In December 1957, I had received a temporary permit to stay and work in Moscow. I was in a constant mood of happiness. I was remaining in Moscow! I had a job in a serious high level Academic Institute and Moscow registration papers! With Lia's help again, I rented a room, with all services for 50 rubles a month. My salary was a microscopic 75 rubles, but my mother agreed to pay my rent.

I entered a big room for a meeting of scholars of the African Department. Though I do not remember the topic of discussion, I cannot forget the faces. I was to work with these people for the next almost 40 years. They were all scholars who had come to this assignment consciously. They were interested in Africa. They loved Africa and wanted to study only Africa. They were extremely well prepared for African studies. All of them were University educated. Most spoke a variety of European languages and even some Oriental and Asiatic dialects. Several, but not all, were specializing in African subjects and knew the appropriate tongues.

Apollon Davidson was among those with a special African education. He stood out from the others because of his brilliant record from Leningrad University, where one can still find the "last of the Mohicans:" Soviet scholars barely touched by the repressions. He was not only erudite, but also—rare among scholars—tall and handsome, with black, curly hair. His first name corresponded exceedingly well with his appearance.

Most of the other African scholars had begun with an Oriental education. Lucy Demkina—a big woman with a loud voice that traveled several floors in the building and narrow slit eyes—had studied India for many years. She seemed to be in a perpetual state of euphoria. Eventually she became a specialist in Indian problems in East and South Africa.

Our department only contained 15–20 people, but the Institute of Oriental Studies was huge, with over one thousand employees. It was one of very few Academic institutions that still preserved the old academic traditions. By comparison with other institutions that had become politicized, our scholars could permit themselves to research not only contemporary economics and sociology of the Oriental countries, they were able to study ancient and medieval history, culture and even numismatics. Some became world famous.

For example, among our scholars who were used to crumpled suits or t-shirts, I encountered one fiftieth European-type man whose pants were always ironed with a razor-sharp crease and whose mustache and beard were always impeccably trimmed. He always wore a fedora and gloves. When I was formally introduced to him, I found out that this paragon of politeness was the son of a famous Russian artist, Nikolai Rerich. Yuri Rerich was a renowned expert on India. He had studied in the Sorbonne, Oxford and Columbia and spoke fluently many Asian languages. As a child, he emigrated to the West with his parents and brother, Svyatoslav. His father opened several galleries around the world, including in France and the United States.

Nikolai, apart from his success as an artist, was expert in Indian philosophy. Yuri's mother wrote 17 books, all of which seemed to be dictated by divine inspiration.

Yuri researched the legends of Shambala. In mythology of South East Asia, there exists a mysterious country somewhere between India, Tibet and China. This is a country not accessible to mere mortals. Here the inhabitants fall into three categories. The first category consists of the spiritual leaders of mankind—Christ, Buddha, and others—reincarnated in order to perpetuate their influence wherever it is needed on Earth. The second category is composed of the great geniuses of mankind who can project inspiration into the minds of others. Thus, for example, the legends feed on light-headed Mozart, who said that his great music came to him by sudden inspiration, or a chemist Mendeleev who insisted that the gaps in his periodic table of the elements were filled by visitation in his sleep. The third group consists of those great figures released into the outer world in order to move mankind in the right directions.

All over South East Asia, people tell these stories. Yuri's father, Nikolai, who was caught in Finland by the Soviet Revolution, realized that if he returned to Russia he would never be able to fulfill his life's dream of visiting India. Moving across Europe and America, he sold his paintings until he had acquired enough money to finance an expedition to the Indian subcontinent. The British suspected that he was a Soviet spy though he had never visited the USSR and did not possess any Russian identification. They attempted to hamper his plans and restrict his movements. Nevertheless, Nikolai painted his vision of the scenes of Shambala. His work helped people who sought the solace of meditation. Then, he vanished without a trace. Just as suddenly, in the 1920s, he materialized in the USSR, moving around the provinces bordering on the Asiatic Soviet Union, studying the legends of Shambala that had spread there. Appearing without travel documents of any kind, he produced a letter from Shambala to the Russian People (which was only published in 1965) and some soil from that legendary country. The evidence was tangible enough that he met with Litvinov, Soviet Commissar for Foreign Affairs. But again he vanished from Russia, reappearing in India, where he opened a scientific research institute for the study of herbs, traditional medicine and other peculiarly Indian sciences.

After the death of his father and the end of World War II, Yuri returned to the Soviet Union. He brought with him his father's art, on condition that they be exhibited as a coherent collection under one roof, in a "Nikolai Rerich Museum," similar to those that already existed elsewhere in the world. Yuri continued his research of Shambala and writing at the Oriental Institute. His life was not easy, for he was considered by some to be a representative of bourgeois science and culture. Communist Party activists constantly criticized him at meetings. Then, one day in 1959, he was listening to a news broadcast when the radio announced, out of the blue, that Khruschev had ordered the Rerich art collection to be split up and distributed throughout the USSR museums. The shock was too much for Yuri. He died of a massive heart attack. Our Institute had lost a world-famous scholar. I remember that his brother Svyatoslav Rerich, and his beautiful Indian dancer wife, came for the funeral. Yuri was buried according to Indian ritual.

I appeared in the Institute at the very beginning of African studies in the Soviet Union. Africa had been under a colonial curtain, both de jure and de facto, since the late nineteenth century. One or other European power, all of which were strictly controlling access to prevent the advent of anticolonialist ideas, dominated each African country. The study of cultural and human problems was regulated by colonial bureaucrats, who were prepared to permit research exclusively by Eurocentric "right thinking" scholars. Their work was aimed, not particularly at greater understanding of African society, but rather at gaining the knowledge necessary for the shaping of policy by the metropolitan authorities in Europe.

Czarist Russia never had colonies in Africa. The only attempt at colonization was made in the seventeenth century, when Peter the Great sent his navy to Madagascar. But that expedition was unsuccessful. One of the first Russians to study Africa was a famous poet, Gumilev (the husband of the poet Anna Ahmatova), who visited the continent four times in the 1920s. He returned with an excellent collection of African ethnography, which can still be found in the Leningrad ethnology Museum. Those Russian scholars who began to study Africa in the 1930s were not allowed to travel there. Some of them, as a result of their interest outside of the USSR, lost their jobs and even their lives.

When I entered the Department, Potekhin was in the process of consolidating the experts on Africa. His role, as he saw it, was to prepare to assist the African peoples in their struggles to achieve independence, and to explain to the Soviet people what was going on in that continent.

One day, Ivan Potekhin invited me for a talk and proceeded to tell me, "On one side, you have a musical education. On the other, you have been trained in history. Why don't you begin to study the history of African music at the post-graduate school in the Academy of Science." Without thinking, I agreed, especially because he said that he would serve as my Ph.D. supervisor. This would be an honor for me since his name was connected not only with the rise of Soviet African studies, but also with the history of worldwide African studies.

Potekhin was born on 1 October 1903, in a remote Siberian village. At the age of 14, he began to work as an unskilled laborer in a local factory. By 1930, he had achieved a place as a student of languages and culture in the African Department of the Oriental Institute in Leningrad. When he graduated, he defended his thesis, "The History of Agrarian Relations in South Africa," and was already author of more than 30 works published in the Soviet Union, the United States, Europe and Africa. In his book, on the *Formation of National Identity of the Bantu,* published in 1955, he analyzed racial, national, social and economic problems of South Africa. In 1960, he published a book entitled *Africa Looks Forward,* in which he showed the modern development of African societies.

In the bright light of *Perestroika,* it is very easy to criticize works that were written in the 1950s and 60s. But I will not do that, because Potekhin as a pioneer of Soviet African studies was compelled to follow Marxist criteria, and apply Marxism to African realities. Though he may not have agreed with all those ideas, he did not have the freedom to stray in his thinking. However, I believe that, in his self-perception, Potekhin was a true Marxist. More importantly, he was preparing and uniting the cadres of educated Africanists. In 1949, on his initiative, a Conference of Soviet Africanists, where the problems of colonial peoples were discussed, was convened for the first time. Ivan Potekhin presented a paper entitled "The Crisis of the

Colonial System of Imperialism, and the Task of Soviet Ethnography."

The first collected anthology of Soviet research in this field, *The Peoples of Africa,* was published in 1954. It was the first time in the Soviet literature that the history of the peoples of Africa, from ancient times, was being presented. The introduction to the book was written by Potekhin, then translated into French and published as a book, entitled *Is the Continent of Africa Backward?* The volume was distributed widely, with great success, in Africa. So great was its political resonance that the book was banned by the colonial powers.

In 1958, Potekhin proposed that I should go to my birthplace, Tashkent, as a delegate to the first Conference of Asian and African Writers. He said that he expected Paul Robeson and Dr. Du Bois, "your friends," to attend. "Try to talk to them about opening of an Institute of African Studies in Moscow. I hope their authority will help us..."

In October of that year, I went to my beloved Tashkent. This trip, of course, was different from those of ten years ago when I was playing tennis after World War II and had traveled by trains that took many days to reach the various cities of the USSR. This time I came by plane. It took only three and a half hours.

Among all the delegations, the Ghanians enjoyed great popularity. First of all, they were representing the first nation of Africa to achieve independence in 1957. Secondly, theirs was the most numerous delegation. They were dressed in colorful kente cloth. But one of the young women, who was extremely beautiful, was dressed in jeans. Uzbek people, in their Muslim Republic, had never seen or heard of such a fashion. I also distinctly remember her French "Ma Griffe" perfume, which I was never able to afford on a Soviet salary. She was of Caribbean origin and had studied in London and Paris. When Nkrumah became President, he had brought his girlfriend to Ghana.

At one point, she asked me: "Why do the Uzbeks look at me so strangely, as if some of them pitied me?" It was difficult to explain. But, as far as most Soviet people had been informed by the mass media, the Africans were poverty stricken, non-educated, deprived of everything. Yet here were Africans who were well-dressed in African and European fashions, who had studied in the best European Universities, traveled around the world and who were apparently much happier with their lives than were the average Soviets, who could not dream of being dressed like their African guests. This conflicted with the stereotypes impressed on them by political commentators who dwelt on the evils of colonialism. I told her about the previous year's Festival of Youth in Moscow when the Russians had been able to see the smart Paris and London fashion shoes peeking out from under the African national robes of dancers. They had expected to see hungry people dressed in tatters. Instead they had met affluent students who spoke several foreign languages, were European dressed and who did not forget their culture.

I became very friendly with John, a member of the Ghana delegation. He was not particularly black or endowed with eyes that would be in place in a Mongolian face. He told me that he had come with the delegation in order to learn about the USSR since he was preparing to become Ghana's first ambassador in Moscow. Not long after the conference, he indeed came to Moscow with his wife and ten children. For many years, he performed with dignity his duties as ambassador of the first country of tropical Africa to achieve independence.

October 1958 was also the month in which Guinea attained independence. On the third day of the conference, an official representative of the new country appeared on stage to be greeted enthusiastically by both Soviets and foreigners. Before our eyes, Africa was gaining freedom. We could never have guessed next year, in 1960, on the initiative of the Soviet Union at the United Nations, more than 30 African colonies would be granted their independence and the year would be declared "The Year of Africa."

Looking back, I realize that we were too naive and optimistic. We really believed that the entire continent would soon be free of colonialism, and that all Africa's problems would be solved automatically. There would be no more wars, no poverty, and no hunger. More than thirty years later, we can see just how deluded we were. But the spirit of self-determination filled the air in the Navoi Theater of Tashkent where the conference held its deliberations.

The general enthusiasm knew no bounds when legendary figures, like Dr. Du Bois and Paul Robeson, appeared in our midst. It is already more than a century since these two were born. On the one hand, there are still discussions about the role and impact of these men. Yet, on the other side, there are already generations of Americans too young to have even heard of them.

Dr. William Du Bois, historian and poet, economist and sociologist, was one of the founding fathers of African American literature. In his books, he formulated theoretical generalizations characterizing the Black history of the United States and of Africa. His pen brought to life many pages of that history that had been forgotten or consciously falsified. He chose as a field of study the problems of race—a subject that was to hold his attention through a long and productive life. His writings encompassed ways to develop continents, problems of war and peace. and struggles for freedom. His books constantly lay open on the tables of all students of Black anthropology and ethnography, history and economics, literature and culture.

Africans and Black Americans recognize Du Bois' activity as extraordinary. Prime Minister Nkrumah of Ghana cited him as a brilliant scholar and a great civil rights fighter. Du Bois fought for the cause of civil rights long before the concept was popular. He was the founder of many organizations that fought for the equality of the African Americans, such as the Niagara Movement and the NAACP. He was the initiator of a series of Pan African Conferences that convened in 1919, 1921, 1923, 1927 and 1945. He visited the Soviet Union in 1926, 1936 and 1948. In 1950, he formed the Peace Center, and became a member of the World Peace Council. In 1951, at the age of 82, he was arrested for anti-American activities. His passport was confiscated and he was forbidden to travel abroad. The minute that his passport was returned, he came to the USSR.

I knew from my mother that my father had known Dr. Du Bois, and he and his generation had been greatly influenced by his first book, *The Negro*, published in 1915. I personally had studied the documents of Du Bois' Pan African Conferences while at Moscow State University. Now, I was very thrilled at the thought that this ninety-year-old sage was coming to Tashkent, and that I would see him. I remember vividly the day that he appeared. A meeting was already in session. Everyone stood up and applauded. From his energy and perpetually sound mind, it was impossible to know that he was in his nineties. He was a short man, sporting a French-style Van Dyck beard.

His skin was almost white, though there was strong pigmentation on his face and hands. For some unknown reason, he was not ushered onto the stage from the backdrop. Instead, he walked through the auditorium and proceeded, to the dumbfounded shock of the audience, to walk confidently up a narrow plank that stretched over the orchestra pit with his arms extended like a tight rope walker's pole. It was a performance worthy of a young, trained gymnast. As he gained the stage and quietly took his seat among the presidium, there was a collective sigh of relief. The applause began again, rising to a crescendo.

I was to meet him several times. He spoke at length about my father whom he remembered and expressed a desire to see my mother, who was still living in Tashkent. One day he asked me to prepare a meeting for him with the writers from tropical Africa. I met all those delegates and invited them to a party with him. We all gathered in a big room, with a round table at its center. At first, the Africans were very shy. They were in the presence of a legend. I had difficulty in persuading them to sit at the table and talk with the great man. The bravest among them was a famous Senegalese writer and film-maker, Sembene Usmane. He began by asking Dr. Du Bois to explain the meanings of the tattoos of many of the African tribes. The party quickly developed into a very significant scientific discussion.

Dr. Du Bois had come to the Soviet Union accompanied by his wife, a famous writer and journalist named Shirley Graham. Her book about Frederick Douglass had just been published in the Soviet Union. Paul Robeson, who had received his passport at the same time as Du Bois—after eight years of travel prohibition—also brought his wife, Eslanda Good. I hadn't seen them since 1937 at the sanatorium in Kislovodsk.

Paul Robeson was very popular in the Soviet Union. He had visited for the first time in 1934, and had returned almost every year up to the outbreak of World War II. In the 1920s, he moved from the United States to England to study the history and culture of Africa at the London School of Economics. Paul could not agree with futurologists who claimed that the development of the African nations would take a thousand years. For that reason, he was interested in the experience of the Soviet Union in dealing with analphabets especially in the north. In 1934, he came to the USSR at the invitation of world-famous film director Sergei Eisenstein. The friendship of these two masters of modern art was based not only on personal liking, but also on shared views and interests. Eisenstein, like Robeson who already knew 25 languages—including four African languages, at least one Chinese and one Arabic—was also erudite and well educated. It was not surprising therefore, that these two could sit all night debating the comparative linguistics of Chinese and the language of the Efik peoples of West Africa.

During his first visit to Moscow, Robeson had met a man who he had dreamed of meeting for many years: the renowned theater reformer, Konstantin Stanislavsky. He also studied the text of *Othello* in Russian, together with the veteran actress of the Moscow Art Theater, Sophie Halutina. He also discussed the staging problems with famous actors Alexander Ostuzhev and Maxim Strauch. He was the guest of Commissar of Foreign Affairs Maxim Litvinov, at whose dinner table he met General Tuchachevsky. He had a lot of opportunities to meet Soviet actors, singers, musicians and filmmakers. He spoke at the Moscow Film Center and at the Society of Cultural Relations with Foreign Countries. There he sang arias from operas and Russian, Chinese and American songs. From Moscow he went to Leningrad, where he visited the Institute for National Minorities. At the Institute he was able to talk to representatives of different minorities, who lived in the north of the USSR and did not have an alphabet with which to express themselves in writing. Like many other Black leaders in the past and even now, Robeson was looking for the alternative to capitalism and was hoping that socialism would be a more appropriate economic system for Black people. Maybe this was a reason why he and many other American communists, from DuBois to Angela Davis, did not want to hear about the problems of Russian people. They did not want to hear about millions of innocent people who lòst their lives in the concentration camps.

Paul visited the Soviet Union several times between 1934 and the start of World War II in 1939. In 1937, Paul was in Spain, singing for the soldiers of the Republic and of the International Brigade. He, like leading writers of the time, including Langston Hughes, Ernest Hemingway, Nicholas Gilyen, Arthur Koestler and others, was acutely aware that the battle against Franco was the world's first attempt to resist the spreading cancer of fascism.

In 1939, well ahead of his time, Paul understood the winds of change that would soon come to Africa. With Du Bois as his vice president, he formed his "Council on Africa." The task of this body was to inform the American public about the so-called "dark continent" and, in doing so, he attracted to its work many Africans, among them Kwame Nkrumah who was destined to be the first president of Ghana. After World War II, the Council sent Eslanda Robeson to the newly formed United Nations to defend the interests and demands of the colonial peoples who lacked their own voice in the UN during that time.

Each time that Paul sang in the USSR, his concerts met with tremendous success. From my home in Tashkent, I watched his triumphant journeys and collected clippings from the newspapers. Recently, I found my collection. In 1949, he came to the Soviet Union for the 150th birthday of the great Russian poet, Alexander Pushkin, who was of African origin. Robeson's first concert on that visit was given on 8 June in the Tchaikovsky Hall in Moscow. The next day, he sang at the Palace of Culture of the Moscow automobile factory. The newspapers wrote that people were even standing among the orchestra and in the aisles. I also found an article that Paul Robeson had written about Pushkin which was published on 11 June in a literary newspaper. There he wrote:

> Pushkin was not only the sun of Russian poetry
> but also of world literature. Familiarizing with Pushkin's
> work brings delight to everyone. For me, as a singer
> and musician, his works were always a fount of in-
> spiration. I discovered the name of Pushkin a long
> time ago. My people have a great interest in the genius
> Russian poet. The Black professor, Dr. Du Bois, who
> studied his works for a long time, wrote a book about
> Pushkin. Because of my interest in the Soviet Union
> and Russian culture, I began to study Russian language
> a long time ago. The first book that I read in the Russian
> language was a volume of Pushkin's poems.

I also have in my collection a clipping with Robeson's last words when he left the Soviet Union in 1949, for they were to play a critical role in his future. He said:

> I am leaving the Soviet Union in high spirits, as
> if wings sprout from my back to carry me to a new,
> more intensive struggle for peace. I take with me from
> Moscow new ideas and new feelings. And I want to
> bid you farewell. I am, I was, and I always will be a
> devoted and sincere friend of the Soviet Union.

This message was to be in the forefront of the anti-Communist witch hunt in which Paul Robeson would find himself trapped. Ironically—and unlike Dr. Du Bois who took the fateful step at the age of 92—Paul never joined the Communist Party. His admiration for the Soviet Union was not political in the conventional sense. Rather, it sprang from his deep conviction that the USSR was devoid of the racial discrimination that then still troubled the United States. At one level, he was dimly aware of the other injustices of the Soviet system but, like many others including my own parents, he was incapable of believing the whispers and rumors about prisons and concentration camps. It was all too easy to dismiss the stories told to him as the bourgeois inventions of enemies of the first socialist utopia. And, in parallel, Senator Joseph McCarthy was involved in purges that, at an intellectual level, were no less severe than the physical ones of which the whisperers were accusing Stalin.

Paul Robeson returned from the USSR to find himself a target. He was not allowed to sing, even in the churches and bars. Acquaintances turned away rather than greet him on the street or in public places. He was summoned to appear before the US Senate Committee on Un-American Activities, deprived of his passport and forbidden to travel. By contrast, mountain climbers in Kirghizia (another Central Asia Republic of the Soviet Union) at that time chose to name a recently discovered peak for him. In Lvov, a city of the Ukraine, a street became Paul Robeson Boulevard. A Soviet publishing house released a biography and an anthology of the songs that he sang. The World Peace Movement gave him its annual award. His appearance at the Conference of Asian and African Writers in Tashkent, in 1958, was the first time that Paul Robeson, and Dr. Du Bois, were able to travel again after the restoration of their passports.

Eslanda Good, Paul's wife, who accompanied him to Tashkent, was an outstanding woman. Her dynamism and fearless energy startled whoever met her. The old adage that behind every successful man stands a woman was invented for her. She was involved in everything, aware of everything and scared of no one—anywhere in the world. Despite her activities in the World Peace Movement, and her peaceful advocacy for the Council on Africa at the United Nations, Eslanda was unwilling to tolerate the existence of colonialism. She viewed the concept as the threat to world peace, clearly understanding that the destiny of that ideal was dependent on the liquidation of colonialism in Africa. This aspect of her character is clearly evident in the documents of the United Nations, and particularly those of the Trust Council that which bore the responsibility for the mandates granted by the world community to the imperial powers. For the colonial peoples, this beautiful and heroic woman, with her sharp sense of humor, was the true defender of their interests. She brought their petitions to the world assembly but, more than that, Eslanda exposed the devious plans of European capitals to delay, by any means, the advent of freedom—or, in the guise of that freedom, to substitute other forms of power and suppression.

Eslanda Good was Black but also belonged to a famous Spanish Jewish family with a long tradition of fighting for civil rights in the United States. Her grandfather, Francis Luiz Cardozo, was one of the first to attempt the education of Black Americans. She had been a student of Dr. Du Bois, the patron of the civil rights movement. Listening to his lectures, she was greatly influenced by his ideas about the liberation of the Black peoples. In the 1930s, she studied together with Paul Robeson at the London School of Economics, majoring in history and culture, anthropology and ethnography of Africa. It was there that she became acquainted with many Africans who were destined to become leaders of their nations, including Nkrumah, Jomo Kenyatta of Kenya and others. In 1936, she went with her eight-year-old son to Africa, on a mission to further her political studies. The result was a book about her travels, published by Ivan Potekhin in the Soviet Union.

This conference in Tashkent was a towering event in my life, and some of its influence still remains with me. I met African and Asian writers who were to become famous figures in world politics and literature. I soaked up the heady atmosphere of the approaching freedom of Africa. I was impressed by the way in which the delegates received their distinguished visitors from America. And, as always, I enjoyed the renewed opportunity to spend time with the Robesons and Du Bois'. With them I went to my mother's home, and from them I learned a lot that I had not known before about my father's life in the United States.

But not all was positive. The head of the delegation of the USSR was a writer named Anatoly Sofronov. Not being in the first rank of Soviet authors, he was secretary of the Union of Writers, and editor-in-chief of a popular magazine. His contacts in the Central Committee and the KGB made him into a big political figure. He was a huge flabby man for whom the conference only represented an opportunity to drink free vodka every evening. This he did at the so-called "friendship dinners." Suddenly he began to show an interest in me. His persistence in chasing me and always attempting to be near me, was a constant embarrassment. Many people noticed it. At one point, three writers from Uganda approached me and asked, openly, whether Sofronov's attentions were disturbing to me. I was surprised, and wanted to know how they had noticed this. The answer was: "Sister, if you get tired of him, just tell us." However, they did not need to interfere. Shortly thereafter his wife appeared. I encountered him carrying her bags, and he muttered through gritted teeth: "I didn't have enough time..."

When I later returned to Moscow, Potekhin called me into his office and whispered that the KGB had received anonymous letters accusing me of spending too much time with the foreigners, rather than the Soviet delegation. For many years, I would continue to have problems in my life because of what were undoubtedly Sofronov's letters. I was considered an "unreliable person." I was not allowed to travel abroad. Correspondence from abroad was not delivered to me. I was forced to write my regrets in response to invitations to attend international conferences.

Meanwhile, the Tashkent conference was immediately followed by the First International Asian and African Film Festival. I decided to stay with Dr. Du Bois, Paul Robeson and their wives for the opening of the festival. I will never forget Paul's concert at Chlopkorob Stadium—which translates from Uzbeki as "Cotton Growers." As in all countries close to the tropics, the sun sets quickly with no twilight. It was still light as we approached the stadium. But by the time we found our seats, night had fallen. In the darkness we could hear thousands of people breathing in the night air and occasionally shouting to each other. Suddenly, all the huge projectors came to life. All pointed to the spot where, in the center of the great stadium, Paul Robeson stood alone. The audience was completely still as, to our surprise, he began to sing in Uzbek language. The air filled with the roar of acclaim. He moved on to American, Russian, Yiddish and Swahili...

Days later, I changed my air tickets in order to fly with the Robesons, Du Bois and my mother to Moscow. Afterwards I heard that the plane on which I was originally scheduled had crashed on take off at Tashkent Airport.

Paul and Eslanda took a large suite at the Hotel Moscow. Dr. Du Bois and Shirley were not far away at the Hotel National, across a square. The Moscow hotel was a recent building of Soviet times, while the National predated the Revolution. But both faced on to Red Square, traditionally the center of the city.

I began what was to be the best period of my life. Each day started at breakfast with Paul and Eslanda Robeson at the Hotel Moscow, and concluded with dinner as a guest of Dr. Du Bois and his wife. These became the habits of an entire year. I was so energized that I can still feel it so many years later. In my conversations with them, I found out more about Africa and the United States than I had in my five years at University. I gained immersion in the problems of contemporary world politics. I was meeting their friends, among them prominent Soviet and foreign politicians, musicians, writers and scholars. But, for me only this quartet was interesting. I was wholly absorbed in my personal contacts with them.

Dr. William Du Bois was always serene, never excited or unhappy, and ever the courtly gentleman. He was never at a loss for a compliment to women. He was constantly drawing on an immense fund of jokes and personal anecdotes. Like those few people who are at peace with themselves, he could raise a laugh at his own expense. His democratic behavior, accessibility and appearance constantly misled me in believing that he was much younger. One day I posed a tactless question: "What is the secret of your longevity? How could you have lived so long, yet have remained so vital and vibrant?" Having asked the question, I was immediately apprehensive at having perhaps crossed some invisible line. But he found nothing untoward, and answered with his customary humor: "You know, for the last sixty years, I have allowed myself nothing extra. Before breakfast, lunch and dinner, I drink cognac. And after breakfast, lunch and dinner, I smoke a cigarette."

When we walked the icy Moscow streets and I offered a helping hand, he rejected it angrily. He never wanted to demonstrate that he was old.

His wife was much younger than he was, being a friend of his granddaughter and the same age as she was. By contrast with Eslanda Robeson, Shirley Graham never looked beautiful, but she was a very energetic woman. With Eslanda, she went in 1958 to Accra, in Ghana, to the first Conference of Presidents of Independent Africa. They returned to tell their husbands what had happened at the meeting. I remember one of the stories, when these two ladies were fighting for the Chinese flag. Since both were endowed with a sharp sense of humor, we spent the evenings roaring with laughter. My time with them was unforgettable, and today I can admit that I have never, before or since, met more interesting people.

Usually Paul ate his breakfast in silence. He responded tersely to Eslanda, and left immediately after the meal. I admired Eslanda, and spent a lot of time with her. For Paul, she was everything—wife, governess, and manager. She stood backstage when he sang, holding a fresh shirt, because he changed after each song. She held press conferences and wrote articles about him. Beyond her obvious beauty, humor and intellect, Eslanda was exceptionally well informed, could speak several languages and had been educated in chemistry, anthropology and journalism. Above all, she was wise. I came to her for advice and explanations about political, cultural and human affairs.

When she sickened with cancer, and was admitted to the downtown Government Hospital, I spent even more time with her. Each morning I brought her newspapers from all over the world, and read to her. Whenever she heard about the actions or speeches of one or another national leader or president, she would dictate to me personal letters to them. On my way to the Oriental Institute, I would drop the letters into the post office. Through long evenings, she told me about her travels and her friends in the different countries of Asia and Africa.

She was always interested in my life. One day, she asked me what I would like to do with my future. I told her of my interest in Black history and about the state of African studies in the Soviet Union: the Academy of Sciences, because of its conservatism, did not want to expand into such new areas. Then I asked her directly whether Paul and Dr. Du Bois could be of help in the campaign to open an "Institute of African Studies." Becoming very excited, she assured me that they would do everything possible. I remember that, at one of our dinners, all four of them were discussing the problem when Eslanda said that they must begin with the head of state, Khruschev. By chance, they were to go to a dinner with him on the very next day. They used the opportunity to talk to him about the idea as if they had been thinking about it for months. Khruschev could not stand against their authority and the energy of their assault. Being impulsive by nature, he decided right then to establish such an Institute. Three days later, the newspapers reported a decision by the Academy of Sciences to open an "Institute of African Studies." In December 1959, I became the first researcher to be employed in the Institute. There was no bureaucratic involvement, which was a measure of the authority and standing of Paul Robeson and William Du Bois in the USSR.

The time had come to introduce my American friends to Professor Potekhin. Dr. Du Bois was hospitalized in Barvicha Government Sanatorium, outside Moscow. He was weak, but they were able to maintain a conversation as equals. So freely did they relate to each other that it seemed as if they were old friends renewing a long conversation. They began by agreeing that the time was ripe to study Africa far more deeply and seriously. Dr. Du Bois became excited, which was very rare for a man whose behavior was usually reserved. They spoke of the future of the Institute of African Studies in terms of making a center for sociology and anthropology.

Du Bois later would write in his memoirs that there had to be a series of research projects based on the one central idea that all the objectives of study must converge into one. History must meet sociology, and culture must converge into biology. Only the complexity of all these findings together could give understanding of the continent of Africa. The main task of the Institute, so Du Bois thought, must be the popularization of the history of the African peoples. This should be achieved by the diffusion of knowledge of that history through libraries and museums, by textbooks and lectures. He argued that lack of understanding must inevitably lead to a popular conclusion that the peoples of Africa possessed neither history nor culture. He also thought that the Institute must offer scholarships to African students and invite scholars to do their scientific work within its walls. It should also open, within Africa, a center for the scientific study of the continent.

Both Du Bois and Potekhin spoke of the future of Africa, as the countries began to develop industry. They agreed that it was the Soviet Union that must give assistance to the new Africa. It would be important to foster the education of the Africans.

Now the time had come to introduce Potekhin to the Robesons. We were invited to lunch at the hotel. And here Paul Robeson explained that the languages of races and nations that are exploited and discriminated against have much in common. The two men began to compare African and Asiatic languages, as Paul demonstrated the different sounds. He made a powerful and convincing case for his theory, though I am far from sure that his basis was correct.

Eslanda later told me that Khruschev had asked her advice on whom to appoint as head of the new Institute. Since she was not familiar with the Soviet scholars in the field, she asked me to characterize them for her. I told that there was only one other man who could be compared with Potekhin. Professor Ollderogge was a scholar, living in Leningrad, who had received a special education in African studies in Germany. A world-renowned figure, he knew several African languages and was familiar with many African cultures. But, if she really wanted my opinion, Potekhin would be the better director for the Institute since his approach was more modern and his understanding of political problems of Africans much deeper. Eslanda studied me carefully, and said: "Okay, let it be this way. But remember, Potekhin

Grandfather Hillard Golden and grandmother Sweet Mama in Yazoo County, Mississippi standing near their house, which was later burned by KKK.

Top left: Oliver Golden (standing, left), with the first group of African Americans who went to Moscow to study in the communist university of oriental workers. Seated is Jane Wilson, his first wife, who died in Moscow, 1924.

At right: This is how Tashkent looked when my parents arrived in 1931.

My father is playing the dutar, a national musical instrument, with his Uzbek friends, 1932.

My parents in the Caucasian mountains. 1933

My mother's mother, Bessie Bialek.

My mother Bertha Bialek, soon after she emigrated from Poland to the United States.

Black agronomists, who came with my father to Uzbekistan on the ship "SS Germany." My father is first on the right, my mother – in the middle with a raised hand. He was 44 and she was 26. November, 1931

Lily Golden at six and a half months.

Lily, two years old, on the way to kinder-garten.

Lily at fourteen months.

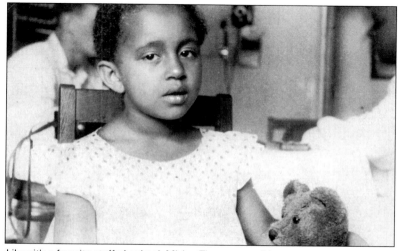

Lily with a favorite stuffed animal, Misha. Three years old.

Top right: Eleven year old Lily with her mother on a Tashkent street. May 9, 1945. Victory day at the end of World War II.

At the opening parade of an All-Soviet tennis championship in Tallinn, Estonia.

Top left: Lily with baby-sitter Auntie Nadya, who spent more than 30 years with our family.

Playing singles at All-Soviet tennis championship in Saratov. 1948.

Yura and Lily. We thought that we shall be happy forever ... 1957

In Batumi, with Rita Emelyanova, a Soviet Union tennis champion in the 1950s.

My first husband Yura Makarochkin plays the piano for our friends. 1957.

My dear friends Galya (left) and Vera (right). Picture taken during our first year at Moscow State University. 1952.

Lily with friends at a student demonstration in Moscow. 1952

I am participating in a motorcycle drive between Moscow and Kiev. 1953

Igor Ter-Ovanisian, an olympic long distance champion. Paris.

The reception at the conference of Asian and African writers. Tashkent, 1959. In the middle dancing is Senegalese writer/filmmaker, Sembene Ousmanne.

At right of Lily Golden is ethnomusicologist from Ghana, Kwabena Nketia. He is an advisor on African music for the UNESCO. Standing with German ethnomusicologists at the International Music Congress. 1961.

Lily Golden at the Graduation party sitting next to her second husband, Abdulla Kassim Hanga who graduated from Lumumba University. 1962.

I am playing the role of a coquette on a Congolese bus who is trying to prevent CIA men from arresting Lumumba, the first Congolese president, in the film, *The son of Africa*. 1966.

Jim Patterson is a naval officer and professional poet. His father came to Russia from the United States with Langston Hughes in 1932. Moscow.

I am playing a role of an African princess with her entourage coming to the 'Death Zone' in the film, *Silver Dust,* 1966.

will never forgive you for this." "Why?" I wanted to know. "Because he is a very strong man, and he will not want to be in anyone's debt. And, he's a very short man and you are too tall. He has to look up to you." I insisted that he had been very kind and helpful to me and, in any case, it was he who had asked me to help him. Eslanda responded: "Lily, I have told you what will happen. But, if you insist, let him be the director..."

The dreams about the future of the Institute were not fulfilled, but Eslanda's prophecy was.

My last meeting with the four of them was at a farewell dinner in Ivan Potekhin's home. I have no recollections about the subjects of conversation. But I do remember that they were all singing. Robeson's bass and Du Bois' tenor, lifted in spiritual, combined into an unforgettable concert...

At the end of their life in Moscow I sensed that something was wrong with Paul Robeson. He looked gloomy. When he smiled, the radiance of that smile could not be resisted, but nevertheless, he was perhaps already feeling the approach of his future sickness, or something was happening in Moscow that was not to his liking. Eslanda once told me of an unpleasant conversation that Paul had had with the Soviet Minister of Culture, Ekaterina Furtseva, who tried to forbid him from singing Jewish songs. There were several other things that happened with him. He found out that his Jewish friend filmmaker Phepher and several of his other friends were killed in the concentration camp. Many Russians were coming to him, asking to use his authority to help to free their innocent relatives or friends from concentration camps. In fact, they approached every Black American leader, asking for help, especially those, who innocently got into American prison, hoping that they understood their problems. All of them refused to help because they were thinking that if those Russians are in prison, it means they are the enemies of the country where there is no racism. Such country cannot be bad. I do not want to mention here the names of those African American leaders, because they were thinking only about Black people, whose main problem is racism.

Robeson was in a state of mental confusion, and one day, in his suite in Moscow, he tried to kill himself. He understood his tragedy. Many people abroad, who were thinking like him, did the same and succeeded.

He was saved, but began to develop a complex of persecution. He got very ill, and Eslanda took him to London. From there they moved to East Germany. In 1966, she wrote me one last letter, saying that "a hot summer" had begun in the United States. They must be there—with their people. She also wrote that she needed another operation for cancer, which she would prefer to have in the USSR, but she must go to America with Paul. Soon thereafter Eslanda died. Paul was taken to his sister to Philadelphia. In 1998 in Moscow nobody celebrated his birthday, as it was usually celebrated every year in April. But there were published several articles about him. One of them was titled: "The tragedy of a Giant." Paul Robeson died in 1974 and several hundred people came to his funeral.

Dr. Du Bois and Shirley went to China, then on to Ghana. He began to fulfill his lifelong dream of publishing an African Encyclopedia. But he died in 1963, at the age of 95.

These unusual people had passed through my life like brilliant comets. I would later meet many outstanding personalities and leaders of Black America and Africa, but would never again encounter such dizzy heights of the human spirit. My understanding of the world had been enriched. My horizons had been widened.

CHAPTER FIVE

My African Husband

As a young woman, I was not particularly worried that I did not have a real home. My possessions amounted to two suitcases, and it was not at all difficult to move from one place to another. When I began my postgraduate studies, I moved into an apartment in the hostel of the Academy of Science. Though most students shared accommodations, with either two or three to a room, the Academy decided to accord me some respect and I lived alone.

When I received my job at the Institute of African Studies, I had to leave the hostel and was again homeless. My mother wrote a letter to the Red Cross, mentioning the work that my father had done in the 1930s in Uzbekistan, some of which had been under their auspices. Though I dismissed the move as being irrelevant, one day they indeed contacted me with the news that the Red Cross was prepared to give me an apartment. For the first time in my life, I had my own apartment, one which actually belonged to me. It was one room, but in a nice building in downtown Moscow near where the Cosmos Hotel now stands.

One evening, there was a knock on the apartment door. I opened it to find a tall, heavily built African. "In spectacles"—which, in streetwise Russian, connoted intelligence. He announced that he had something serious to discuss with me, and had actually been seeking me for three years. I invited him in. Once inside, his first words shocked me: "I come from Zanzibar. My name is Abdulla Kassim Hanga, and I would like to marry you." Not believing my ears, I said, "At least tell me something about yourself." I sat all evening listening to a fascinating story. Mostly he spoke of the history of Zanzibar, and about his family. From his words, I was given to understand that the island of Zanzibar is, beyond a doubt, the most beautiful place in the world. Abdulla told me the history of his people, insisting that they deserved a better life. He explained that his country was now fighting for independence, as a result of which they had many problems... I was impressed that here was a man who knew his purpose and headed straight toward it. His determination to free his people and create a new life gave evidence of seriousness and commitment. And, of course, he was an attractive, vigorous, powerful and handsome man. Finally, he announced that, "I am the General Secretary of the Afro-Shirazi Party. Our Revolutionary Council has decided that, when we win independence, I will be the President of Zanzibar."

At this juncture I began to laugh to myself. Each African studying in University believed that he was destined to be President of his country. But Abdulla continued, "The Council proposed that I should study in Oxford and marry you." "Why me," I asked innocently. "There were many candidates: African women from all over the world. But the Revolutionary Council voted unanimously for you as my wife," he answered. "And how did they find out about me? Where are they and where am I..." Abdulla mentioned a Zanzibar delegate to the World Festival of Youth, in 1957, in Moscow. "He had noticed how you helped all the African delegations, and how they had come to lean on your support. Now, that delegate is a member of the Council. He told them about your activity. He also said that you were very beautiful. And your figure is like one barrel on another."

This unexpected story amused me greatly. In some way it was even flattering. But I could not give him an answer on the spot. First, I was still thinking all the time about Yura and I could not forget him. I was not yet ready to bring another man in my life.

Abdulla insisted and I did begin to think about the positive and negative aspects of his proposal. Zanzibar was a Muslim country where men had a right, given by the Koran, to marry four wives. With my sociable instincts, I would have difficulty playing the role of a Muslim wife. But, from another point of view, I could sacrifice my lifestyle, and leave my scholarly research, to help him and African people. It was my duty to go to the native land of my ancestors. Then what would I do with my elderly mother? I could not leave her all alone in the Soviet Union without relatives.

I told Abdulla that I wanted to postpone the continuation of our conversation until I had a chance to discuss my future with my mother. Openly, I said that the more we talked, the more I liked him. But I could not make such a decision "standing on one foot." He told me that all my fears were without base. There would be no other wives. Not only that, he was willing to transfer from Oxford to the newly opened Lumumba University in Moscow so that he could be with me while I reached my decision. Eventually, he did indeed transfer. He graduated within two years, receiving the first degree awarded by Lumumba State University.

Meanwhile, my life went on as before. As I have already mentioned, this was a period of slight thaw in the Soviet Union. A few people were beginning to travel abroad. However, even in those years, there was no way I could contemplate going anywhere except to Soviet controlled Eastern Europe. Not even in my wildest dreams could I think of visiting the United States or the capitalist countries of Western Europe. Even to go to a socialist country, permission had to be given by at least seven or eight different bodies at different levels of the Communist Party and KGB, from the workplace, the city district and the national Soviet authorities. Then, a person needed to be in a group under the supervision of the KGB. Before leaving, the group would be lectured by a KGB officer on where they could go, how they must dress, who they could speak to—and who they may not. Above all, the group must stay together and avoid any provocations, especially from Americans.

The easiest permission that I could get was for a visit to Bulgaria. In those years, there was a Soviet joke, "The hen is not a bird, and Bulgaria is not a foreign country." For me, Bulgaria looked like some of the places in the Crimea or Caucasus, only worse. Their Black Sea coast was inferior to ours. Bulgaria was reputed to be dusty, dirty and undistinguished by mountains, forests or sites in comparison with Pitzunda in Soviet Abhazia—where ancient Greek legend had placed the Golden Fleece. When we came to the resort Golden Sand in Bulgaria we realized that tourists from America or West Germany were housed in adequate quarters, the Soviet visitors were thrown into poor accommodations. Although Bulgaria was a socialist country, they were already, in the 1950s and 1960s, capable of differentiating between the respective values of the ruble and the dollar.

On our first night in Bulgaria, our KGB escort gave us a list of prohibited restaurants where Americans were likely to go. Of course, forbidden fruit is sweeter. With three of my girlfriends, I went to one of the listed bars. All the money that we had been allowed to exchange in Moscow for Bulgarian currency was little more than enough to pay for a bottle of lemonade. But we felt adventurous, we were in a foreign country, sitting in a foreign bar, surrounded by American spies and provocateurs. However, none of the faces looked American. When we went to the bathroom, it was filthy beyond description. One of my companions cursed in loud Russian, sure that Americans do not understand Russian. After all, the place was prohibited for Soviet citizens, and occupied by Americans. Peals of laughter rose from all the booths. Clearly, the KGB list had ensured the bar a huge Russian clientele.

The women in our group were mostly from distant places of the USSR and knew no other languages other than Russian. They were scared to stray far from the hotel. Their shopping expeditions were restricted to stores that could offer very cheap articles, for there was no money for more. They sat on the benches near the hotel, chewing sunflower seeds, watching me enviously as I passed by on my way to some new adventure. My only objective in the shops was Ma Griffe perfume, which I still remembered from the time of meeting the girl friend of Kwame Nkrumah, and, if it was to be had, the price was way out of my reach. I went to the bars, traveled to the attractions, and generally behaved like a tourist abroad. The language presented no problem. I could understand the dialects of the locals because of my Uzbek upbringing which has Turkey and Arabic roots and I could speak German or some English as well.

The teacher's unions had mostly financed my companions from the villages on the tour. Few of them would have been able to pay for such a trip themselves, and fewer were lucky enough to have had University education. They had envied my playing the piano and my ability to speak other languages. As far as I was concerned, their attitudes and envy were the result, not only of their own inclinations, but also rather of the Soviet social structure that was so restrictive. So I could not be angry with them, but I also could not forsake the experiences of travel abroad to comply with their fears and hesitations.

Bulgaria is an agrarian country with strong Turkish influences. Many of the Bulgarians speak a Turkish language. I strongly believe that you can learn much about the history of any people from watching their dances and listening to their music. For example, there is in some African countries music with Arabic influence, as a reminder that Arabs enslaved Africans. Bulgarian dances include distinctly Turkish steps, especially when the men dance, with arms extended around shoulders. To my joy, the local coffee was also Turkish. I was a heavy smoker those years, and needed plenty of real coffee—a commodity virtually unknown in Moscow. Moscow natives drink like Americans, just black water. Turkish coffee demands a special attitude to be prepared. The local dress and attitudes toward women were clearly influenced by Muslim practices. I quickly concluded that Bulgaria was a big Turkish village.

On my second trip abroad, in the next year, I went to East Germany. Again, I was in a group. Again, the KGB was supervising us. And again we had to listen to the lectures on what was permissible, and what was forbidden abroad for Soviet people. Germany was an interesting country because, in every city, I could feel the traditions of a European culture. I didn't see villages like the ones to which we were accustomed in Russia. The Germans had no villages of which to speak. There were cities—smaller or larger, sometimes very big—all with everything you could possibly seek: shops, galleries, schools, churches and museums. Their standard of living was much higher than that of the Soviet Union, though the East Germans told me that it still didn't compare with West Germany.

The Germans were a very standard thinking and respectable people, which I found boring. First in their list of priorities was *das ordnung*— "order"—, which must be in everything: work, study, love and recreation. These were the traditions worked out over centuries. *Das ordnung* flowed in the veins of every German. It was widely known that the proportion of suicides in Germany was higher than elsewhere in the world. To me the explanation was plain. Life will not always conform to that kind of order and many Germans were unable to cope with any nonconformity. Several years ago I came to Germany at Christmas, an important family occasion for Germans. Berlin was still divided by the wall, and many people had relatives on the other side. The son of one of my female friends had succeeded in crossing the Berlin Wall. She missed him all the time, but especially at the family festival. And so, at Christmastime, because her son could not cross the wall and come to visit her, she killed herself.

The mother and husband of Sigrid, with whom I studied at Moscow State, also, committed suicide. Her mother spent a long time in the concentration camp and of course her mind could not stand this. The story of her husband was different. One day Sigrid came to see me in Moscow. She wanted my advice. Her husband, who was a surgeon, decided to go to work in African country. Sigrid was happy that he would have an opportunity to work together with doctors from different socialist countries in the hospital which was built by all socialist countries together. They felt they would become friends, and would visit each other and together helping Africans. I was not excited about this opportunity and I told her, that I doubt that her husband would develop such friendship because Soviet people are not allowed to visit foreigners at home, even if they are from the socialist countries. What happenned? This enthusiast went to that African country. Of course, neither Russian doctors, nor even doctors from other socialist countries were willing to have friendships with him. More over, they would steal the crutches, medical instruments, and other things in the hospital and sell them at very expensive prices to Africans. But what his German soul could not stand was that he had to do operations without sterilized medical instruments, without hot water and electricity. He got mentally sick, was brought back home, put in the hospital and one day killed himself.

On that first visit to Germany, I found it very easy to communicate with Germans. In the 15 years that I had studied the language, there had been no opportunity to speak or hear German. For the first three days in Germany, I was speechless. Then, as if a light had been turned on in my brain, it all came back and I was conversing freely. I had even surprised myself.

I respected the German people for their discipline and capacity for hard work. Now I began to understand many things about Sigrid, who had evoked in me envy and inferiority complexes as she rose early for her energetic exercises while I cowered in bed in our room in the hostel of Moscow State. I had been surprised that she was able to preserve her German traditions of *das ordnung* in the disordered atmosphere of Moscow. Russians are not famous for their order.

My next expedition beyond the frontiers of the USSR was to Hungary and Czechoslovakia. It was memorable, not only because of the beauty of the two countries, but also because of the behavior of our KGB escort. We began as usual, with the lecture on how to behave. From there we proceeded to a long series of confrontations with the female comrade from the KGB. These became so intense, and so much a part of our daily routine that all the group's energies were expended on her and we saw little of the landscape. All that I could say about Hungary and Czechoslovakia was that we could feel the influence of European culture, especially German.

The group leader from KGB was a huge woman with unnaturally blonde hair. She was completely devoid of ceremony and utterly convinced of her rectitude. Daily, even hourly, she reminded us that her husband was high up in the ranks of the KGB. Officially, as she introduced herself to the locals, she was an employee of the Institute of Slavic Studies. Invariably she concealed her function as our controller from the KGB. Naturally, particularly in Czechoslovakia, people wanted to discuss Slavic issues and problems with her. She was so abysmally ignorant that we blushed with shame at being associated with her. Her ignorance also extended to politics and culture and her perpetual questions to our guides kept our attention riveted on her for fear of some new stupidity instead of on the sights through which we passed.

For some unfathomable reason, she took a liking to me. Whenever we had "official" talks as representatives of the Academy of Science of the USSR, she deemed it better that I lead the proceedings. Consequently she announced that "Lily will be the chairman." She told me, "We are two bosses, so we must live in the best rooms in the hotel."

The first scandal struck on the shore of the famous Lake Balaton in Hungary. I had gone to swim. When I returned, a group of Austrian women—who crossed to work each day in Hungary as cleaners—were gathered at the door of our shared room, screaming in voices that could be clearly heard from across the lake, "Russische schwein!" (Russian pigs!) I rushed into our room to find that, in her ignorance, she had used the bidet as a lavatory. Having been found out by the cleaners, she was standing, hands on hips, shrieking: "I did this in revenge for Hungary's actions on the side of the Germans during the Great Patriotic War."

In Prague, she didn't allow us to leave the hotel alone. We could only get out in groups, with her, and must return early in the evening. Needless to say, we all escaped one after the other. She spent all evening in the lobby, compiling a list of the hours at which each of us returned. At 10 p.m. she felt too fatigued.

As she retired for the night, she asked the Czech doorman to continue the list.

All this was too much for us. The group decided to go to the Soviet ambassador, to protest and elicit exact information on the rules of travel abroad for Soviet tourists. I was asked to join the delegation because I was able to ask in German for directions to the Embassy of the USSR.

The ambassador was very polite, but advised us not to go out alone. He reasoned that the Czechs retired to bed early, and after 8 p.m. we would be unable to get guidance to return to our hotel. He did not make a very convincing case. As for her attempts to control us, he admitted that it was not very nice, but he admonished us for not returning early enough. After all, we were causing great concern to our escort, who was only worried about our welfare.

In sum, the entire trip revolved around our escort's behavior. We were in a constant state of excitement; our nerves were frayed. Eventually, she fell in love with our young Czech guide, and we had immense problems trying to keep her out of his room.

Prague is one of the most beautiful cities in Europe. On the day that we were due to leave the city, we could feel that autumn had begun. It was mid September. The trees were losing their multicolored leaves. Prague's famous small bars, each with two or three tables, looked very cozy and inviting. We did not want to leave. It was sadly that we said goodbye, but it was a sadness alleviated by the beauty of autumn descending on an exquisite city.

I was never allowed to go abroad again. The KGB sent a letter to the Institute, accusing me of bad behavior abroad, and of heading a group that had fought against our escort from the secret police. Moreover, the group had accused me, so said the KGB, of instigating the visit to the ambassador. According to the letter, the group had not wanted to go to the Embassy, and had only followed me because I was their chairman.

In the following year, the same group—with the same escort— went to Yugoslavia. But the KGB did not give me permission to join them. I was not particularly worried. The East European countries were all too obviously dependent satellites of the Soviet Union, and as such had lost much of their appeal for me. Although their standard of living was higher than that of the Soviet Union, my trips had convinced me that all these East European countries were very provincial. As for going to the capitalist countries, I did not conform to the requirements of the KGB. I was a foreigner by origin, though born in the Soviet Union. I was unmarried, which meant that I might marry abroad and remain there. I was not a member of the Party and, lastly, I did not have good contacts in the KGB. For people like me, the door to the West was always closed.

The prices of any tour abroad grew by leaps and bounds. Such trips quickly became beyond the reach of anyone earning a normal Soviet salary. In any case, my visits to Germany, Bulgaria, Czechoslovakia and Hungary had taught me that I had no stomach for being part of a herd. I wanted to be free to go where I desired and to talk to whomever caught my fancy. I believed that the experience of being abroad meant walking the streets of an unknown city, maybe even getting lost and finding one's own way out, to spend an evening in someone's home, to discover what people thought about their lives. These "socialist" trips provided none of those satisfactions.

After all these ventures beyond the frontiers, Abdulla Hanga was still waiting for me. We were meeting more often. I introduced him to my friends, both White and Black. He became friendly with George Tynes and other families of African origin. We often went to films and theaters, but he did not like ballet. In his view, ballerinas were improperly dressed and there was too much touching of bodies. In fact he demanded from me to stop going to ballet, and I promised even though it was something that I enjoyed very much.

Though there was much of Islam in his lifestyle, I could sense no fanaticism. There were mannerisms from the everyday life of Muslims. He was perfectly at home sitting in African fashion on the floor and eating with his hands. When he shook hands, it was Muslim fashion with one hand gripping the other arm.

I introduced Abdulla to Ivan Potekhin, the director of the Institute of African Studies. Ivan was happy to meet him. To me he said that, if I was to marry Abdulla, I could be of great help to him at home. Several times he told me, "Hanga is a very honorable man, who could give his life for the freedom of his people."

My mother was also favorably disposed to this marriage. She told me, "My dear daughter, you must marry him. It is your duty. Remember that

I also left America to go with your father to help Uzbekistan. We have the same genes. Abdulla is worthy of love. This is a man ready to sacrifice himself to an idea. You will need to forget many things in your life, but he is worth it."

I married him in 1961, not realizing that my marriage would stir such a reaction around the world, including in the Soviet Union. Suddenly, there was interest from all kinds of institutions and people. The House of Commons in London held debates about me. The British Secretary of State for Foreign Affairs, Douglas Home, stated: "There is a red under each bed in Zanzibar." As an example, he spoke about me. Home even hinted that I was a Chinese spy. The magazine *West Africa* was deeply offended by that allusion, and responded: "Nothing of the kind! Lily Golden is an American spy!" A Kenyan newspaper wrote that I had been kicked out of Kenya. The London *Times* wrote that I was deputy director of the Institute of African Studies and, at the same time, Khruschev's right hand in African affairs. The Times stated flatly that I was the leader of the anticolonial movement in Zanzibar. The *Daily Telegraph* wrote that I had concealed the fact that my husband was educated in China. The *Nationalist* in Zanzibar asserted that I could not get a visa to come to the island because of my membership in the Communist Party. The *East African Press* maliciously gloated that Abdulla Hanga had refused to confirm that I was a Communist Party member.

From all this, my head was spinning. My God, why did I deserve all this? I had been sitting quietly in Moscow, minding my own business, and suddenly everybody in the world wanted to know whether I was a spy and a member of the Communist Party. Obviously, they all knew little about the Soviet Union if they believed that I would be allowed to join the Party. Even I became interested in finding out what it was that I could conceivably sell or what the espionage services of other countries could hope to get from me.

The funniest thing was that I began to feel the same interest coming from the KGB. One after another, my friends would come and tell me, in deepest confidence, that KGB had interrogated them. The main question was, invariably: "Why did she marry a foreigner?" Truthfully, I was among the first in the USSR to marry a foreigner. And the KGB was consumed by the question of whether I had done so in order to leave the country to sell the Soviet

Union's darkest secrets. In this entire story, what worried me was what I could know of such immense value that the KGB was speculating about me.

For me, the real problem was not espionage or defection. I had other problems. I needed a larger apartment. I was expecting a child and I wanted to bring Mother and Mamanya to live with me. Apartments could not be bought in the Soviet Union. The government, to be precise, Moscow City Council, usually gave them free and people waited for them for several years. I did not expect to receive a new apartment, but I could exchange my mothers' apartment with three rooms in Tashkent and my apartment with one room to a bigger apartment in Moscow. And here, there was a new problem. A greedy neighbor, in a typical Soviet scenario, reported on me to the KGB denouncing me for wanting to defect with the intent of selling my apartment to my mother. The KGB promptly forwarded a copy of the letter to Moscow City Council, which appointed a 50-member commission to inquire into the behavior of the "famous American spy." I was summoned to appear before them. In tears, I tried to explain that, I was married and loved my husband; nothing was further from my mind than absconding to Zanzibar; I had a doctoral thesis to defend at the Academy of Science. Among the 50 were many women and they supported me. A miracle happened! I was allowed to exchange and recorded the fact that my accuser, the greedy neighbor, would never have the right to aspire to a new apartment. This story reminded me of the book *Twelve Chairs*, where the authors Ilf and Petrov wrote: "The apartment problem spoiled Soviet people."

With great difficulties, I began the adventure of changing apartments. In the beginning, I had found someone who was willing to trade one room in a multi-family building in a remote district of Moscow for my mother's three rooms in Tashkent. Then, I could trade her one room and my one room apartment, with the help of the City Council, for a two-room apartment in Cheremushki—a new district where housing was just being built. Underground did not yet reach that far. On the day that we moved, the daily paper noted the sighting of a wolf in the streets of the suburb.

Abdulla was in Zanzibar, preparing for Revolution. I very much wanted him to be in Moscow when I delivered the child. Like all women, I needed his help and compassion. I read all the Zanzibar papers, avidly following his deeds, understanding all the while that he had a big role to play in the political life of Africa. I regretted that I was not alongside him.

He came back to Moscow in April 1962. I was happy that we were together again. He said that, after his son was born, we would go together to Zanzibar and I must prepare for the long trip. I packed all the books that we had in English, many of them brought by my parents in the 1930s from the United States. I also packed all my silverware and everything else that was precious, and dispatched it all to Zanzibar. I had seen these possessions for the last time in my life.

One day we were both invited to a government breakfast in the Kremlin. The participants included Abdulla and me, the Minister of Education and the minister of Foreign Affairs of Zanzibar and some other ministers who had come with him. We sat around a great table, together with the members of the Soviet government. Abdulla was at the other end of the table, while I was wedged between the Soviet Minister of Fisheries, Ishkov, and the Deputy Minister of Foreign Affairs, Kuznetsov. During the breakfast, to my surprise, it did not occur to them that someone among the Zanzibar group could understand Russian. I was especially happy that Abdulla, who spoke perfect Russian, was seated too far away to hear how the two Soviet dignitaries were discussing me. He was consumed by an almost pathological jealousy, and their remarks, in his ears, could only have resulted in an international scandal.

Ishkov and Kuznetsov were discussing in detail my female attributes. I was so interested in listening to what they were saying that I barely touched my plate. When the waiter wanted to remove the plate, I said in my best Muscovite Russian: "Leave it here. I haven't finished yet." I expected that the two of them would be embarrassed, or would at least have the decency to blush—but nothing of the kind. Kuznetsov turned to me and bragged: "You know I have been in Africa. I met Kenyatta..." The talk flowed on politely as if the previous conversation had never happened. They were particularly complimentary about my Russian language. Meanwhile, I was thinking to myself: "God help us. These are the rulers of the USSR. They don't even have the grace to apologize." As we left, we were invited to join the government on the saluting platform at the traditional May 1st parade.

I had seen such occasions on TV several times and it had always been interesting to see the foreign guests, leaders of different countries on the dais. Now I had a chance to be there myself.

But it was not to be. Early in the morning of May 1st, when thousands were marching to Red Square, I was taken to the delivery room of a hospital. They put me in a big room with many expectant mothers. All the doctors and nurses were seated around a television in a neighboring room. They were so excited at the spectacle unfolding in Red Square that they did not even look at me.

I was very nervous, and when I'm nervous, usually I begin laughing hysterically for the slightest reason. A young, very heavy, pregnant woman was jumping from bed to bed, cursing all men. She was listing all the men who might have gotten her pregnant, and enumerating the sexual characteristics of each in a language such as I had never heard in my life. I began laughing so hard that I almost rolled off the bed. My laughter was contagious. Soon, the whole roomful of women was roaring with laughter. One woman, who had been in labor for three days, and was just approaching the moment of deliverance, rocked herself back to starting point.

The mass hysteria at last penetrated the deep concentration of the doctors in the next room. They rushed into our room, and one shouted: "What's the matter with you? We're trying to watch the parade! You're distracting us!" An interrogation began, aimed at identifying the instigator of the disturbance. And they descended on me, with a hypodermic syringe, to speed up my labor. Evidently they had decided that I should be disposed of as quickly as possible. To be on the safe side, they then moved me into an isolated room. They left, and my labor began. I shouted, and I shouted, but no one came. I became scared. The pain intensified and I began to think that I was dying. Suddenly, an old nurse appeared and began to calm me with soothing words. Her kindness did the trick, and I delivered my child. I vaguely heard someone say, "What a beautiful girl!" I was very surprised! Abdulla had adamantly insisted that he was going to have a son. I was too exhausted to argue. As I fell asleep, I resolved to sort it all out in the morning.

Next day, I felt physically and spiritually drained. There was a note from Abdulla saying that my mother had disappeared. I wanted to run from the hospital to look for her, but was afraid to leave the child. Somebody handed me a mirror, and I could see that my eyes were bloodshot. It would be several days before I found out that, rushing through a rainstorm to my bedside, mother had fallen and broken her arm. She had been taken to another hospital.

When I left the hospital, with my newborn baby, a group of friends were waiting for me. Abdulla was also there. He said, "I will never forgive you for producing a daughter instead of a son." He turned away and walked off. I was doubly upset. It is a Russian tradition that as mother and child leave the hospital, the father takes the baby in his arms. Ed Theodorovich, my friend from the time I lived in the Lux hotel, saved the situation by taking the child in his hands. This was how he became my daughter's godfather. Yelena Parker, Ralph's adopted daughter, said, "I give her my name." And Yelena became godmother.

This was a difficult year for me. Abdulla went off to Zanzibar and was ordered arrested by the Sultan. I was left with a newborn baby and a sick mother. The child suffered from sepsis, and I was afraid to leave her even to cross the street to buy bread and milk. I was totally unprepared for motherhood, and furious with a government that invested no effort in giving the right preparation and training. Amid all the anguish over my sick mother and daughter, the care for both of them, my daily work at the Institute and writing my dissertation, I was also busy in helping Abdulla to get out of prison. I was sending letters to the United Nations, UNESCO, and the president of the United States and other world leaders, to obtain Abdulla's release.

As if this was not enough, it was turning into the worst year in the climate of Moscow's history. There was not one single day without rain or snow. Just before my daughter's first birthday, the pediatrician told me that, if she was to live, I must take her away from the city: "She needs fruit and vegetables. She needs to see the sun. Otherwise, she is in danger of developing rickets." Yelena couldn't lift her head from the pillow. She couldn't yet sit up, though she should have taken her first steps already.

What could I do? I decided to go to Batumi, the capital of the Soviet Republic of Adjaria on the border of Turkey. It was the only place in the USSR to enjoy a subtropical climate, with hot weather almost all year. On May 1,

1963, I flew to Suhumi, a small town on the shores of the Black Sea. There I boarded a ship, *Peter I,* and sailed to Batumi. Nobody on the ship could ignore Yelena. I had always thought, from the first day of her life, that she was very special and not an ordinary child. Other children were born with wrinkled and indeterminate features. My daughter was born with smooth skin and a fully formed face and body. The first time that she opened her eyes, she looked around with an apparent intelligence as though already seeing and understanding the world. I told this to my mother, eliciting the response, "You sound like a real Jewish mother!"

Be that as it may, Yelena grew taller and broader, but her features remained exactly what they had been on the day she was born. Her character had also formed immediately. She was always stubborn, very well behaved and very virtuous—and so she was to remain. But the voyage on *Peter I* was her first real encounter with strangers. They were all enchanted with her. The people of the south are usually very temperamental and fiery, especially Georgians. One of the Georgians begged me to give away him my child. He offered anything that he possessed for her. Proclaiming that he had fallen in love, and could not live without her, he protested that he couldn't understand my refusal. Others showered her with little presents and chocolate. Since she could not possibly eat all of it, I began to gain weight.

In Batumi, I took a room in a hotel on the beach which had been built long before with balconies and balustrades, columns and flourishes. The management also fell in love with Yelena. Daily they made expeditions to the marketplace to buy fresh fruit for her. They cooked special dishes which they brought to our room. And they wanted no payment for any of it. I made a lot of friends in the town, among them a fascinating man from Somalia. Mr. Cook had come to the Caucasus with an Italian circus, while he was still a small child. When the civil war began in Georgia in the 1920s, he was lost. Found by the authorities, he was sent to an orphanage. He studied sports, and became a light athletics coach. Cook married a Russian woman and his daughter in turn married an African, like so many other Black Soviet girls, and went to Africa with him. She stayed in Tanzania longer than most of the Soviet girls, but eventually she also returned—alone and with her son.

Mr. Cook had many students whom he helped reach significant

achievements in sport. Some became champions of Georgia, others of the Soviet Union. A thin man, as is typical of Somalis, he was black to the point where he almost seemed blue. From him, I found out that many Africans were living in the mountains not far from Suhumi and Batumi, in places to which they had been brought as slaves by the Turks 300 years earlier.

The Batumi sun was good to Yelena. Within a month she was sitting up. Two months later she was already running around the promenade, pausing at all the people who admired her.

Then I received a telegram from Abdulla. He had been freed and was waiting for me in London, where he was holding talks with the government about the future of Zanzibar. He was working on a constitution for an independent country.

I lost no time. Buying a ticket on a plane to Moscow, I went to a farewell party with Cook. There, Mr. Cook introduced me to an old Armenian woman. Cook told me that she was a fortuneteller who could read coffee dregs. He tried to persuade me to drink coffee, then turn the grounds upside down on my saucer. I protested that I didn't believe in such things, but finally gave in. The old woman studied the remains of my coffee and then announced: "You are married to a man who has long been walking with bowed head. Soon he will straighten up, and stand taller than all his people. I see him seated in a large automobile. With him is a woman." I interrupted, "Yes, that must be me," I said with absolute certainty. "No," she continued, "she looks like you, tall and not too black—with a boy. You will never be there." Announcing that this was foolishness, I said: "Here's a telegram saying that he's waiting in London. I'm on my way to Moscow, where a visa is waiting for me at the British Embassy." Her response was: "I don't know about that. I do know, the cup never lies..."Having heard enough, I said goodbye to Cook and left for Moscow.

In Moscow, to my great surprise, I was quickly given an exit Soviet visa from Moscow authorities. But, at the British Embassy, I was told: "You are late. Parliament decided several days ago that people of African descent will not be allowed into England, unless they have papers proving that they have a job there." For the first time in my life, I was meeting with discrimination because of the color of my skin.

I tried several times to go to Zanzibar. Each time something interfered: my mother was sick, or Yelena was ill, or I was preparing for my postgraduate exams. An astrologer friend told me, "Jupiter is watching over you. There may be danger for you in Zanzibar, and he is saving you." He was probably right. Abdulla came often to Moscow in an attempt to persuade me to return with him to Zanzibar. But I had responsibilities in Moscow, and Abdulla was not yet in a position to offer a stable life. As a revolutionary, part of his existence was underground. Between the British protectorate, and the Sultanate that followed it, he was often imprisoned and always courting arrest.

One night, early in 1964, like most Soviet citizens who wanted to know what was happening in the outside world, I was discreetly listening to the prohibited *Voice of America*. Suddenly I heard that there was a Revolution in Zanzibar. Among those who had come to power, the announcer mentioned my husband. I was laughing so loudly that I woke my mother, who was sleeping in another room. She asked what was so amusing in the middle of the night. I told her, "You won't believe... Abdulla won, and I never believed it would happen."

Zanzibar united with Taganyika to form Tanzania. Abdulla was appointed Minister of the Union and Minister of Mines, Industry and Energy.

On 18 August, a Tanzanian government delegation that he was leading came to Moscow: Rashid Kababa, the Vice President; Trade and Cooperatives Minister, Jeremy Kasambala; Education, Information and Tourism Minister, Idris Abdul Vakil; Economics Minister Nsilo Swaii; the Parliamentary Secretary to the Industry Minister Mahani Kundia; and a secretary of the Minister of Agriculture Ahmad Rashid. I moved with Abdulla to a large "residency" on Lenin Hills. Beyond the knowledge of Muscovites, there exists in the Lenin Hills a conclave of luxury buildings for members of the Soviet government and very high-ranking guests.

KGB border guards were everywhere. Two Chaika limousines, usually reserved only for very high level members of the government, were permanently by our door with four drivers in attendance. We had so many servants that it was hopeless trying to remember all their names. They were extremely well trained and virtually invisible. I could never understand how they managed to materialize at my elbow before I had summoned them. How was it that they anticipated our needs so supernaturally? I had never imagined that there could be such kind Russian servants. It would have been interesting to know who trained them—and who employed them. The answer would be KGB. But I didn't have the nerve to ask them.

The house had two floors, though I suspected that there were at least two more below ground. There was no visible heating, yet the floors were so warm that we could have walked barefoot. In the bedroom we had a large movie screen, and we were able to use the bedside phone to order any film that took our fancy. The walls and furniture in the dining room were of oak, and a bowl of tasty candies always stood on the table. To my amazement, the candy was Soviet-made, though I had never seen the likes of it in any Soviet shop. In the garden were beehives and four tennis courts. A representative of the Ministry of Foreign Affairs was permanently seated in the entrance lobby, waiting to fulfill our every wish. The food was excellent. Though I was, as always, trying to lose weight, it would have been sinful to reject these delicacies—so my diet was indefinitely postponed.

There were many such houses around us. It would have been fascinating to know how much of the government's money was being spent on the upkeep of such residences. Closer to the Moscow River, the buildings were taller. It was there that the top power echelon of the USSR was living. The buildings were so carefully hidden that ordinary citizens could pass by on the street, never suspecting the different life and world that existed behind the fences.

Abdulla had changed. If before he had been obliging and sociable, ready to discuss all sorts of problems with me, now he told me that these matters were not for discussion with women. He stopped visiting my friends, explaining to me that he was afraid of being poisoned. Maybe the fear was well founded, because that technique for removing political opponents was widespread in Africa. But I couldn't believe that any of my friends would do such a thing.

From time to time, he spoke to me about the way in which a Muslim leader's wife must behave, according to the laws of Islam. I was ready to agree with him that if the wife did not behave that way, the people would not believe in their leader. True, Abdulla did not expect me to wear a veil. However, he no longer permitted me to sit at the table when we had male guests. I understood that he needed to satisfy his nation. None of these restrictions worried me, because I saw my way of life as secondary in importance to his. After all, I would survive.

At the next stage, he stopped me from going out into the streets of Moscow. When he was leaving the house, he would lock my door and I could be out only when he came back. Once he went to meet his friends at the airport. The plane was late and he spent all day there. Of course, I could call servants and they would open the door and free me, but I was ashamed that I tolerated being treated this way. Playing tennis became a forbidden pursuit. And then, he stopped me from going to the Institute. Fortunately, Ivan Potekhin knew enough about the ways of Africa to understand what was happening. He did not mind that I was absent from the work place. In any case, he liked Abdulla. But with time passing, I was beginning to think about my role in Zanzibar. Abdulla wouldn't discuss with me the situation of women in Zanzibar, though I was writing for publication an article called "Women in Africa," which shortly appeared in *Moscow Magazine*. When he read this article he told me that with my ideas about the role of women I could get killed in Africa.

I was becoming convinced that Abdulla's views were sometimes too radical. Africa, in my mind, was not ready for widespread nationalization of small businesses. He wouldn't talk about it with me.

All this was unimportant compared with the problem of what I would do with Yelena in Zanzibar. I dreamed of giving her the best possible education with opportunities in music and sport. But Zanzibar, with its Muslim traditions and restrictions on the freedom and equality of women, was hardly the appropriate place compared with possibilities in the Soviet Union. It was difficult to discuss this with a devout Muslim who truly believed what he said "We respect women so much that we do not even look at them."

One day, after Abdulla returned to Africa, I was sitting in the Institute library, looking through the Zanzibar *Nationalist* issue of 20

January 1965. On the first page was a photo of Abdulla with a woman. The caption read: "The Minister of the Union in the President's government, Mr. Abdulla Kassim Hanga, came yesterday to Dar es Salaam with his new brunette wife from Guinea..." Not believing my eyes, I picked up another paper, only to find a photo of Abdulla and the woman in a limousine on the streets of Zanzibar. In an American newspaper, I read that Hanga rides in such a big car that it is barely able to turn in the streets of the city. Now I remembered the words of the old Armenian woman in Batumi. She was right, the coffee cups never lie.

One month later, Abdulla again came to Moscow. I was expecting some talk about the new wife. Several days passed, and he was silent. As always, he was kind, nice and tender with me. I could no longer stand it. Asking about his new wife, I reminded him that he had promised not to take other wives, even though the Koran permitted. He said: "You don't understand. It is not a wife. It is a present!" I asked what he meant. "You see," he said, "I went to Guinea and President Sekou Toure liked me so much that he gave me a present. That is their custom."

As a student of Africa, I had, of course, read about such customs. But I never thought that such a thing would happen to me. There had even been a story about one famous Austrian artist who had married an African and become his fourth wife. But that was literature, far distant from my reality. As a side issue, what was I going to explain to my daughter when she discovered that I was not the only wife of her father. Abdulla was explaining to me that there was no official marriage. He just could not refuse to take this "present." He repeated several times that this woman had nothing to do with him personally. This Sekou Toure's "present" so angered me that Abdulla promised me to send her away, and we never spoke of her again.

One after another, my girlfriends of African origin were marrying Africans. Ella and Ina Ross followed hard in my footsteps. After them Amelia Tynes, and then Victoria Rudd. Yelena, Parker's adopted daughter, became the exception, marrying a man from India. All followed their husbands. Soon, one by one, they began to reappear again in the Soviet Union. This was no mean feat, for in those years the Soviet authorities deemed anyone who married a foreigner to be "a traitor." Visas to return to the USSR were not easily obtained, but some of them were prepared to face prison in order to return. Some could not even bring their children with them. The family of Ina's husband, for example, would not relinquish her child. She had to leave Ghana in such a hurry that she could not fight it. For thirty years, she was unable to see her daughter.

This was a fascinating phenomenon. The Black Soviet girls were marrying Africans in the conviction that, by going to that continent, they could be of some help to their husbands' peoples. And yet, they were all returning. Now, I know that there were similar cases, and similar outcomes, in the United States. We had believed that our education would enable us to contribute, especially in the 1960s as one country after the other gained independence. As men and women of African origin, in the Diaspora, we were feeling solidarity with our brethren who were fighting for, and gaining, their freedom. It was a time of oneness of all Black people around the world.

One of my recently returned friends enlightened me on the complexities of their situation. The Africans, who studied in the Soviet Union, or for that matter in Europe and America, were getting an education in high technologies and sciences for which Africa was not yet prepared. Despite their education, and that of their wives, they were jobless when they returned. Some of the men took to drink. Many of the others forgot promises easily made and resorted to polygamy. This was not a life for Black women coming from Europe or USA. As a marginal issue, a husband who brought back a white woman as his wife suddenly found that his social standing was enhanced. Banks were willing to make loans for home or business. Their company was sought and welcomed everywhere. If the wife from the USSR or America was black, they were just another African couple. And their education was of no help in changing their social status.

Abdulla disappeared. For several years, he did not return to the Soviet Union and he did not write. Nobody—not Soviet nor Tanzanian officials—could tell me what had happened to him. In fact, they were reticent about talking of him. It was only in the 1970s that I discovered that he had been assassinated in Zanzibar, as a result of political intrigues. I was unable to conceive any situation in which Abdulla could have acted dishonorably. He never thought of money or personal power, but only of his people. I think that

I would perhaps have divorced him had he lived. But not because of any disrespect for his character. All that stood between us was the difference of lifestyle. In my mind, he was one of the most outstanding of African leaders in those critical years.

CHAPTER SIX
Life's Harsh Prose

Immediately after the creation of the Institute for African Studies, new developmentments began. The people whom Ivan Potekhin brought with him from the Oriental Institute were well qualified academically, versed in foreign languages, some African dialects among them, and—above all—were enthusiastic about Africa. But new people started to appear—employees who had no background in the subject and knew nothing about African Studies. They were former Soviet spies whose cover had been broken, forcing their withdrawal from the stations abroad. In practice, they needed a sanctuary in Moscow, where they could sit for a few years before being reassigned to the outer world. Their former employment had been as bureaucrats from the Foreign Service or the army. The majority had been educated in one or other Party Academy far from the standards and quality of Universities. A Soviet joke calls these establishments "likbez"—a contraction of "liquidation of illiteracy." There were common denominators for all these people. They were exclusively Russian nationals and Communist Party members. They all lacked formal higher education.

At the time, anti-Semitism was especially widespread in the Soviet Union.

When I lived in Tashkent, that racial prejudice had passed me by as no more than a figment of "cosmopolitism." I had never had cause to think about the meaning of that word. Perhaps Tashkent was too far from Moscow. Maybe I was too young to know many things. I did know that my mother had lost her job the but official excuse was that it happened because the Institute of Foreign Languages had not accepted her American degree from Rodes University.

When I came to Moscow, everyone was speaking about the "doctor poisoners." The reference was to another of Stalin's typical Soviet scenarios. A Russian woman medico, Timoshenko, in seeking career promotion, had written a letter to the Communist Party Central Committee stating that there was a conspiracy of Jewish doctors aimed at poisoning all the Communist leadership. The Committee had referred the matter to Lavrenti Beria, Head of the KGB, who responded that it was "foolishness." The letter was filed away. As the years went by, Stalin had exiled many minority populations from the Caucuses to the outer fringes of the USSR, but still lacked a solution for the country's Jews, whom he considered to be members of the greater Jewish international conspiracy. Timoshenko's letter was unearthed and turned against the medical professions, who were mostly Jews. Many Jewish doctors were arrested and sent to concentration camps. Senior Jewish Communist Party officials were forced to write letters to Stalin, ostensibly asking him to exile them and their compatriots.

Though I was so busy with my work, studies and romantic life, I did grasp that it was yet again a ploy particularly used against Jewish intelligentsia. On the streets, there were plentiful comments: "Hitler didn't have enough time to burn all of you in his ovens..." These were the words I heard thrown at one old, weak Jewish woman. To me this was a shock. I had never conceived that such things would be said openly on the streets of the city.

At Moscow State University, there was no problem of anti-Semitism, for no Jews were admitted. According to one classic response: "No, we have no anti-Semitism, for all the Jews have already been eaten..." Very possibly there were Jews here and there, but only because their identity documents did not correctly reflect their nationality. In order to avoid persecution, many Soviet Jews had adopted the names of their non-Jewish husbands or wives, rather than record obvious names.

The Institute became the flag bearer in the crusade of anti-Semitism in the Soviet Academy of Sciences. It began in the early 1960s when the Institute's Scientific Council denied two employees—Goncharov and Tretyakov—the position of "senior researchers." Tretyakov had been Soviet Ambassador to Ghana and Guinea where he had vigorously pushed Soviet interests till one day he was declared persona non grata and given 24 hours to remove himself from Africa. This was how he, and others like him, materialized in the Institute of African Studies.

Now, these two complained to the District Committee of the Communist Party, charging that they had been denied their rightful status because Jews dominated the Scientific Council. Of the 25 Council members, only two were Jews. Nevertheless, the complaint was discussed in the Party Committee of the Institute and was recorded in full in the minutes. As word spread around the city, people came from all sorts of institutions in Moscow to study these minutes. It was the first time that anti-Semitism was revealed so straight and open. Usually, such things do are not allowed. Such documents were not normally available for outside perusal. Very quickly, these pages "disappeared" from the protocols, but not from people's memories. The Institute acquired a citywide reputation for anti-Semitism.

Soon a group of like-minded employees of the Institute coalesced on the basis of their anti-Semitic beliefs. They targeted Potekhin, contending that he had collected too many Jews around him. The members of this group sought for their own the leading positions of Communist Party secretary of the Institute, scientific secretary and the chairs of all the departmental heads. The Institute was growing quickly, already having passed 300 employees, so the departmental chairs were becoming significant. To have a good life in the Institute, it was necessary to pay lip service to this group. Their favorites were rewarded with better salaries and permits to travel abroad.

When I began my struggles with them I had said plainly and loudly that their behavior was terrible. I was told openly that I could never expect a pay raise in the Institute and would certainly never be sent abroad by this Institute. That indeed was what happened.

I could of course approach Potekhin and my friends to support me, but I couldn't take the first steps in that direction. It was my conviction, because of our former relationship, that first he must come to me. He was aware of my situation, but was waiting for me to broach the subject. When the situation became particularly acute, Potekhin's assistant quietly assured me that Potekhin was ready to do whatever I asked of him. Still, I could not marshal the will to go to him. My pride stood in the way. To supplement my meager income, I wrote articles for the press, for radio stations and for news agencies. The articles were placed abroad, in Africa and elsewhere. This was enough for survival.

One day, Potekhin invited me to his office to talk about my dissertation. As always, I was happy to discuss the details of my work for he was very knowledgeable in African problems. Suddenly he asked me, "What is your salary?" As if he didn't know. I answered, and he promptly asked: "Is it enough to live on?" I was silent, out of fear of showing my feelings. I felt so bad that my head began to ache. This was uncommon for me. Why should I have to tell him all my worries? No allowance from Abdulla, since he believed that I was living under a just socialism; my mother's tiny pension necessitated a supplement from me; and I was financing my daughter's travels for tennis championships and the need for her and my mother to spend two or three months a year in the warm south. I answered, "My salary is enough for me." He was angered by my answer. So was I. But I couldn't behave differently. I know it was stupid, and that others were getting raises because they tearfully asked for them. I still haven't learned how to beg. This was my last talk with Potekhin. How had Eslanda Robeson known to prophesy this.

He became the first Soviet scholar allowed to travel to Africa. He went to Ghana, where he wrote a book portraying Kwame Nkrumah in a positive light. This necessitated a struggle with the Communist Party Central Committee over publication. The Party had no interest in anything that supported Pan-Africanism, which they considered a form of bourgeois nationalism.

Next, Potekhin went to Tanzania, where he contracted a tropical disease. He was still infected when he returned to Russia in 1963. One by one, his organs ceased functioning. First his lungs, then his feet and then his left arm. But he continued to write his last book. As he inserted the last period, his right arm stopped functioning. Potekhin was placed in an artificial heart and lung machine. His daughter, Gera, also an enthusiastic student of Africa who had written a book about African literature, came to me. She begged, "Ask your husband. Maybe he knows how to help my father. The sickness, after all, began in Tanzania." Abdulla responded that he did indeed know the disease which was widespread in Tanzania. He was prepared to bring a witch doctor to Moscow to treat Potekhin. The Soviet doctors, though they knew nothing about the treatment of this disease, were not going to allow a reputed Soviet scholar to be treated by a witch doctor. I do not know whether the shaman could have helped, but even as a last resort it should have been tried. On 17 September 1964, in the 61st year of his life, Ivan Potekhin—the pioneer of Soviet studies of Africa—died.

His death opened all the doors to his opponents. They had already seized all the leading positions in the Institute, and had been preparing a candidate for the directorship. Ksenia Kremen was at the center of the group. Ironically, it was widely believed that she was of Jewish origin. However, the phenomenon was not unknown in Russian history even from Czarist times. Jews who had converted to the Orthodox Church became anti-Semites, perhaps as the logical conclusion of the process, much like Catholic converts tried to be "more pious than the Pope."

Ksenia fell into that category. As a long time member of the Party, she had worked for many years in the Central Committee of the Soviet Union, then transferred to the Committee's Academy of Social Studies. She was Secretary of the Scientific Council of the Institute, the Party Secretary of the Institute, the Secretary of the International Relations Committee and so on. None of her Party or Academic positions had required doing any research or scientific work, or writing any papers. Much of her energy was devoted to keeping the director of the Institute who followed Potekhin under her control, and to keep Jews, Armenians and other "undesirables" out of positions of influence. She kept up her policies for more than thirty years, during which the Institute succeeded in ridding itself of its most talented and capable scholars. They were quickly made to understand that they would receive no promotions or career opportunities in the Institute. One by one, they transferred elsewhere, receiving their doctorates from other institutions and Universities and rising to high positions.

Meanwhile, my situation was becoming increasingly menacing. Because of Abdulla, I had gotten to know many people in high places in the government and in all walks of Soviet life. My friends pushed me into going to see Arzumanian, the Academic secretary responsible for all of the Academy of Sciences' institutions of social studies. He was a wise Asiatic and a nice, approachable person, despite his high rank. He listened very attentively, even laughing a little at my tales of life in the Institute of African Studies. Finally he said, "Don't worry. None of that group will get the directorship. I will send to your Institute an internationalist for the job."

Soon his appointee appeared. Vassily Solodovnikov had been Soviet ambassador to the United Nations. Maybe there he had been an internationalist, but that aspect was not noticeable in his work as our director. During his tenure, the number of anti-Semites grew as he hired all those who had been fired from other institutes for just that reason. For example, the director of the Oriental Institute, who had kicked a number of "scholars" out because of their intrigues and anti-Semitism, though the official pretense was somewhat different, once told me: "I would like to take you to my Institute, instead of those people. But there are so many people that I need to save, and you at least have a protective umbrella over your head." In preparation for "D-Day," one of the newcomers began to compile a list of open and covert Jews. From time to time, we heard him shouting at Solodovnikov, who fearfully appointed him chairman of the Department for the Study of Anti-Communist Movements.

But the man was a drunkard. Though we hadn't spoken to each other for years, he approached me one morning with a request for some coins to buy "the hair of the dog that had bitten him"—to cure his hangover. Though I know not why, I gave him my loose change. He said, "Oh, you seem to be a nice person." I could only respond, "And you thought I was a bad person?" "Yes, I reported you many times," he confided. "To whom," I wanted to know. "To the KGB, to the Presidium of the Academy of Science, everywhere!" I asked: "Why? For what reason..." He said, "When you lived in the hostel for post graduate students, I was very drunk and tried to get into your room. You pushed me down the steps and I have never forgiven you."

I had no recollection of the incident. But I never drink, and I detest drunkards, so it could be.

The KGB and Party organizations frequently received reports about me. A large part of the archives of the Soviet Union apparently related exclusively to me. And the peak, for the report writers, came when I was elected to the Trade Union Committee of the Institute despite their vehement opposition. My function in the committee was to arrange tickets for events, exhibitions and cultural functions in the Institute with the participation of famous actors, singers and ensembles of African students. My parties became so well known in the city that people from outside were constantly trying to gain access to them. I invited poets like Bella Achmadulina and Yevgeny Yevtushenko, who were periodically banned from public performances, without applying for Party permission. This was a time when poetry was even more popular than usual in the USSR. The poets were the first to speak openly about the faults of the Soviet Union. Outside they were banned, like Yevtushenko, but I brought them within our doors. For this I was, of course, highly criticized by the members of the group around Ksenia.

On one occasion, with some friends, I staged a play entitled "School For Informers," which satirized the stool pigeons in our Institute. Next morning, I was summoned to the District Committee of the Party which had already been informed by some energetic "stoolie." I had been giving lectures to factory audiences about African culture. The Party Committee of the Institute ordered me to stop, on Ksenia's contention that, as a person of American origins, I did not have the moral right to talk to Soviet audiences. The Institute of Asia and Africa of Moscow State University invited me to give seminars on Pan Africanism. After three months, I was told that the Institute of African Studies did not recommend that I be so employed by the University. Whatever I did, the group tried to hamper my activities.

For years I had struggled to complete my doctoral thesis, "African Music—the Tendencies of Historical Development." It could not be written in the Institute because of my research on its behalf. In the evenings at home, I had to tend my sick mother and daughter. And, in addition, Potekhin, who had been my supervisor, was no longer alive. There was no one in the Institute conversant enough with African music to guide me. Beyond our walls, there were no other Soviet scholars in this area of expertise.

In 1964, the thesis was finished. I took it to the chairwoman of the Department of Russian Folk Music in the Moscow Conservatory. Professor Rudnieva was expert on *chastushka*—which could best be described as a type of Russian rap music. To my surprise, she did not even want to read my dissertation, on the grounds that it contained quotations from foreign literature. For my part, I deemed this quite normal. Many American and British scholars, and African musicians themselves, had written in English, French and Spanish about African music, but there were no Soviet sources in Russian language. I told her that I was willing to translate the quotations into Russian, but she answered, "Why must I believe your translations?" This was, of course, a hiccup left over from the recent campaign against cosmopolitism. What could possibly be evil in my translation of an article about African drums? Did she think that it would constitute a major political mistake if I made an occasional error in translation?

I went to Leningrad, to the African Department in the Museum of Ethnography, headed by the most famous of Soviet Africanists, Ollderogge. He gave me a negative response, but not personally. Instead it came from an assistant who happened to be a very good personal friend of mine. She had spoken out at the conference. I asked her why she had changed her views, when she had been most complimentary about the work one week earlier. She replied, "Don't ask me anything. It has to be this way."

Returning to Moscow, I went to the Institute of Ethnography, which was well known for its tolerance and breadth of vision. Telling the administration what had happened, I asked whether they would agree to me defending the dissertation before their Scientific Council. They agreed. Now I needed two "devil's advocates," conversant in the subject, who could act as opponents in the proceeding. There would have been no problem in finding historians specializing on Africa, but no one in Moscow knew anything about African music. Altogether, from the moment of finishing my thesis until the completion of preparations for its presentation, three years elapsed. At last, the *Moscow Evening News* announced that my thesis would be defended before the Scientific Council of the Institute of Ethnography at 2 p.m. on February 27, 1968.

The leading opponent was Professor Sergei Tokharev, a world-renowned scholar and my former instructor at Moscow State. In his opening, he said that I had taken upon myself an important and honorable task in exposing the legacy of musical culture of the African peoples—something for a long time unknown to Europeans. Three musical critics, who had some acquaintance with African music, supported me.

The defense went well. But for a few unimportant observations, there was no negative criticism. The hall was full with several hundred people. To my surprise, most of the members of my Institute came for the event, which took place in a location on the other side of the city. But come they did, and they sat through the entire proceedings despite the heat and discomfort of the auditorium. Some of them were obviously waiting for my defense to

collapse in the face of the devil's advocates. When it was over, the administration of the Institute of Ethnography told me that they had never before
seen so many anonymous submissions as contested my right to the doctorate. Several years later, I met Ollderogge at a dinner party in a friend's house.
He asked permission to kiss my hand, then said, "I am so sorry that I refused
to be your opponent in the dissertation proceeding. Some members of your
Institute misled me. Now I understand this, and I like everything that you
have published. I consider you the most representative of scholars in African
subjects in your Institute. Forgive me if you can, and consider me your
friend." I did not need to ask him who had misled him. I could imagine what
his answer would be.

As a result of the successful defense, my salary began automatically
to increase. As time went on, I received automatic raises as prescribed by law,
and supplements for my knowledge of foreign languages. Financially, I no
longer had problems—and there was nothing that Ksenia's group could do
to stop it. Many scholars in the Institute of African Studies remained in the
same situation that I had been, with no hope of salary raises. They struggled,
they begged and they demeaned themselves in the attempts to get a living
salary. All is fair in love and war, and this was a war in which they denounced
friends and resorted to any tactic that offered hope. I did not want to be a
part of this struggle. I did not want to dirty myself. I had made ends meet by
my published articles, by film-scripts that I had written, and even by acting
in some of those films.

I got my first film role when I was six. During the war, Moscow filmmakers came to Tashkent to make a movie about Hadja Nasredin, a famous
Uzbek clown and sage. Dressed in a gold suit, I stood out from the crowd
around a Bukhara emir who I was fanning with huge feathers. The fan was so
big that I was almost falling down with each stroke. The money that I made
from this film was of great help to my mother.

When I came to Moscow, I began to participate in every Soviet
movie that needed a black face. Sometimes, the producers would ask me to
recruit more extras of African descent. In effect I became a talent scout for
Soviet films. The task took me to other cities and to Universities in the Soviet
Union where Africans were studying. To the best of my recollection, I acted

in more than ten films. I wouldn't make any great effort to remember them because they were mostly very bad movies. If there were Blacks in the film, it meant that the film was used for blaming the USA, but it did not help Blacks. At the same time these films were far from reality. This was exactly what they were trying to do with Langston Hughes in 1932.

Among the good movies was *Thirty-Three*—the first Soviet satire, but few people know about it because the regime frowned on the showing of a film that criticized them. The plot was very simple. A man living in a small town was suddenly discovered to have 33 teeth, instead of the normal 32. He was brought to Moscow where he acquired great fame. Eventually it was decided to send him on a space mission. Meanwhile, another man having 33 teeth was discovered in the same town. For him there was no great honor or respect. He became jealous, took a crowbar and, one night, tried to destroy a monument erected to his predecessor. The story was not the main purpose of the movie. It was merely a portrayal of everyday Soviet life, and it ridiculed all the aspects about which the country's citizens did not, and could not, speak.

For example, in one scene, the hero, a famous actor named Leonov, goes to his wife and family in a village to ask their permission to participate in a space flight. This alone contravenes the Soviet stereotype in which only the Party decides such matters, and it is a big secret even in the family. The audience sees a convoy of official limousines, escorted by motorcycles, traversing a dusty, potholed road to a ramshackle farmhouse, where the wife is hanging washing. Leonov climbs out of the car, followed by an obvious caricature of a KGB agent, walks up to her and whispers in her ear. She responds by hitting him with wet laundry, whereupon he returns to the KGB agent and says: "The family agrees." That somewhat simplistic scene had poked fun at a number of sacred cows, including the way that Soviet officialdom appeared in public, the ubiquitous KGB presence and the secrecy that surrounded cosmonauts. Public laughter was more than the KGB could endure. They banned the film.

My role was that of an African woman, with a child, who explains to the hero how teeth are treated in Africa. Again, to a Moscow audience, the situation was hilarious.

There were two passable movies in which I acted together with my daughter. In one, *Black Sun,* written about Patrice Lumumba, the first President of the Congo, I played the role of a coquette who tries to help him escape from his opponents and CIA. For this film, I wrote the script and acted as advisor on Africa. The second was *Black Like Me,* an American story. Speshnev, a famous Soviet film director made both these films.

In 1966, I was invited to the studio of a documentary company. The First Festival of African Culture and Art had just taken place in Dakar, Senegal. There was no official Soviet participation, since the organizers were demanding an entrance fee of two million dollars and the USSR did not have that kind of foreign currency to spare. But two Soviet cameramen were there, by sheer coincidence, and they succeeded in persuading—with the help of some bottles of vodka—an Italian film crew to let them shoot scenes together with them. They returned to Moscow with masses of footage. I was asked to help them piece together their material into one coherent film. We made one film of one-hour length titled *The Rhythms of Africa* in which we tried to show all aspects of African culture—dance, music, songs, theater and plastic arts. I invited a famous Soviet art critic, Vil Mirimanov, to serve as a consultant. He used to work for my Institute, but such talented people were not desired here and Mirimanov had to leave. Vil is generally regarded now as the leading expert in African art in the world. He has published books on African art and is the Vice President of the International Society for the Study of Art. He liked the film and said that he had found no mistakes in its conceptions.

One day I received a phone call inviting me to Friendship House where a group of experts were gathering to discuss the film. I could not understand why Friendship House, which was only known for expert KGB agents who controlled everything relating to foreigners, would be involved in film discussion. When I arrived, I was even more surprised. The entire Ksenia group from the Institute was there. After Potekhin's death they had become even stronger. Nobody among them was conversant with African art. In addition, Muhidinov, a member of the Political bureau of the Communist Party Central Committee, was also present. Clearly, my enemies had called in heavy guns.

A representative from the Institute opened with a declaration that I had made a "pro-American" film. Challenged to prove the point, he said that he had counted the flags shown around the festival hall and that there were more American than any other. Further, there were no Soviet flags. I responded that Liberian flags also looked like the Stars and Stripes and, if there were no Soviet flags it was because the USSR was not a participant. Muhidinov then delivered a heavy pronouncement, "I have been to Africa. I have seen that they have nothing to eat or wear. Yet, you show them singing and dancing. This is a distortion." I explained patiently that the material had come from a Festival of Culture where people obviously demonstrated native dances and were dressed appropriately.

Beyond those two responses, I realized that it was better to remain silent. I couldn't find responses at the stupid level of the criticism, so I allowed them to expend themselves unchallenged. The scene was reminiscent of the purge atmosphere of 1937, and talk of this kind could result in my arrest. Particularly disturbing was the fact that some of the experts on Africa, whom I knew to be decent men and women, were also remaining silent—presumably out of fear. The shock was so great that for several days I did not go to the studio. Then I got a phone call from Serov, the cameraman who had brought the material from Dakar. He wanted to know: "What happened to you? Are you disillusioned by the criticism? Aren't you familiar with the proverb about the dog barking while the caravan continues on its way? Let's continue. I have more material. You will write the story, and I will make the film." We made two more films. One was called *The Folk Art of Senegal,* in which we showed ritual dances, wooden sculpture, musicians, actors and singers. The second was named *The Centuries of Africa Speak.* Here we compared the traditions of ancient times with modern African art.

I have already mentioned that the Communist Party Committee of the Institute had stopped my lectures in factories. In 1974, the International Year of the Woman, gatherings were discussing the situation of women in the USSR and outside. The Moscow House of Scientists, of whom I was a member, held an Academic seminar on the subject. They were unable to find a speaker on the situation of African women. I had already published several articles in the Soviet press. I was approached by the Presidium of the Academy of Science and the Society of Knowledge, which is responsible for recruiting Ph.D. level lecturers, to tour the Soviet Union with lectures. It was requested that I should make a report to the seminar.

The first speaker was Tereshkova, the first woman cosmonaut. After returning from outer space, she was appointed chairman of the Soviet Womens Committee. She read a dull, toneless paper that bored the audience. On the spot, I decided to drop my notes (in fact I never read from my paper when I lecture) and give a totally different presentation. Making it as vivid as I could, I interjected humor and gave examples from my own experience of being a Muslim wife. The auditorium was awake and attentive. They laughed at the right points, then applauded loudly when I finished. As a result the Society of Knowledge invited me to give a series of lectures across the USSR during the Year of the Woman.

My tour, to a number of Siberian cities and some of the remote republics of the USSR, was a great success. I received much press attention and I became the subject of many articles. Upon my return to Moscow, the Society of Knowledge asked me why I was never on the list of speakers submitted to them by the Institute of African Studies. I told them about the situation in the Institute and the internal Communist Party Committee, which would only list its own favorites. The Society representatives responded that they were affiliated directly with the Central Committee of the Communist Party. If they chose to invite me, no minor Party Committee in a mere Institute could interfere. And they admit that my style of speaking they need very much.

In the first years of my association with them, I was sent to lecture in almost all the big cities of the USSR. Later, I was elected Secretary of the Scientific Council on Culture and Literature of the Society. This gave me the opportunity to visit those cities of the Soviet Union, which were particularly interesting to me yet difficult to access for most citizens. Thus I was able to see places like Kamchatka, Yakutia, Sakhalin, Taimir, Yamal and others which were forbidden to foreigners and to ordinary Soviet citizens. I was also able to travel in an unaccustomed comfort. In areas where there were few hotels and restaurants, if any, I would be met by official drivers and taken to comfortable homes, with good cooks. All was provided, and all was paid for—in a country where the shops were empty and salaries were usually meaningless. My work for the Society gave me a view of the USSR far beyond that of most other people. I met interesting people, saw beautiful sights and visited places the existence of which was not even common knowledge. I saw Lake Baikal, which is famous for having the purest water in the world, the Budhist temple at Buryatia, the Kamchatka volcanoes, the Caucasus mountains and the Black, Caspian, White and Japanese seas. I traversed from the icy cold of the North Pole to the burning southern deserts and from the fringes of Europe to the Bering Straits facing Alaska.

Traveling around the country, it was noticeable that people far from Moscow were very different from those in the capital city. They were simpler, kinder and much more open. I was constantly surprised by their tolerance. Many of them lived in ruined houses with inadequate food and clothing. These people were subject to eternal need for ration coupons in order to get minimal supplies. Yet these people, living in abject poverty, were located in areas of the Soviet Union that were rich in oil, gold and diamond deposits and so on.

Wherever I went, I was met with open arms. Often I would be asked to speak to audiences five times a day. They were so obviously deprived of news and information about the outside world that I ended up talking about anything and everything: Russia, the USA, music, cinema, history, literature, and foreign policy... It was interesting to watch their reaction to my black skin. Most of them had never seen a Black man or woman in their entire lives. My audiences always began with the assumption that they would not be able to understand me. With my skin color, it was obvious that I couldn't speak Russian or if I did speak, it will be with strong accent. Then they began to grasp that my Russian was even better than theirs. By the time that they had puzzled out how it was that I spoke the language so well, the lecture would be almost over. Each time I watched this lengthy process take place in the expressions on their faces. I could even see how their brains were stirring. As I opened the meeting to questions, the first was invariably: "Where did you learn such good Russian?" Invariably, I ended up giving a potted biography of my life. I had to do this so often that I now have recall of every tiny detail.

By nature, Russians tend to be kind and open people. But too many years of living in a totalitarian regime had done its damage. One current theory has it that the national genes are changing and that Russians will not in the future be what they were in the past. There was a time when widespread belief held that the nation had a mystical soul which expressed itself in kindness, compassion and self-sacrifice. However, more and more negative characteristics have materialized under the influence of threatened genocide, hunger, denunciations, and the awareness of concentration and forced labor camps. In a society where each watches the other, and informing becomes a way to survive, kindness and compassion are doomed to extinction. Arrogance, suspicion and jealousy become common coinage when the ruling Party is both corrupt and absolute. Nevertheless, among the common people, outside the ranks of the regime, hospitality and human kindness can still be found.

My travels around the USSR also helped me to understand the situation of those minority nations that were in the last stages of their survival. In Moscow, there were no sources of information about these nations. Even Academic discussions about the minorities were held in conditions of secrecy and participants needed KGB clearance. That was why, on a trip to the east of Russia, I took time out to visit the Karyak people of the Kamchatka Peninsula, in order to study their art and culture. It took 12 hours by plane from Moscow to Petropavlosk on Kamchatka, then another three to fly north to a point where a helicopter picked me up for the last two hours. The entire population of the village came to welcome the helicopter. It was their only contact with the outside world. In addition, the Russian pilots sometimes smuggled forbidden vodka, which they traded for reindeer antlers. Sadly, the majority of these nations are dying a slow death from drinking vodka.

When I emerged from the helicopter, the Karyaks were in shock. Maybe they had never seen anyone as tall as me. Like the populace of nearly extinct nations, they were small. Or, perhaps, they had never before seen black skin. As they recovered, they began to laugh. As I walked down the only street of the village, they followed, still laughing and very friendly. Laughter was apparently so much a part of their lives that any question was first answered with a laugh, and only then with a verbal response. There was nothing offensive about the mannerism. They brought me to the village hall where I talked to them for a few minutes, then invited questions as usual. To my utter astonishment, a woman stood up and said: "What about Mona Lisa? How is she?" It was my turn to laugh. In the frozen wilderness too far away to know anything about Kamchatka, with no radio or television, this was their question. Afterwards I discovered that the woman was a Communist Party member who had been sent to a city to learn Russian reading and writing. She had picked up the name, yet knew nothing about Leonardo's mysterious woman.

It was not an easy encounter. My talk was punctuated by constant coughing. Later I would learn that they suffered from a 99% incidence of tuberculosis. Additionally, it was quite a problem to know what to say to such a strange audience.

Stone built homes provided by the regime had replaced their deer hide homes which had adequate warmth in winter. The stone built homes were terrible and offered no weather protection whatsoever. One old tent dwelling still remained, perhaps to permit the Soviet officials to brag about how the people's lot had improved. Descending to my knees, amid my hosts' constant laughter, I crawled through a low opening. The interior was infinitely warmer that the wooden or stone huts. It struck me that I might have discovered one reason for the tuberculosis that was rife among them.

I was brought to the hall of the Village Council, and offered a bed on a table under a giant portrait of Lenin and a red flag in the corner of the room. Throughout the night, the entire population of the village watched me through the window. The next morning, I decided to seek out a bathroom. Told that one had been built for the entire population in the center of the village, I was escorted there by a huge crowd. When I arrived at our destination, I discovered that it is good idea to build them a toilet, but it is also a good idea to explain how to use it. There was no way that I was going to plough through yards of muck, so I walked out of the village, still with an escort, to one of the low hillocks that made up the terrain. Eventually I had to draw on all my athletic abilities to run so fast that I could gain a few minutes alone.

Under Soviet law, women and children were not allowed to accompany the men of the family to work. When the men shepherded their deer flocks wherever there was sparse pasture, the children were taken to Russian cities for education. The women, left at home with nothing to do, took to drink. When they went to the cities to visit their children, there was a yawning communication gap. The children no longer knew the Karyak language. Some of the mothers couldn't understand their children's songs and stories. After ten years in Russian orphanages, the younger generation had little desire to return to their native villages. Those that did found no jobs, nothing to do, and no way to pass the time. They too began to drink.

Their culture had revolved around the reindeer. They sang about them and their dances were modeled on the animal's movements. In the nineteenth century both men and women had worn garments of deer skin, beautified by colorful embroidery. Some of the garments had been exhibited in Paris and London, and had won prizes for their design. Now, Communist Party officials no longer allowed them to take deer skins to make clothes. To get what had been theirs by right, they were now expected to buy at exorbitant prices in the shops of nearby towns. Those successive generations of the Karyak people had lost their language, their songs and dances—and even the craftsmanship that had enabled them survival in the frozen wasteland. Mothers no longer wanted to keep their children at home. Orphanages and vodka had become norms, and the deer, which had contributed so much, was no longer a central factor in their lives. I do not think that Paul Robeson would like to have seen this when he came to the Soviet Union in 1934 to collect information about minorities.

I had been lucky in organizing my expedition to the Karyakis. In Sakhalin, my pressure and energy were to no avail. I could not get official permission to visit, in the north of the island, the Ainy people, from whom by tradition the Japanese are descended. To console me, I was invited to the local television station to watch an archive film about them. It was a beautiful propaganda production. Women dressed in exquisite skins were dancing a legend about the deer. I said that I had not noticed women dressed that well in Sakhalin. In fact, the local dress was mostly torn and grubby European. My courteous hostess explained: "We sewed the dresses especially for the film." "And you left them the dresses as a present," I mused. The answer: "No. How would that be possible? They would have sold them to buy vodka."

I went to Taimur, to see the living conditions of the Nganasyan and other nations in the far north of the USSR. Soviet "civilization" had transported them from their traditional fertile pasturelands to the outer islands of the White Sea. The precious pasture became littered with old rails, empty oil barrels, torn tires and the other debris of the twentieth century. Now the landscape is one of oil derricks. Unfortunately for the Nganasyan, they had been living over a natural reserve of oil and gold. None of the benefits of the modern age were available to them. They didn't see doctors from one year to the next.

I became interested in the lives of these people because of the many years that I had spent studying African races. Many of the problems were common. For example, both African tribes and Soviet minorities shared a limitation of language. Lacking a local alphabet, they were compelled to rely on the language of the regime, whether colonial in Africa, or Russian in the USSR. They were caught between the devil and the deep blue sea. If they remained with their own dialect, they maintained and even enriched a native culture, but lost contact with the outside world. If they opted for the advantages of external and wide communication, they gave up their cultural roots and perhaps even lost the value system that had kept them alive. How can the problem be solved? I wish I knew. If there is an answer, I haven't yet found it. And the same problems very obviously exist through music and filmmaking. If it is necessary to adopt European musical instruments, for instance, in the effort to reach communication then the music has been changed... and so on.

In my work, I was trying to reach some kind of scholar approach to these problems. But my Institute would not allow me to write about such subjects. I had to publish tedious papers: "The Spread of Marxism in Africa," "Trade Unionism in Zanzibar," "The Year of Marx in Africa" (whatever that may mean) and "The Liberation of Women in African Countries Having Socialist Orientation." The Institute had no interest in African culture. Later, they would open a Department of Culture," it was based on ideological lines that had little to do with the subject matter.

I am thankful for Ivan Potekhin's advice to study African music. The studies helped me to understand many aspects of African culture. In addition, concentration on music as a main theme kept me out of the ideological conflicts that were always going on inside the Institute of African Studies. I spent more than thirty years researching the music of Africa, beginning with the thorough work on my doctoral thesis. My main objective was to demonstrate the influence of historical trends on music. This includes colonialism which destroyed much of the traditional musical culture; the influx of Arabs and Islamization of Africa which brought about a lot of changes as two different forms of music blended into each other; the conversion of many Africans to Christianity and their exposure to European music. A major late influence was the first encounter between Africans and the military music of World War II armies. As they adopted the instruments that they were hearing, they tended to move from a pentatonic scale to a diatonic.

I was lucky in that I had access to the archives of von Hornbostel in Leningrad. He was a German anthropologist who had harnessed the possibilities of the new cylindrical recording machines of the early 1900s to the needs of his research. Von Hornbostel used every opportunity to convince acquaintances travelling in Africa, including missionaries, merchants and doctors, to take along a "dictaphone" and record the music that they heard. He eventually acquired 15,000 recordings from all over Africa. With the rise to power of Adolf Hitler, von Hornbostel fled to America. His archive remained in Germany and was taken, after World War II, to the Pushkin Museum in Leningrad, where it remained for almost forty years until it returned to Germany. During those years, it was sealed off from public eyes. Few people even knew that it existed, and even fewer were allowed access. Professor Olderogge, who had now become my "best friend," obtained for me the necessary permission to work with von Hornbostel's material.

Another source was the performances of African ensembles in the Soviet Union. These became much more frequent after the advent of independence on the African continent. And whenever a group visited the USSR, I reviewed their presentations for the Soviet and African press. Though three or four other people began to study African music, I was the first to enter this field in the Soviet Union. As a result, I became a contributor to the *Soviet Encyclopedia,* the *Encyclopedic Dictionary of Africa* and, in several instances, the *Encyclopedia Britannica.*

The study of African music developed my interest in other spheres of culture beginning with literature and religion—which was vital because of the focus of music on cults—and eventually taking me to cinematography. Every two years, I went to Tashkent to the International Festival of African and Asian Films. Ironically, Tashkent happened to be the best place in the world to see African films. Distributors across the African continent were far more interested in showing American and Indian movies. And, in any case, the paucity of technical resources had limited the filmmakers to narrow reels, which meant that their products were not suitable for the 35-mm projectors of large cinemas. At Tashkent, the larger halls were taken up with Japanese and Indian films, and the Africans were shown in smaller halls to smaller audiences. From early morning to late at night, I sat watching the small screen. Eventually, and not by design, I had become the first, and perhaps only, Soviet expert on the African film industry. Consequently, I wrote film reviews for the press in addition to my music columns.

As a historian, I was very interested in the contacts between Black Americans and Africans. I published articles: "Marcus Garvey and his Influence on the National Liberation Movements in Africa;" The "Ideas of William Du Bois and their Influence on the Liberation Movements in the United States and Africa;" The "Role Played by Black Americans and Africans in the Communist Internationale in the 1920s and 30s."

None of this was within the strict lines of my job description at the Institute. For me, it was a hobby rather than the full time occupation that paid my salary. After Potekhin's death, my visits to Tashkent and Leningrad were mostly on my own time, on weekends. Though the Institute of African Studies had opted to devote its energies to politics, economics and its own theories about "the socialist orientation in Africa," and frowned on my spheres of interest, I found that my writings were in demand. The Institute constantly offered articles and papers to the African press and, invariably, their contacts were rejected the stuffy writings about politics and instead published my articles about African culture. To my amazement, I discovered that a paper called "The Contribution of African Culture to World Civilization"—which I had written, then forgotten—was being serialized in newspapers across the whole of Africa. Though I published more than a hundred articles and Academic papers, my greatest success was a small book entitled *Africans in Russia,* which was a history of a previously undocumented but highly significant aspect of Russian life.

CHAPTER SEVEN

Africans in Russia

I have already mentioned Apollon Davidson, but his role in the development of my life as a scholar deserves more detail. Even during the lifetime of Ivan Potekhin, it was Apollon who became my mentor and the motivational force behind my research. He was the one who pushed me into publishing on various subjects. Every session with him stimulated interest in new areas.

Apollon was born in 1929. He graduated with distinction from Leningrad State University, and quickly became a distinguished scholar of African studies especially in relation to South Africa. He was one of the first senior researchers to join the Institute of African Studies. Ksenia and her group had ascertained that Apollon's father had been exiled during one of Stalin's purges. They used that, supported by the fact that he never joined the Communist Party, to raise every conceivable obstacle in his professional and personal way. His life became difficult. Nevertheless, outside the Institute he achieved a position that was unassailable. Whenever Soviet politicians or functionaries went to attend international conferences about Africa, they took Apollon along as their consultant, though he did not conform to any of the standard requirements for such delegations.

His reputation and independent standing infuriated Ksenia's group even more. Apollon, however, was far too proud a man to attempt a defense against the rabble yapping at his heels. Eventually, he left the Institute to become the Head of the Department of Africa in the Institute of World History and a Professor at the Institute of Asia and African Studies at Moscow State University. Our relationship remained close, and he was constantly giving me new ideas and directions for my own work. One day out of the blue, he suggested that I should write about Africans in Russia. I was, of course, aware of a Great Russian poet of African origin, Alexander Pushkin, and had heard Mr. Cook from Batumi tell me about Africans in the Caucasus, but had never thought of creating a coherent account as an identifiable historical problem. I decided to go to the Caucasus to take a look at this phenomenon, about which nobody had ever written.

In 1965, I came to Batumi, Adjaria and checked into the same hotel where I had been two years ago with my baby daughter. A day later I got a phone call from the Central Committee of the Communist Party of the smallest Republic in the USSR. A very officious voice announced that the General Secretary of the Party wanted to see me. I was amazed to find that this high functionary already knew that I had come to his domain. Curious about the whole episode, I went to the Party's pompous headquarters, located in a huge building, complete with ornate pillars and surrounding palm trees.

The Secretary, a brown haired, blue eyed Adjarian, sat in an immense office with windows opening to the sea. He very carefully tried to ascertain where I had come from, where I lived and for whom I worked. I asked him whether he knew about the African people living in his Republic. He declared: "I am hearing about them for the first time in my life. But I ask you, if you go to look for them, do not do so without an escort of my people." Returning to Cook, I reported the conversation. Laughing, he commented: "By the way, one of the Secretary's drivers is an African. Don't listen to him. I'll give you names and addresses and you should try to get to them by yourself."

I had a constant feeling that the eyes of the first citizen of this exotic republic were upon me, though I couldn't understand why. It wasn't long before I got another phone call from him. He said: "Why don't I see you at the beach?" I told him that I tried not to be seen too much on the street, because a crowd of local men always followed me. One occasion, when I had gone to the beach, I took a dip, then lay down on the sand and closed my eyes. When I opened them again, I was surrounded by a group of macho types, who were heatedly discussing my figure. The Secretary asked: "Did they say anything bad about you?" "On the contrary," I replied, "but I don't feel comfortable with all that attention." "Excuse us Adjarians. It's not long since we achieved literacy here. I would like to invite you to the government's private beach."

He sent a car and driver for me. The beach looked like heaven. Across the pebble beach, from the changing rooms to the water, extended a red carpet. All the servants wore immaculate white uniforms. Each guest had, not a wooden deckchair, but a couch upholstered in silk fabrics, and by each one stood a personal telephone. The few bathers were ministers of the Adjarian government. They became excited when they saw me. I was something different from the women they normally see. And all this luxury was mere yards away from a crowded public beach, where it was impossible to reach the water without treading on bodies. There, amid the thousands, you could drown and nobody would notice. I liked neither government beach, mainly because there were no women whatsoever. It was my first and last visit to the Secretary's private beach resort.

The Secretary had not forgotten our talk. Each morning, I emerged from the hotel to find three cars waiting for me, and an escort of well built, athletic men, all dressed in white nylon shirts and black ties.

On the first day, we came to a village, where there was a tea plantation. People were working in the fields but, as our convoy approached, they fled. The same event was repeated at the next village. We spent several days in this fashion, only stopping for lunch at one of the villages. I noticed that whenever we sat at table, the company was exclusively male. Finally I asked why there were no women at the table. I was told that they had already eaten. I declared that I would not sit at the lunch table if there were no women there. My companions started to "trap" women and seat them. Each time they set out to catch another, the previous one would bolt. I realized that it was hopeless. There was no way that I could beat decades of a pattern imposed on the Adjarians by Turkish Muslim tradition. And so, I compromised my principles and adjusted to being the only woman eating in the company of men. From their viewpoint, it was permissible because I was not one of their women, but rather a foreign guest.

When we returned to Batumi, I asked Mr. Cook why everyone ran away when we appeared. He said that a black government car always meant bad news: new taxes or somebody was about to be arrested. I knew wouldn't get anywhere, or talk to anyone, traveling in this company.

One evening in the hotel, I met a young student from Mali. He was destined to become, much later, the ambassador of his country in the Soviet Union. I told him my story and asked him if he was willing to travel together with me, in preference to the government entourage. Next morning, like in a detective story, we evaded the escort by sneaking out a back door of the hotel. Reaching the road that ran up into the mountains, we began to try our luck at hitchhiking. To my surprise, the first car stopped. The driver was Armenian. I asked him if he knew where there were Africans. He said that of course he did, and he would be willing to take us, but on condition. First, we must come to his village to see how the Armenians lived.

The Armenian village was high in the mountains, situated on a rocky slope. The scene was amazing. Orange trees, tangerines, lemons were growing on terraces between wild flowers and cultivated gardens. What an effort must have been invested to wrest soil for gardens and fruit trees out of these rocks! We spent two or three hours being entertained at a rich table, groaning under the weight of delicacies, though we had been unexpected guests. We didn't want to leave this extraordinary hospitality.

Our Armenian host took us to the next village, and here I met my first African. He was short, stocky and very shy. But his wife was not afflicted with the same problem. She was a very tall talkative Tartar woman with red hair and Mongolian eyes. She had produced ten children, all with black skin, Mongolian eyes and kinky red hair! An unusual crossbreed!

I left Batumi and moved on to Suhumi, the capital of Abhazia, another miniscule subtropical republic. Here again, my hotel was on the beach, near a seaport. From the window of my room, I could see a constant stream of ships bearing the flags of different nations. The air was constantly vibrating with loud Italian music. It only stopped late at night.

In Abhazia, there were many descendants of two African sisters who had been brought from Turkey in the late 1800s. I met two of their daughters, Nutza and Tsutsa. Nutza was inhospitable and hostile: "Many journalists and writers come and ask me all sorts of questions, but no one helps me get an apartment and a telephone." By Soviet standards, she had little cause to complain. Educated in Tbilisi, a capital of Georgia, she became a gynecologist, acquired considerable respect and fame, had been written about in many articles and had been elected to the Supreme Soviet of Abhazia. One day she received a letter from a Russian who had read about her in a newspaper. They corresponded, met and married. Soon there was a daughter. Of course she had problems, but they were typical Soviet problems. Her husband became a drunkard. There were difficulties in getting a bigger apartment.

Tsutsa was a waitress. She lived in a beautiful, big, two-storied house among orange trees and tangerines. From time to time she took her fruit to Moscow, sold it in the city's markets and made a lot of money.

Some of the Africans had a difficult life in the Caucasus. High in the mountains of Abhazia, on a tobacco plantation, I visited one African family who was living in a bare hut, with no doors or windows. They got into their house by crawling through a small hole hacked in one of the walls. They had neither electricity nor running water. Their children did not attend school.

There, in the mountains, I met an African family, the head of which was an old man named Toupania. That year he was 102, but his memory was remarkable. He could still describe how he had been caught, as a child in Africa, and shipped north to Turkey by the Arab slave traders. From Turkey, he had been taken to Abhazia.

It is not easy to relate to the people that I met in Adjaria and Abhazia as typical Africans. For two or three centuries, there had been intermarriage with Abhazians, Adjarians, Georgians, Armenians and Russians. Their skins were paler, their hair had straightened and the color had become a strange mix with local characteristics. Yet, there were some that had remained constant to their anthropological type, and all of them remembered that their roots were in Africa.

I could not leave the Caucasus without meeting Shamba from Tbilisi, about whom I had heard wherever I went in the area. Tbilisi is a beautiful city sitting on the Georgian hills above the rapidly flowing Kura River. In the taxi from the airport, I asked the driver whether he knew of an African called Shamba. "Of course I do," he relied. "Everyone knows him in Tbilisi." All the way to the city, the driver talked about him. Shamba had been born in Congo. At the age of eight, Arabs brought him to Iran with his parents. There, he was separated from his family and sold to a British officer, who took him to Turkey. In Istanbul, the Englishman lost him in a game of cards to a Georgian officer, who brought him to Tbilisi. Shamba had participated in the revolution and the civil war. Afterwards, he became fire chief of the city and a local hero. A book and many newspaper articles had been written about him and a bust of him occupies a place of honor in the city's history museum.

Shamba received me very hospitably. He was a burly, very black, dignified man with a typical African face and a shaven head. He wasn't very talkative. He was obviously in love with Tbilisi and very proud of the city. His first remark to me was that he wanted personally to introduce me to the city. Walking with him on the street was next to impossible. People were constantly rushing up to embrace him, kiss him, and thank him for having saved their lives or their close relatives. All wanted to invite him home or to a restaurant, which in Georgia is a unique experience. Georgians sit around a table and drink but, unlike the Russians, they can drink all night without getting intoxicated. The proceedings begin with the selection of one of them as "tamada"— the chairman of the table. Only he can say when it is permissible to drink. Without his permission, no one can speak. He points at whomever he chooses, and the lucky man must then make a flowery toast, and perhaps even sing it. Anyone unable to carry that off has no place in such company.

Shamba took me to the most beautiful spot in the city on the banks of the Kura. There, in a cave, there was a cozy little restaurant that served marvelous Georgian food. We talked about his life in Africa, but with incessant interruptions by temperamental locals who wanted to show their love and respect. He told me that he had married a Russian woman and his son was a policeman. He had three grandchildren, all of whom looked typically Russian: blonde with blue eyes.

Upon my return to Moscow, I decided to do a literature search at the library for any evidence of the Africans in the Caucasus. I found newspapers from before World War I, which had published sensational accounts under headlines like "Black Russians," "Batumi Negroes" and "Suhumi Negroes." The audience response was so great that *Caucasus*, the daily paper of the region, had established a regular feature entitled "More about Batumi Negroes." There were articles by the first Russian scholars to study the subject, among them Vradi, Elius and Kovalevsky, who had written that the entire African descent population in the Caucasus numbered no more than 500 people. They were well assimilated, spoke the local languages and wore the regional dress, but differed in their anthropological features and, of course, the color of their skins. The majority of them lived hard lives as unskilled laborers. For example, Elius wrote, in the Petersburg *Argos* magazine:

> It is so strange to encounter such a phenomenon as a village of Negroes, so close to a big city yet the citizens have never heard about them. To encounter such a phenomenon which seems to be a subject for attention and research. All this is so unique that I have never, in my life, experienced such joy of discovery as at the moment when I saw with my own eyes the existence of Black people in the Caucasus.

He finishes his article with the conclusion:

> The fact of existence of Africans in Russia must become known and the subject of scientific attention. We in Russia can find more oddities and unexpected things than you, my readers, might think.

Caucasus declared on 16 March 1913, before the Batum region joined Russia, that Africans lived in the swamp near Batumi. They lived in clusters of farmsteads. There were apparently thirty such families. When the region became a province of Russia, some of them went to Turkey, where their families can still be found near Trabizon and other Turkish cities.

Professor Kovalevsky wrote about the amazing revelation that there was an entire village of Africans in Abhazia. It is known that the Caucasus, from early times, had been at the center of international events that concerned West and East, the Black Sea and Mediterranean, Africa and Asia. There are theories that trade with Egypt had brought contingents of Africans to the Caucasus as early as the first Pharaonic dynasties. Ancient Greek mythology speaks of the sailors on the *Argo* seeking the Golden Fleece, which was guarded by a dragon. After a long series of adventures, they came to Kolhida, situated at exactly the spot where Africans presently live on the Black Sea shores. With the help of Queen Medea, they fled but were trapped by Kolhs. The historian Heroditus, in the fifth century, believed that the Kolhs of Kolhida were in fact Black men from Ethiopia.

The legends surrounding the Africans of Abhazia have persisted through many centuries. Ancient Greeks, Romans, Arabs and Genoese all maintained their colonies and trading stations on the shores of the Black Sea. Starting in the fifteenth century, Abhazia was subjected to three centuries of domination by Turkish sultans, who developed the slave trade even further. At the beginning of the nineteenth century, Abhazia united with Russia and some 70,000 people migrated from Abhazia to Turkey. On their way south, some stayed in Batumi that was still a Turkish possession. Abhazian feudal overlords arrived with their slaves, and this is how many of the present African population reached that part of the world. How many Africans are in that region now? Nobody knows because we do not have race statistics.

But there were other ways for Africans to appear in Russia. One of them involves the activities of Czar Peter the Great. He sought to reform Russia, and bring the country into line with the European standards of those days. In doing so, it was of no concern to him whether those who could help were Russian or foreign, yellow, red or black. Swiss friend, Franz Lefort, stimulated his interest in Africans. In a series of unpublished letters, written by Lefort to the Czar when he was traveling incognito in Europe and which I discovered in the Russian National Archives, Lefort insisted that there were Africans at every European monarch court and these Africans are famous for their good work. Each letter ended with the admonition: "Peter, my friend, don't forget to bring Africans!" In one exchange, Peter replied, "What kind of Africans do you want me to bring?" Lefort responded, "Big ones..." I also found documentary evidence of Peter's continuing interest in the Africans who did come to Russia, in the form of Peter's instructions to provide education to one or another of these Africans. He even wrote in detail about the clothes that should be bought for them.

Peter the Great's agent in Turkey, Count Savva Raguzinsky, was usually engaged in finding wines and other items that the Czar desired. In another unpublished letter to the Minister of Foreign Affairs, the Count reported that he had purchased three African boys. The first he was sending to the Minister, the second he asked to be delivered to his own household, and the third—"which is the worst"—should be taken to Peter the Great. Peter loved Abram Hannibal, adopted him, and taught him Russian and mathematics, then sent him to France to study artillery. He returned to Russia as a lieutenant, having participated in the Franco-Spanish War. Then, it so happened that "the worst" of the Count's purchases became the most famous general of his generation, commander in chief of the Czarist armies. Hannibal sired eleven children, some of whom also attained the rank of a general in the Russian army. His great grandson Alexander Pushkin a genius poet, was to make a major contribution to Russian and world culture.

Usually, racists declare that people of African descent are not able to accept European culture. Pushkin proved that Africans not only can accept European culture but even more, they can influence it.

It is known that the average student knows 20–25 thousand words, and the average professor—30 thousand words. The scientists concluded that only two people have existed who knew more than forty thousand words: Pushkin and Shakespeare.

In Russia there are hundreds of societies and thousands of writers that study the life and works of Pushkin. Russians know everything about him, including his relations with his friends and women. More than 200 years after his birth in 1799, many publications about him are introduced yearly. That is why I am not writing about him here. You cannot write about Pushkin just on a few pages.

In 1966, I published *Africans in Russia* in Paris and London. That year, there was the First Festival of All African Arts in Dakar, Senegal. Official participation by countries cost a fee of two million U.S. dollars, a sum that the Soviet Union did not feel able to devote to an African subject. Instead, the entire printing of my book was sent to Dakar, where it was distributed to the African participants free of charge. No copies remained for distribution in the Soviet Union or the United States.

The book had been handled, in common Soviet practice, by an official literary agency that made all the deals with foreign publishing houses. Upon receipt of the manuscript, the chief editor of the agency discarded my chapter on Pushkin. When I protested, he said: "I consider Pushkin to be a Great Russian poet—not an African!" He went on to hint that I was a "nationalist," which in Russian parlance was a very strong and even dangerous curse. In his book *American Dilemma* Swedish author Gunnar Murdal wrote that in

Russia there is no racism, except anti-Semitism. To prove his statement he writes that in Russia Pushkin is a Great Russian poet but in America he would be a 'Negro'.

I needed to come to the United States to hear great grandsons of those Africans who were brought from Africa into slavery still described as "African" Americans. Another thing that I found out in the United States, and which confused me no end, was the term "Caucasian" applied to people of European origin. This is definitely not a scholarly term. Anthropology has no record of such a definition, and I can confirm on the basis of my travels in the Caucasus that no white people originated from there. By American standards, the peoples of the Caucasus are decidedly "colored" or of olive color with black hair.

There were several other themes which I developed under the influence of Apollon Davidson. One of them was about African and African American communists that came to the Soviet Union in the 1920s. I mentioned them in the first chapter of this book. It took me a lot of time working in the archives, and interviewing with these people. Among those working with *Communist International* was Marx from South Africa, and B. Patterson from USA and several others. They helped me to finish my article "International Trade-Union of Negro Workers", which was published in Moscow and many other countries, including the USA and Gayana. Only Marx was thinking that such research is not needed. But I answered him, that history gives us positive and negative lessons. If we shall know them, we shall not make the same mistakes. From Apollon Davidson I developed interest in "white spots" in history. For many years I studied the history of African people, and my articles and one book appeared in many African countries.

Dr. Du Bois was very kind to spend a lot of time talking to me, although I was very young then. I still remember our talks. One day I wrote an article about him which was published in many countries, including *Presence Africain* in Paris.

CHAPTER EIGHT

Faces and Masks

I have always been blessed with many friends. Some I acquired through common interests in music, sport, history or politics. Others I acquired because of simple human chemistry. The majority have remained friends throughout my whole life, even when we have been separated by great distances. For example, Ola Romanova, Anna Shumilinska, Ella Plotnikova and others remain from my schooldays in Tashkent. From my studies in the University, I can still count Ola Tschernischova, Vera Arvan, and Galia Davnaya. The days of glory, traveling around the USSR to participate in tennis championships, gave me friends in Tbilisi, Mziya and Givi. Lera lives in the Ukraine and other tennis players are in Lithuania, Latvia and Estonia. In the light of recent political developments, I can now visit old friends "abroad" in the newly independent countries.

One day in 1952, when I first arrived in Moscow, I met Rita Yemelianova in the Metro. We had met for the first time at the 1947 tennis championships in Saratov. She became champion of the Soviet Union in that year. Blue-eyed with high cheekbones, parted blonde—almost white—hair, carefully braided, Rita played semi-professionally, a prohibited status in Soviet sporting concepts. But she was really a student in art school. We became friends because of peculiar circumstances. She won the championship, but I got all the media attention, though I hadn't played that well. Rita sought me out to understand why the journalists surrounded me and not her. Fortunately, it was not jealousy, just curiosity. After a chance encounter in the Metro, we began to meet frequently. Her fiancé, Igor Ter-Ovanisian, world and Olympic gold medallist for the long jump, was my neighbor.

Igor was exceptional for an Armenian: he was both good looking and tall. Apart from his sporting prowess, he was an excellent dancer, a good painter and very skilled at languages. In fact, he picked up fluent English just by virtue of his visits to the United States to participate in sports meets. Since coming to America, I have met many people who still remember Igor and his appearances in the 50s and 60s. At the climax of his competitive career, he became a coach of the Soviet Olympic team and a member of the leading sports bodies. Perestroika affected his life, as it did others. Igor is now Deputy Minister of Sports in the government.

My friendship with Igor and Rita deepened during the two years that Abdulla lived in Moscow, waiting for me to agree to marry him. We four became close friends and, ultimately, we married on the same day. Whenever Rita was due to deliver a child, Igor had to travel to participate in some competition. And so I looked after his children, and they became "brother" and "sister" to my daughter.

Rita and Igor built a country house, using the construction plans prepared for the former president of Finland, Keikonnen, who was a personal friend of the couple. My daughter and I were frequent visitors. The house was always full of Olympic athletes from all over the world and there was never a problem to find partners for tennis or for a swim in the lake.

My daughter and I both loved animals and often spent Sundays in the homes of friends who had dogs, cats or other pets. My daughter especially liked the house of Ira, who was a famous singer with a remarkable family background. Her uncle, Count Vitte, had been Finance Minister in the last government of Csar Nicholas. She was also a distant cousin of Madame Blavatskaya, the founder of the International Theosophical Society, which is now headquartered in Chicago and Madras. Ira's husband had been a priest, and a dissident, who had been expelled from the Russian Orthodox Church, at the insistence of the KGB. After his death, which followed years of persecution, he was named to sainthood by that same church which had rejected him. From our point of view, Ira was the owner of a rare treasure: a private house within the city of Moscow full of antiques. Inside the walls of that estate, on the banks of the Moscow River, she kept horses, dogs, cats, goats, chickens and parrots.

Many a beautiful summer evening was spent around the fireplace in that home. Our hostess sang "Ava Maria," accompanied on the piano by me or her son, with candles standing on the piano and a brilliant moon peering through the window, over the head of a white horse that stood looking in the window and nodding in time to the music. But perhaps Ira's greatest treasure was a cross-eyed St Bernard dog. One evening, Ira phoned and said we must come over to her immediately. Breathlessly we arrived and watched Ira as she asked the dog time and again, "Who is your mother?" Obviously there was no response. But, later, as we sat at dinner, the dog came up to me and, peering through his cross eyes, said with a perfect French pronunciation: "Maman!" This is not a joke! I know there will be people who will not believe this story, but—you cannot throw away the words of the song.

One day I met Tatyana who worked in the Radio station of Moscow University. She gave me a lot of news. Our common friend, Luba, had died. Tatyana herself was living in Leningrad and married to the son of Count Alexei Tolstoy.

I had fallen in love with Leningrad, or St. Petersburg as it is now called, having reverted to its name from the times of Csar Peter the Great. I went several times a year to visit the Hermitage Museum which was headed by my friend Academician Piotrovski, who had spearheaded the battle to preserve the Russian heritage and culture. He had on one occasion literally taken his career, and perhaps his life, into his hands, for the sake of the museum's treasures. The Party Secretary of Leningrad, a man who bore the name Romanov like the last Csar of All the Russias, ran the city with a high hand reminiscent of his namesake. When Romanov's daughter was to be married, he instructed Piotrovski to hand over the dinner services of the rulers of Russia for the wedding reception. Piotrovski refused and, seeking support for his defiance of the "commissar" of Leningrad, he cabled to the Party Central Committee in Moscow. The Party Secretary's instruction was withdrawn and the priceless plates and glassware remained in the Hermitage. I loved also the other museums of Leningrad. In the Russian Museum, for example, I found paintings by Chagall and Kandinsky whose works could not be exhibited anywhere else in the Soviet Union.

I was especially interested in the opera and ballet in the Kirov Theatre which was more to my taste even than the Bolshoi. Kirov maintained the classic Russian ballet, but also ventured into modern interpretations. The city's architecture was superb, and its museums and cultural life outstanding by any criterion, though Leningrad was poverty stricken, provincial and bureaucratic. The city's buildings had not been repaired since the devastation of World War II. Many of the structures needed plumbing and other "conveniences" which had not repaired from the nineteenth century, or at best from the time of the pre-Revolutionary era. Leningrad was considered "the cradle of the revolution" but, ironically, the strength of the Communist Party in the city had resulted in iron-fisted repression and purges, coupled with a lack of imagination and initiative. This, on top of the 900-day siege of the city in World War II when thousands died of hunger, eradicated the genius for which Leningrad had been famous. The writers, artists and intellectuals were replaced by peasant stock flocking in from villages destroyed by war.

It had become difficult, if not impossible, to locate traces of the aristocracy and intelligentsia for which the city had been famous. And in this cultural wasteland, Tatyana's husband, Dimitri Tolstoy, was a rarity indeed. His father, Alexei, though not as famous abroad as his cousin, Leo Tolstoy, was more celebrated in the USSR for his historical novels. After the revolution, Alexei had immigrated to Germany, and later to France. Dimitri was born in Germany. Then, to the incredulous shock of the Russian émigré community, Count Alexei Tolstoy returned to the Soviet Union. Stalin, perhaps seeing himself in the Csarist giants about whom Tolstoy wrote, was very fond of the Count. That fondness gave him access to the highest echelons of the Communist Party and society, though he was not a member. Dimitri in fact told me that Stalin had been in the habit of dropping in on Maxim Gorki's literary evening parties. Whenever he did so, his security men would enter first and go round the room saying who could stay and who must leave. Alexei Tolstoy was always among the "survivors" of this intellectual screening. Russians, who are fond of inventing jokes, had one about him. Somebody came and asked for him. The manservant said that his Excellency the Count is at the meeting of communists.

Countess Tolstoy, the mother of Alexei's two sons, Dimitri and Nikita, was a famous poet in her own right. But when she married the Count, she stopped writing and devoted herself entirely to him. When I knew her, she was already old and blind, but still very beautiful and perfectly coifed. After World War II, which the Tolstoys spent in Tashkent "in the same house where I lived" he divorced his Countess and married his young secretary. The Countess promptly resumed her writings.

Meanwhile, the Tolstoy family was living after World War II in very reduced conditions. Dimitri wrote operas that were not often produced because he lacked the necessary Party influence in his music. What little income he had came from lessons that he gave in the Conservatory of Music.

Dimitri was thoroughly conversant with the history of Russian literature, poetry and music. Eventually he published his memoirs, and proved that he is even a stronger writer than his father. He is an original thinker and has to his credit a series of essays on time, space, and the cosmos. The writings are deep in their content and full of revelations in their philosophical viewpoints.

Dimitri lived always at a distance from Soviet reality. Dimitri was one of the few who succeeded in saving himself from the classification of "homo Sovieticus," and preserving the human characteristics and values that were so easily lost in a Communist environment. For him, there could be no compromise with a system that demanded continual worship in order to achieve the few doubtful rewards that were available to devotees of the regime. Dimitri was incapable of understanding all this. Consequently, he often seemed abnormal to those of his acquaintances who did conform. He never stood in the bread lines, nor did he join in the constant retrace to achieve better salary or housing. Whatever needed to be done to survive, Tatyana did. Dimitri's mind was off in outer space, far from reality. She gave him the support that allowed his intellectual flights into philosophy and literature. She in turn was supported morally by her elderly mother who had been educated in an Academy for daughters of the aristocracy before the revolution. Her behavior and deportment were perfect into her old age, though they in no way hampered her in the daily struggle for crusts of bread.

Stalin had given count Alexei Tolstoy a mansion in Moscow where he lived with his second wife. After he died, most of the family wanted nothing to do with the widow, who had inherited the entire estate, money, and gallery of art. Dimitri was the sole exception. Because if his kindness, from time to time, he visited her in her lonely luxurious home near the monument erected to Alexei Tolstoy. After she died, unaware that she had left a lot to Dimitri, I invited Tatyana and her husband to dinner in a restaurant. When the bill arrived, Dimitri wanted to take it but, knowing, so I thought, how hard a time they had making ends meet, I insisted. Tatyana intervened in the exchange to inform me, "But Lily, we are now millionaires."

I loved the Tolstoy home and family, and would go to Leningrad just to spend a few days with them. It was in their house that I met some of Russia's most interesting and greatest writers, composers, singers and actors. On one occasion I met there a red-haired, green eyed, rather short woman who was dressed very simply and whose eyes reflected the immense pain of knowledge denied to others. Her name was Svetlana and she, like me, had come from Moscow to visit her friends, Dimitri and Tatyana Tolstoy. She was interesting to talk to, and we quickly became friends. That evening, Tatyana said that she wanted us to accompany her to meet a family friend, Professor Manuylov from Leningrad State University. He taught nineteenth-century Russian literature and was writing the libretto to a ballet by Dimitri.

Manuylov was a very special person. He lived in one room in a communal apartment, but he often had to stay with friends or relatives for his room was occupied by a student of his who was sick, poor or homeless. His entire salary was spent on food and clothing for the poorest of his students, though few people were aware of this. Like Dimitri, he was a remnant of the earlier richness of pre-Revolutionary intellectual Russia. Though he was not feeling well when we arrived, he played the perfect host, making tea for us and speaking about the old days of St. Petersburg. Suddenly, in a change of mood, he said: "Show me your hands! Sometimes I have success in palm reading." I was not impressed with what he said about my palm. It seemed that he found little inspiration there. But he became very excited as he looked at Svetlana's hand. He said that he had never seen a hand like it: "This belongs to an extraordinary person. Your life divides into three periods. The first, finished long ago, was one of cloudless bliss. Your present period is difficult. You are fighting to get together with a foreign prince. And you will succeed in bringing him into your home. But soon he will sicken and die." Manuylov even supplied the date when the disastrous event would happen. "Then you will begin the third period, when you will cross oceans and travel far away."

I stopped listening. It was becoming far too personal for this woman whom I barely knew. Tatyana and I walked out to the balcony while Manuylov continued in a near trance. Turning to Tatyana I asked, "Who is she?" Tatyana answered: "Svetlana Aliluyeva, the daughter of Stalin." It was difficult to place this simply dressed, modest young woman in the family of the man who had brought so much evil to the Soviet Union, amid the horror that must surround her life.

Much as I tried to put myself in her shoes, to understand her trauma, I could not succeed. People do look at me when I walk in the streets of Moscow, but it did not worry me. This was just the curiosity of people who had never before seen a Black person. Though she was not immediately recognizable to everybody, when Svetlana walked out into the city, and someone did know her face, she encountered eyes that reflected hate and contempt for her and her father. She told me about an attempt to find a job and work like other people. She applied to the Institute for World Economics and International Affairs. Svetlana actually worked there for a few days, but every few minutes the door would open and someone would stare in with undisguised hate. The fact that the raw emotion was directed against her father was unimportant. Nobody wanted to know how she felt about the man who had killed her mother and many of her close friends and relatives and millions of people. She decided to work at home translating books from English into Russian.

Svetlana lived in "The House by the Riverside," a famous house near the Kremlin which had been inhabited by high Party officials, the majority of whom had been arrested and assassinated in 1937.

Her first boyfriend had been a Jewish film producer whom the dictator sent to a prison camp. Then she had married another Jew, but Stalin would not let them live together, though she had already given birth to his son. Then her father had forced her to marry Zhdanov, the son of his close associate, in an obvious marriage of political convenience. The match was hell, and Svetlana had escaped from the house in the middle of the night, carrying her newly born daughter in her arms. Svetlana then married a colleague of mine at my Institute. He was Vano Svanidze, the son of Stalin's brother-in-law by his first wife, who was Georgian. Vano's field was agriculture in Africa, a subject in which he had gained his Ph.D. Svetlana was very fond of Vano's father, who had been the first director of a Soviet bank, and especially his mother—a Jewish woman from Georgia, and an outstanding opera singer. A portrait of this extremely beautiful woman, who had been like a mother to her after Stalin executed his first wife, hung in Svetlana's bedroom.

The dictator's murderers also assassinated Vano's parents, but he survived because his nurse insisted that the boy was her son. Then, the nurse and her "adopted son" were denounced by some acquaintance, and Vano was exiled to Kazakhstan where he was forced to live in inhumane conditions. Though talented and capable as a scholar, he had been slightly deranged by his experiences. At the time of his childhood he had been considered a "wunderkind." Now he was super-sensitive to the suggestion that he was Jewish by origin. Indeed, when they married, he removed from the walls all the portraits of his mother, who he blamed for his Jewishness. Svetlana, upon meeting Vano in Moscow, had deep feelings of guilt over the deaths of his parents. She had been convinced that he too had been killed. Perhaps it was the guilt feelings that led to a very quick marriage. But he was impossible to live with, and he hated her Jewish son by an earlier marriage. They split up after a few months and shortly thereafter Vano died.

Svetlana and I became firm friends after our return to Moscow. Indeed we shared common circumstances. I was waiting for my husband to come from Africa, where he was again imprisoned. And she was waiting for her "foreign prince" who lived in India. Svetlana met Singh originally when he was hospitalized and she was visiting a friend, the very famous actress Ranevskaya. Immediately she felt that he loved her as Svetlana, and not because she was the daughter of Josef Stalin. Upon his release from hospital, Singh had to return to India. These were the 1960s. Foreigners were never at liberty to stay at their discretion, and she would never be allowed to leave the USSR. When we returned from Leningrad, Svetlana decided to initiate her campaign to have him allowed back into Russia. Though she could have used her privileges and contacts as Stalin's daughter, she rarely did so. I know of only two occasions when she did approach her father's old colleagues. One of these cases concerned me, the other her friend Singh. When she found out, after the assassination of my husband in Africa, that I had no "widow's pension" or support, neither from the USSR nor from the Tanzanian government, Svetlana used her influence to get me a monthly allowance. Though it only totaled 50 rubles, in those days it was a very welcome addition to my income.

To get permission for Singh to return to and stay in the Soviet Union —Svetlana went to the top, to members of the Communist Party Central Committee. Help materialized from the longest surviving Committee member, Anastas Mikhoyan. In a world where Stalin had imprisoned the wife of his Foreign Minister in order to keep Molotov toeing the line, and had killed many others, Mikhoyan had used all the flexibility of his Armenian ancestry to walk in the political rain yet remain dry. Incidentally, he was well remembered in the USSR as the Minister of Trade who brought back from a visit to the United States the idea of hot dogs and "Eskimo" ice cream on sticks. Though he was no longer very powerful, he did get Svetlana the permission that she needed to bring Singh back to Moscow. There was no recognizing Svetlana. The eyes always shrouded in all the pain and suffering of her world, suddenly radiated happiness.

She was so much in love with Singh that she could spend hours just sitting and looking at him, punctuated by occasional breaks to open or close a window if the draught bothered him. It was so overpowering that, at one stage, he asked me, "Lily, can you please find a job for her?" Her main concern became how to marry him officially. One day, they went to register their marriage. That evening I received an urgent call from her, "Lily, come quickly!" She told me that the Registrar, recognizing her name, had refused to take note of the marriage. He had immediately picked up the phone to call the Communist Central Party Committee. That same day she was "invited" to meet Suslov, the "gray eminence" of the Communist Party. Though he never held the position of number one in the Party, Suslov pulled all the strings.

She could not hold back the tears as she told me about their conversation. He harangued her about the dirt and decadence of India, about the Indians selling their wives into slavery, "The country is wild—so wild that no one can live there. I have been. I saw it. We will never permit you, the daughter of Stalin, to go and live in that backward country. And I will never allow you to marry him officially. You will stay here forever." The blow for her was terrible. Singh contracted dropsy and had to be hospitalized. Svetlana spent days and nights at his bedside. But the treatment was of no avail. He deteriorated, then died. The date was exactly that predicted by Professor Manuylov in Leningrad.

My daughter, Yelena and my mother, Bertha. 1963.

Yelena and Lily in Moscow. 1987.

Yelena, age 13.

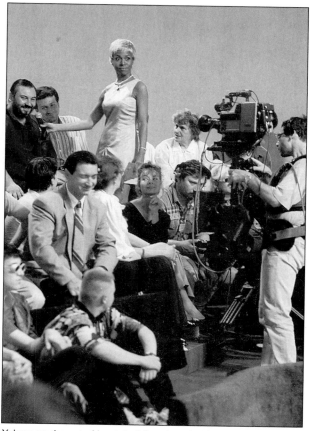

Yelena on the set of her television show in Moscow. 1998.

At top: Eslanda and Paul Robeson. Paul Robeson just received an Honorary Degree at Moscow State Conservatory.

This picture of black-american actor, Aira Aldridge, was drawn by a great Ukrainian painter and poet, Taras Shevchenko who was also his best friend. 1856.

Marian Anderson with a great Russian reformer of theater, Konstatin Stanislavsky.

Marian Anderson with actor Wayland Rudd and singer Korreta Arle-Titz at a railroad station in Moscow. 1936.

Ollava Golden my half-brother with his mother, Anna. 1956.

This photo of Svetlana Allilveya, the daughter of Stalin was taken before she defected from the Soviet Union.

Majory Scott, a black ballerina performing in Bolshoy theater. Moscow, 1969.

I am seated next to the sculpture of Alexander Pushkin at Pushkin Museum. 1999.

Ivan Potekhin, the first director of African Institute in Moscow, 1958.

Aram Cook of Somalian origin with his daughter, Rina and wife, Talia their grandson and their son-in-law from South Africa, in Batumi, Adjaria, Georgia. 1969.

Kamancha Shamba and her sister, Sofia Abash (photo at right) were the oldest living people among Africans brought through the Arabic slave trade.

African descendants
in an Abhazian village.

Ella Ross, a singer.

Grand-daughter of Abash-Nuza is a
doctor. She was elected alderwoman
in the city of Suhumi in Abhazia.

A descendant of African
slaves originally brought to
Caucasian mountains in the
16th century.

Sharon Tennison, (middle) the president CCI brought me to the United States several times to help to locate family there. Barbara Rinnan (left) was hosting me in Chicago and brought my relatives to meet me in Moscow.

Lily reuniting with long time university friends, Olga and Kolya.

Musician and composer Count Dimitri Tolstoy with his wife Tatyana.

My third husband Boris Yakovlev, a writer on a trip to Bulgaria in 1977.

At top: Meeting my eldest cousin Mamie and other relatives at O'Hare airport in Chicago, 1990.

Middle: My mother's relatives found me through an article in Los Angeles Times. Long Island. 1991.

Yelena with daughter, Liza

Some of my father's relatives at the naming ceremony for the "Dr. Lily Golden" Conference room at Malcom X College in Chicago.

On the evening of the day that Singh died, I came to Svetlana's home with a common friend, the wife of the Egyptian Ambassador, Mrs Ghaleb. Ambassador Ghaleb, a very cultured and intelligent man, was a trained medical doctor. He would later become the Foreign Minister of the Republic of Egypt. His wife was a rarity, both beautiful and kind. We sat together in the bedroom, looking on the man whom we had considered "a foreign guest." Svetlana was sad but silent. Suddenly she said: "How am I to live now? What can I do now?"

I had one of my sudden and crazy brainwaves. "Go back to Mikhoyan. Tell him that Indian custom demands that Singh's ashes be thrown on the waters of the River Ganges. You have nothing to lose. Maybe he will help." I do not know whether something had changed in the Soviet government, or whether it just happened to be an opportune moment. Whichever, Mikhoyan and the Ambassador of India decided to take personal responsibility for her. It was decided that Svetlana could take the ashes to India. Anastas Mikhoyan was always kind to Svetlana. Just before the Twentieth Congress of the Communist Party, he invited her to his home to see a copy of the speech that Khruschev intended to make denouncing Josef Stalin and his deeds which were being officially exposed for the first time. Mikhoyan's gesture was designed to give Svetlana time to prepare herself psychologically.

Her background had always worried me, yet I was unable to speak easily of it. On the one occasion I let something slip about her father being a tyrant and killer, she suddenly lost her usual free and open manner. As though girded in steel, she stated dryly: "It was not his fault. He was a true communist. He slept on a soldier's cot with no mattress. All the terrible things were done by Lavrenti Beria [the Minister for Internal Security]." The message was clear. This was a subject best not discussed with her. It was too painful. I pitied her and was careful not to touch the open nerves. It was enough that she was totally different from Josef Stalin. Where he was ruthless, cold and hard, she was kind, warm and sensitive. There was no meeting point between those two images.

The day of her departure arrived. The evening was cold, windy and snow swept. We called every half-hour to the airport only to be told each time that the flight was cancelled. Svetlana later wrote in her book that I was chain smoking and very nervous. True, I was smoking two packs a day back then, but she was the one who was nervous. All the time a beautiful young Tartar woman was flitting around the apartment. I asked Svetlana's children who she was, and was told that this was their mother's KGB escort for the trip. The woman herself suddenly started to tell us that they had been allowed, that same day, to go to GUM, the department store with a special section for Party functionaries. There, anything from anywhere in the world could be bought for rubles, and very cheaply. She and Svetlana bought whatever they wanted. She continued to chirp happily while cavorting in front of a mirror, changing new hats. Svetlana made her entrance. For the first time I saw her in a rage; and, for the first time, I had a clear image of her father and could see the family traits. "Don't forget that we are going to a funeral, not a party," she snapped at the Tartar woman, who suddenly cringed in a corner. We didn't hear her voice again.

Finally, Svetlana announced that we would wait for the plane at the airport. She was right. As we arrived, they announced that the plane was ready to leave. She went straight into the customs hall. She had little luggage apart from the two hand-carried urns of ashes of her beloved "Indian prince." The parting was brief. She disappeared through the painted glass doors. Her last whispered words to me were, "Lily, please don't forget my kids. Keep their intellects alive and developing." At the time I didn't think about the implications. She was going on a two week trip and was nervous. As it happened, I couldn't keep up the contact with her children. Later, it became obvious that Svetlana knew she wouldn't return and had planned for it. Nothing had been further from my thoughts.

Svetlana Stalin disappeared from my eyes, but not from my life. The entire world was watching as she escaped from India and appeared in Switzerland. One day I received a call from that country. I was happy to hear her voice. She said: "Is anybody in your home?" It was a rather foolish question. Every espionage agency in the world had to be listening to her phone calls, at least the KGB and CIA. Nevertheless, I answered, "Nobody is at home, not even my mother." She began to list all the names of the government and the Communist Part, and gave all their crimes and terrible deeds that she had learned about them abroad and about her father. I stood, holding the phone, numb with terror. Any and every phone call from abroad was monitored. But all I could think was, What did she mean by "anybody in my home?" Had she so quickly forgotten Soviet realities?

Several months later, she phoned again—this time from New York. Nobody in Moscow received phone calls from New York. In those years, nobody would dare. The Russian operator announced, "New York wants to talk to you." Very interesting! What could New York want from me? The operator said: "Wait a moment!" I waited more than half an hour. Suddenly she said, "The caller doesn't want to talk to you." This was becoming even more interesting. Who had called whom? And why did the caller not want to talk? I guessed that the call from Switzerland had prompted a permanent monitor on my line. The KGB was now controlling my telephone calls.

Meanwhile, Svetlana began to publish books about the Soviet Union and to meet with some success. However, I was not impressed. From my intimate knowledge of her, I could always see what Svetlana had written, and what had been ghosted by others. Roughly divided, the malicious kitchen-style gossip that related to her friends was her own work. Just one example of this was her claim that Dimitri Tolstoy's operas were so bad that the Soviet government had to send soldiers to fill the auditorium seats. I will not repeat all her remarks here, but they were decidedly impolite to someone at whose table she had broken bread. Historic or economic facts and statistics were clearly contributed by others, like former American Ambassador Kennan.

I was listening one day to the BBC, our main source of news about the Soviet Union. They were interviewing Svetlana. Wasn't she afraid that the book she was publishing would cause harm to her friends? She answered, "No! Many things have changed in the Soviet Union." She was mistaken. Her book first of all did untold harm to her relatives and friends. The Communist Party had just begun to allow certain people to travel abroad. All the names that she mentioned were put on a list of people banned from traveling. For example, she mentioned outstanding scholars and scientists who were on a secret list because they worked in security establishment research installations. They lost their jobs. She was no more polite or generous to Mikhoyan and the Indian Ambassador, who became the Minister of Foreign Affairs of

India, and who had helped her to leave the USSR.

True, she wrote good things about me, but they were used against me. For example, she wrote that I was clever enough to be "Minister of Culture," and that I knew African culture better than anybody—yet the Director of the Institute, "a foolish and ignorant man," went to the international conferences instead of me, simply because he held a Communist Party card. The director at the time, academician Solodovnikov, a former Soviet ambassador to the United Nations, could hardly be expected to like that comment.

It was a time when many faces around me were covered by masks, each playing a role to suppress me. I was followed and watched. If I went to the library, the time was logged. I was clocked in and out by ever-watchful eyes. My opponents were trying to find faults that could be used to kick me out of the Institute. My former friends were induced to join in the persecution. I discovered that "a friend" was checking on the books that I had consulted in the library. Another friend was censoring all my mail, incoming and outgoing. My best friend was checking on all my meetings with foreigners, and constantly inquiring about our conversations. I was banned from the library shelves where foreign books were kept.

The noose around me was tightening. Underlying it was my feeling that something held them back in their efforts to be rid of me. Perhaps it was because I was the only person of African origin in an Institute devoted to studies of that continent. Perhaps it was because my name had become too well known outside of the Soviet Union. I could not be dismissed without some comment coming from African presidents, friends of my late husband, or from American senators and congressmen who knew my father and me. Suffice it to say that, when I eventually arrived in the United States for the first time, I was invited to speak in the U.S. Congress. However, meanwhile the situation had become so tense that I decided to take a vacation on the Baltic Sea.

When I returned to Moscow, one month later, I discovered that my department had been closed. My work colleagues had been forced to leave the Institute. It was made clear that the move had been taken in order to remove me without being accused of "racism" or "discrimination." They had made their mistake. According to the laws of the country, nobody could be dismissed while on vacation. My colleagues had suffered for no good reason. I did think about leaving. But, on reflection, I was there for a good reason. I was here for something that had been considered important by Paul Robeson and Dr. DuBois, and by the first director of the Institute, Ivan Potekhin. I was hoping that maybe things in the Institute would change for the better and I would be far away, regretting not being there. So, putting my doubts aside, I stayed. My adversaries understood that they could not force me to leave, but they tried to isolate me.

Then I began to feel the presence of the Central Committee of the Party and the KGB even more than ever before. One day I was visited by one of my friends. He had a strange story to relate. He visited somebody in the office of the Communist Party Central Committee office of Manchkha, the Chair of the Committee responsible for Africa. Manchkha had previously been responsible for relations with Albania. His work in that section had resulted in a rupture in the relationship between the two countries, one that still persists to this day. He was transferred to African affairs, and relationships with Africa began to deteriorate. The Soviet Union was actually losing friends among African countries that wanted Soviet backing. My friend had overheard daily conversations between Solodovnikov, Director of my Institute, and Manchkha, the gist of which was: what to do about Lily Golden. They wanted to get rid of me, but feared international repercussions. In earlier days, the answer would have been simple. In the 1930s, a quick execution, or later a few years in the Gulag or a psychiatric hospital. But this was the 1970s, and something had changed.

I decided to put a good face on all this. I appeared at work wearing a new dress everyday, and well made up. I smiled at former friends and laughed a lot as if nothing untoward was happening in my life. It caused confusion and bewilderment as people began to wonder, almost visibly, what cards I had up my sleeve. Then, one day, I was summoned to Deputy Director of African Institute Starushenko, who was famous for his theories on the maintenance of socialism in Africa. He told me: "We found out that you have foreign friends. You are not to meet foreigners any more. And, if you do, you are to report the details to me." I asked, "Who decided this?" His response was, "The Minister for Foreign Affairs of the USSR." I was amazed at the suggestion that so august a man or institution could be interested in my affairs. Had he said the KGB, I could have understood far more easily. On the other hand, he obviously could not mention the secret police.

After a few seconds of reflection, I responded to Starushenko, "Are you unable to understand that I cannot do this to my friends? How can I tell the Chairman of the American Communist Party, Henry Winston, who had been like a son to my father, or the Egyptian Ambassador Murad Ghaleb, or William Patterson who had written a book on genocide of African Americans and considered me to be his daughter; that they could no longer talk to me or I would have to report on them? And what about the African ambassadors and politicians who had known my husband? What am I supposed to do about invitations from the presidents Kwame Nkrumah, Sekou Toure and Jomo Kenyatta"? He answered that he had given me an order. I neither discarded my friends nor did I report to him. It was clear that Starushenko and his ilk could do nothing to me.

However, I always knew that the KGB was watching me. My first real intimation was soon after I arrived in Moscow as a student. There was one famous Uzbek restaurant where I could go to eat the fruits and dishes of my former homeland. One evening a man whom I did not know greeted me with a bear hug. He was obviously happy to see me. Between the kisses and hugs, he told me details about my parents and myself that few among our friends would have known. I asked him who he was. "What? You don't know! I am the KGB officer who was responsible for watching your family all those years in Tashkent!" We sat together chatting about old times. Then he told me that he had been promoted to a job in Moscow. One of his duties was to sit in this restaurant keeping tabs, every evening, on the Uzbeks in town. He said that, to keep his table without too much suspicion, he had to keep ordering drinks: and he was becoming a drunkard. I found myself sympathizing with his problems. We parted as firm friends, but now I knew that the Goldens had been watched by the secret police since the early 1930s. I was to pick up the traces of the family role in the KGB dossiers.

The first time that I felt personal surveillance was when I married Abdulla. With the devious and twisted minds of secret policemen, they needed to speculate on my reasons for being one of the first Soviet citizens to marry a foreigner. Was it because I wanted to leave the country? Or maybe I had been recruited to serve foreign intelligence? The simple concept that we married for love was not in the KGB lexicon. They called in all my friends and acquaintances to ask them and each one dutifully reported back to me that the KGB was interested.

Whenever I found new friendships, they were promptly interrogated about my political views. Sometimes they sent people of their own, in the hope that I would become friendly with their informers and enable them to control me that way. The ploy was done with such a lack of finesse that my true friends would warn me, "He's trying to be your friend, but watch out..." I always responded that it didn't worry me. I had nothing to conceal from the KGB or anyone else. My life is an open book, and I never conceal what I think.

Soon after my marriage, I acquired a new friend—a tall, blonde, good-looking girl, who always smiled. She made no attempt to hide the fact that she had worked previously for the KGB, and that her husband was a colonel in that organization. She told me about her spy work in Turkey and Albania, and about her experiences as an interpreter during KGB interrogations. She had lost her job, so she said, because she fainted during sessions where interrogees were tortured. She stuck like a leech. If I went to the library, she came too. If I went to a meeting, she was there. If I took a vacation, she turned up at the same place. And all because, as she said, she found me to be the most interesting person she had ever met. She had been in depression until she met me, and now she couldn't live without me. I would not have minded so much, but her behavior was embarrassing to say the least. I would be invited to places like the Black Sea resorts by organizations or prominent people, and she would be there sleeping around with any available men. It reached a point where I was ashamed to be seen with her on the street. Finally, after she entertained what seemed to be an entire army during a riot of Abhazians in Georgia, I told her that I didn't want to be associated with her anymore. On her knees, she cried and begged me to stay with her. I relented only to discover later that the lady could not hold her drink very well. And whenever she was drunk, she talked. Bit by bit, I learned the KGB's innermost secrets.

Then, one day, in a drunken ecstasy, she gave me the list of all the KGB informers in the Institute for African Studies. On one occasion, she invited me to a very expensive restaurant. When she was intoxicated enough to talk, I asked her where she got the money for such a restaurant. She said that the KGB was giving her the funds to get me drunk so that I would tell her what anti-Soviet books I was publishing abroad anonymously. A book damaging to Soviet interests had recently been published in the West, and they suspected that I was the author. She drifted well away from reality when she asked me to draw up, for her, a list of the books that I had published abroad under *noms de plumes*. I told her, "You are getting paid for this, not me. You go to the library and compile the list."

Finally, at one of our restaurant rendezvous, she was drunk enough to let it all out. She said, "I don't like you at all. In fact I hate you. Everything I told you about admiring you was a lie. I am reporting on you to KGB. I had a lot of problems. My husband was about to lose his job. My brother is a drunkard. I have to get a good education for my son to keep him out of the army and find him a good job. Every time I took my problems to my high level friends, I had to pay for their help by bringing information about you. Now my problems are solved. I don't need you." After this catharsis, I felt much better. The game was over. But I now needed to be alert to catch whoever would be next. Truthfully, that didn't require much effort.

My immediate superior was also a proponent of building socialism in Africa. He was a man remarkably free of complexes, a coalminer who had acquired his academic degrees in an institution for Marxist indoctrination of workers. He was thirsty for knowledge and would latch on to new buzzwords, which he invariably used out of context. In a moment of truth, he said to me, "Lily, why didn't you come to the meeting? I spoke." I asked him why he needed me there, and his response was, "Whenever I speak, I watch your face and know immediately whether I am saying something foolish." His doctoral supervisor admitted to me that his biggest mistake had been to let my superior defend his dissertation which he did successfully on the third attempt. It turned out that the man did have some sound instincts. His scholarly achievements were dull and uninteresting. My interest in him was solely to record that he was the man assigned by the KGB to report directly on my activities within the Institute.

In comparison, Kuskov, the KGB "rezident" in the Institute, was remote from any scholastic or academic interests. He loved to attend our meetings, where he listened intently without understanding the topic. On one occasion I sat near him during a discussion of the political situation of the Ibo in Nigeria. When he heard that many of that nation were pilots, scientists, musicians and writers, he turned to me and asked, with a perplexed expression, "Are they Jews?" This question amused me. That summed up perfectly his scholar level. And this was the man empowered to strike my name off lists for library permits or participation in conferences abroad. And whatever he did, was done in consultation or collusion with my supervisor.

Once every five years, the Scientific Council of the Institute convened for the purpose of "reaccreditation" of researchers, based on their publications. Out of the blue I was told that I would have to go before them for a new accreditation. This was a shock. I had been through the process a few months before, and had come out of it with high commendations and the belief that I had another five years till the next one. Nobody could explain the reason. The best that I got was "There are new laws..." I had to comply. My friends warned me that this was no accident. The session of the Council was being convened especially for me, and I must be very careful. The powers that be were "preparing for an execution." There seemed no cause for worry. I had met every criterion, and had even published three times more than the quota.

They were all there. Solodovnikov, who could not forgive me for Svetlana's comments about him. Starushenko, who only recently had told me that I wasn't behaving like a true Soviet, and must stop meeting foreigners. Kremen, the secretary of the Party in the Institute, who though a Jew was the biggest anti-Semite in the place. Curiously enough, though Black, I was, to her, Jewish. They were happily interrupting each other with accusations that I hadn't written, and that I hadn't "registered" my articles (there was no such requirement). Starushenko saw all my articles because I could not publish them without his permission and had in fact received just several days before my paper entitled "Women in Somalia" which I had written for him. He had told me that it was the best-researched and written piece that he had seen, but now he stood up to announce that he never saw my writings. The Council ruled that I must not be permitted to write on ideological issues, and that I was being reassigned as an editor of one of the Institute's journals.

I quickly realized that this was a good place to work. My new boss, Pokrovsky, was both intelligent and decent. Like many Soviet intellectuals, he had decided to hide his light under a bushel. The atmosphere of good, solid and unobtrusive labor suited both of us. My only regret was that I had to read the as-yet-unpublished manuscripts of my Institute colleagues. Previously I had seen their work in print, after editors had worked on them. Now I was seeing the paucity of writing skills first hand—and these were the people who were telling me that I could not write when work of mine had been published in respectable journals worldwide.

There is never any way to predict for tomorrow. Within months my situation had reversed itself. It all began with a book, *The Working Class in Africa,* published by the Institute and edited by the Director of African Institute Solodovnikov and Manchkha from the Central Committee of the Communist Party. All of Moscow listened every morning as the BBC quoted from the book and made appropriate comments. It was hilarious. Other radio stations across the world picked up on the game, among them the Voice of America. Reviews began to appear in newspapers and magazines, and all were negative. This was fast becoming the foundation for a new scandal on the international scene.

One day I received a phone call from Solodovnikov. "Have you heard about the scandal?" he asked me. Working hard to hold back my laughter, I blurted, "Yes, I did." "Something has to be done. I approached several American magazines asking them to review it, but they all refused, saying that they don't know Russian and the book is too thick." I said that there was nothing I could do to influence them. "But the editors of American magazines told me that if you write the review, they will publish it. They will not refuse you..." What could I do? I contemplated how to make a purse out of a sow's ear. The book was, after all, junk. But some of my friends had written good papers for the volume. The trouble was the editors' introduction written by that prize pair, Solodovnikov and Manchkha. Maybe I could review just the good parts of the book. Forgetting Starushenko's instruction that I was not to mix with foreigners, I used my contacts to place the review in American media and it appeared within days after Solodovnikov's request.

Nobody bothered to thank me. But, ten days later, I was again invited to the Scientific Council for accreditation. Again I didn't have to wait five years between appearances. Solodovnikov made a brilliant presentation: Lily Golden is the best scholar that we have and her writings are published all around the world. All the superlatives were at the same level of intensity as the negatives voiced only weeks earlier.

Shortly thereafter, in 1973, Solodovnikov had to face his own accreditation before the Presidium of the Soviet Academy of Science. In preparation for the confrontation, Solodovnikov published a bibliography of his own writings, with an autobiography. We discovered that he was the son of a farmer, and had joined the Communist Party in 1942. Ten years later, he had presented a thesis for his MA on the subject "The Expansionism of American Monopolies on the Cotton Market." In 1966, he defended a doctoral thesis, "The Export of American Capital after World War II." The lesson was simple: for an easy academic career, publish papers critical of the United States. I counted 284 works listed in the bibliography. But close investigation showed that the same work was often published under different names. Some listed papers only consisted of one or two pages. He had spent many years fighting, on paper, American capital "in the cotton fields," "in export markets," and so on. He eventually had begun to write about Africa, but mostly in small articles in newspapers of the outlying republics in local languages, which were unlikely to get into the hands of scholars in the metropolis.

None of it helped. The Presidium ruling was that Solodovnikov did not possess the academic qualifications for his position. A letter backed up the decision from two deputy directors of African Institute stating that he was not scholarly equal to his position as director of a research Institute. The Minister of Foreign Affairs, Andrei Gromyko, recognizing his rank of ambassador, sent him to Africa. He was replaced as director by Anatoly Gromyko, by no coincidence the son of the minister.

We were delighted. At last, so we thought, we would have a strong director with a powerful name, who would not be afraid of the anti-Semites and Party bureaucrats who had ruled the Institute. Kremen and her friends were quiet, perhaps while they learned the foibles of the new boss. Before, Andrei Gromyko had worked for the state radio, then published a book about the assassination of John Fitzgerald Kennedy. The book met with negative reaction in the United States where Anatoly had spent many years while he majored in history and his father was an Ambassador. He had never been interested in Africa, and knew nothing about the continent.

At my next accreditation, Kremen said that I was writing and publishing too much abroad, a very negative trait. Anatoly Gromyko, at best very melancholic, drawled, "If they publish her, it means that she writes very well!" Kremen did not persist in her discussion. But as time went on she took over the management of the Institute, including of the director. Anatoly's father had meanwhile become President of the Soviet Union. Arguably it was within the son's power to make changes in the Institute. So we waited while trying to explain his behavior as concentration on preparing his doctoral thesis—something of which he was clearly scared.

While we sat and waited, Kremen and her friends were gaining in strength to the point where one of the deputy Directors, Igor Belyaev, was forced out. Belyaev was then a journalist who worked for many years in Egypt with another journalist Evgeny Primakov, who became a head of KGB and later a prime minister of Russia. Both co-wrote and co-defended for their doctoral thesis a book about the president of Egypt, Gamal Nasser. Belyaev came to the Institute on the strength of his experience in Africa, and an extensive knowledge of the African continent. His independence grated on Kremen. Belyaev was sent as a Soviet representative to the World Peace Committee that convened in Finland. At the end of its deliberations, the Committee secretariat began to receive anonymous letters stating that he had been stealing galoshes when he was a secretary of the *Komsomol* cell in the Institute of Foreign Relations where he had studied as a young man 30 years ago.

Starushenko, another deputy director, survived Kremen's reign of terror simply by flinching and sidling away every time he encountered her.

Anti-Semitism was growing in the Soviet Union throughout the 1970s and early 1980s, and this was what was reflected inside the Institute. One of Kremen's friends wrote a book, *Africa and Israel*, where his anti-

Semitic views were so virulent that the Institute had to refuse to publish the work. He applied to the courts and got a ruling that the Institute must publish. Another of her friends killed his wife in the belief that Jews were using her against him. He chopped the body into pieces, made a bonfire in the alley by his home, and threw the pieces into the flames. He was arrested, but was sent for psychiatric evaluation and committed to hospital for two or three years. He is now at liberty, and an energetic leader of the anti-Semitic *Pamyat* society.

While all the attention was on these earth-shaking events, Anatoly Gromyko was awarded his Ph.D. and became an associate member of the Soviet Academy of Sciences. Though the situation in the Institute was not changing, the country was. Gorbachev was instituting Perestroika in the Soviet Union. People started speaking more openly; we began to feel the wind of freedom. In 1988, a reputed academician, Shklovsky, published a paper in the magazine *Chemistry and Life* in which he enumerated the children of members of the Communist Party Central Committee. He showed how their careers had advanced thanks to the influence of their fathers. Anatoly Gromyko was obviously among them. Meanwhile, Anatoly was bursting with energy. He traveled every month to somewhere else in the world, further and further from Africa. And the Institute continued on as always.

Kremen was "buying" friends and followers. Her best friend, Natalie Wissotskaya, was getting frequent monetary awards of the kind given for outstanding writing. Other friends already occupied all the high positions in the Institute. Those whom Kremen disliked were doomed never to be more than low ranking researchers. Many of the best of them were forced out only to make rapid career promotions in other institutions and universities. Apollon Davidson left, and promptly received many high positions. Vil Mirimanov defended his doctoral thesis elsewhere, and progressed to become a world level expert on African art—something that would have been out of the question in our Institute. Ovanes Milikan left a very junior post in our Institute and eventually became deputy director of another Institute. The gist of it was that academic and scholastic development and deepening was blocked by intrigue and petty power struggles. Anatoly Gromyko had no interest in being involved in the daily life of the Institute.

Kremen's control was absolute and no one had even contemplated direct resistance. But there were indications of a growing bravery. An election for trade union organizer put in place a quite unorthodox communist named Margo Kuznietsova, who saw her mission as defending the workers. A small gray woman with the figure of a young girl, Margo was full of energy. For the first time, Communist Party secretary Kremen could not dominate the trade union leader in the Institute. Margo arranged access for us to one of the few groceries that actually stocked food. Somehow she acquired land just outside Moscow on which to build cooperative houses for Institute employees. She rented a house on the shore of the Black Sea so that we had somewhere to go for vacations. For the first time, somebody who cared for others occupied a high position in the Institute, and not for the moneys that could be siphoned into her own pockets. I tried to help her where I could. Using my contacts outside, I brought musicians, composers, poets and artists to speak or play under trade union auspices. Most of the interesting members of the intelligentsia were subject to KGB supervision. Poets in particular had come to be regarded as dissidents. Whenever I got into trouble for inviting someone, Margo would defend me to the KGB.

Margo went a step further. She began to research Kremen's activities, and particularly the financial documents of the Institute. Very soon she had proof that Kremen was using Institute funds for her own personal benefit and that of her friends. Moneys were being diverted to pay for trips abroad for her followers and favorites. Kremen began to campaign against Margo. She brought all her power to bear on the campaign for the next year's election of union organizer. Rumors began to spread about Margo's misuse of funds. The Director offered no support as the classic ploy surfaced: "Margo Kuznietsova is not fulfilling her quota of work." Her salary was reduced. Though she was obtaining for us things that should have been Gromyko's responsibility, he did not lift a finger to help her. There was even talk that she would have to face criminal proceedings.

Though she was not young or inexperienced, Margo had a streak of naivete. She believed that her record of good works would convince people. But the fight against Kremen's corruption was turned against Margo. Once again, the majority voted where the power to influence their salaries lay.

Kremen's reign finally ended after 30 years. Help came from an unexpected quarter—a diminutive, myopic, uncomplicated woman called Tania Tonkonogova. Tania was so quiet and self-effacing that many people in the Institute didn't even know her name. But one day she got so angry with Kremen's antics that she wrote a letter to a strange organization called "District People's Control Office," a kind of public complaints bureau, which lacked power until the advent of Gorbachev. A commission of lawyers appeared in the Institute and began to investigate Kremen. The result was that she lost all her high positions and power. The moral of the story was that you never know on which stone you will stumble.

Kremen was powerless, but the Institute didn't change, it merely faded away. At first, it filled up with young, energetic researchers who were free of all the past complexes and obsessions. They had not experienced the fears and dogma that beset our generation. They chose relatively easy subjects for their doctorates—subjects that did not require knowledge of languages or history, but which did conform to the current interests of the political echelons. For example, many were studying aspects of the political situation in South Africa, which now commanded the attention of the Central Committee of the Communist Party. Nevertheless, the intellectual level of the Institute did not rise. The newcomers lacked the depth of background shared by some of the first generation researches.

Perhaps the most obvious symptom of decline was the presence in my department of Manchkha. Yes, the same one from Central Committee of the Communist Party. After many years of fighting American imperialism, and me, from behind a Central Committee desk, he was ejected because of a drinking problem. In fact, he had been found in a drunken stupor on the floor of his office. After Gromyko "inherited" him from the Central Committee, Manchkha behaved to me as though he could not do enough to assure my comfort. Life sometimes plays delightful tricks. He made tea for me, he brought candies every day, and he changed the flowers on my desk every morning. He told hilarious and sometimes ridiculous stories about his past and his love affairs. When he was asked to prepare a small article from his doctoral thesis, "Communists in Africa," he astonished all of us by asking: "Where is the Lenin Library?" Any schoolboy would have known that, and this man had apparently gained a doctorate and guided foreign policy without ever entering a library. However, there were days when Manchkha neither contributed to the levity of the Institute, nor brought candies and flowers to me: he had urgent business at home with bottles.

Public funds were no longer available. Like other research institutes, African Studies is now expected to pay its own way with its publications and other activities. But no publishing houses are interested. Detective stories and spy thrillers sell better than heavy tomes on the unimportant facets of African life, such as the historic development of the use of fertilizer in Burundian agriculture. Anatoly Gromyko, on his travels around the world, developed affection for Greece, and decided to stay there with his family and the gallery of art bequeathed to him. The new director, having a personal history of involvement in the Arab world, puts all his efforts into conversion from "African" to "Arab" studies. To stay alive, since the Institute cannot support itself adequately by publication, he has begun to rent out parts of the building to companies, shops and all kinds of suspicious organizations. The researchers still in the Institute have to wait sometimes as long as four months for their salaries. The only ones left there are those who could not find other jobs. The others have moved out, some to other countries.

So ended the brilliant conception of Dr. William Du Bois and Paul Robeson, endorsed by Nikita Khruschev, to have an Institute of African Studies in Moscow. Perhaps the idea was doomed from the start. Like all the other regional research institutes, we became the servants of the political needs of the regime. The Institute's studies had to support the policy views for Africa of the Central Committee of the Communist Party and the KGB, and salaries were dependent on that output. Culture, history, art and music —the fields of Davidson and myself, among others— were irrelevant compared to Soviet policies.

CHAPTER NINE

Perestroika and Glasnost

I accepted *perestroika* and *glasnost* with great enthusiasm. In 1985, when Mikhail Gorbachev came into power, one of his first moves was to announce *perestroika,* "reconstruction" of the Soviet Union's political and economic system. It was only then that I began to understand what had prevailed previously in the USSR. For sure there had been things that I didn't like, but I had seen no obvious correlation with the evils of the regime. The purges and persecution of dissidents; The inefficiencies of the economy; The ever present pressure to belong to the system; The constant hunt for scapegoats—cosmopolitans, Jews, doctors—and the role of the Communist Party and the KGB; had all seemed wrong, yet there had been no connecting link in my mind. Now the connection was clearly established.

Under *perestroika,* the newspapers began to write the truth about past events. It was called *glasnost*—"openness." Under the new freedom my friends and I founded a theater in the House of Moscow scientists where we were able to produce a satire show. In the beginning, we staged shows that contained criticism of Gorbachev and Yeltsin, with one ear constantly cocked for the heavy footsteps of the KGB. The KGB are still there but the fear has receded. Indeed, while other theaters in Moscow are failing, ours is always mobbed. I cannot name all our productions or begin to list the fifty members of the group, but I must mention a few of the scholars who have distinguished themselves both in science.and on the stage. The initial enthusiasm was supplied by a mathematician, Valeri Kanner. He did everything from writing scripts to painting sets and stitching costumes for dancers. His one limitation was an indifferent ear for music. Andrei Petrov, a physicist, wrote scripts, all in verse. There was to be no prose in our theater.

We have three brilliant pianists, all capable of virtuoso performances, from classical music to jazz and blues: Olga Sucharevskaya, a physicist, Dima Goltzof, a mathematician and Genia Oganisan, the Deputy Director of the Insitute for Children's Defects. Gordina Luba has a cupbord full of awards for chemistry and for her singing. She and the other soloists are ably supported by our choir of doctors of the exact sciences. Though I was not the best singer, dancer or actress, I derived considerable enjoyment from being in this group. We were friends and creating collectively and happily in a world that was gloomy. And our reward was the laughter and applause of our audiences.

My membership of the Moscow House of Scientists also led me to found an organization named Women of Science, all the members of which were again doctors in the exact sciences—except for the president, myself, a mere historian. The first conference, convened to discuss the problems of women in the age of *perestroika*, attracted 700 people, including a goodly number of men. The first elections to the new parliament had not produced many women members. Each of us. From our different viewpoints, wanted to reach a consensus on the problems that needed to be raised in parliament.

However, the years went by and, for all the talk, little actually changed. Mikhail Gorbachev was, so I began to understand, a product of the very system that he sought to change. As a result, the man was the model of a dichotomy in which all his training and background fought against his instincts and intellect. Nevertheless, in my eyes today, he was not to blame. There are leaders, some who can only destroy, others who can only build. He had shaken the very foundations of a monolith that had seemed impervious to change, even though he had been incapable of instituting the desired replacement. For what he had achieved, he deserved the admiration and gratitude of the Soviet peoples. Gorbachev deserves a place of honor in the history of the Soviet Union and the world, despite the inability of his own people to grasp the greatness of his contribution.

Our first intimation of Gorbachev's sincere intentions came with his phone call to the city Gorki. The new ruler of the USSR called to inform the country's foremost physicist and dissident, Andrei Sacharov, of his freedom. Even the very reactionary Academy of Science of the Soviet Union had refused to denounce him although it was pressed by the KGB and the Communist Party. Though, on a later occasion, Gorbachev grabbed the microphone from Sacharov's hand during a session of the Congress of Peoples' Deputies, he was still the man who had brought the great scientist back home.

Another indication of the new atmosphere was the freedom to travel. True, a Soviet citizen still needed permission from the Communist Party and the KGB. True, the cost of tickets in rubles was prohibitive. But, in theory, we were free to come and go.

The changes began to affect me. At the home of a politician who was active in women's organization, which was still under Party auspices, I met a group of American women. In a world where meeting with outsiders was still proscribed, I was amazed that our hostess would take such a risk, until it dawned on me that her Communist Party affiliations were precisely the reason why she could entertain twenty or so foreigners.

Among the group was a lady called Sharon Tennison, who was in the USSR for the second time. Though of my age, she looked very beautiful and much younger. A petite woman, with bright eyes, she had worked much earlier—so she told me—as a registered nurse. Patients had told her that they didn't understand why she bothered to treat them when the Russians were going to throw atom bombs any day. So she decided to see the terrible monsters for herself. Sharon had prepared very carefully for the trip. She bought a dictionary and a phrase book. Refusing the services of a guide, she went out onto the streets of Moscow by herself. Constantly referring to her source books, she talked with people in the subway, in the shops and on the streets. Deeply impressed, like many Americans of that generation with Khruschev's declaration that "we shall bury you," she asked ordinary people why they hated Americans enough to kill. And, of course, she discovered that the average Russian "man or woman in the street" had no such feelings or intentions. Armed with this slightly different view, she had returned to America and spoken out. She began to bring American groups to Russia to gain the same experience first hand.

It was the beginning of a chain reaction. People that she brought from different cities in the United States, returned again with groups that they had put together. Sharon by this time was coming to Moscow six times a year. Each time, based on our first meeting, she called me and suggested that I should invite members of the groups to my home, to hear my story. My story did not strike me as interesting enough, but if Sharon was convinced, I wasn't going to refuse. Then she started to invite Russians to visit the States.

At first she brought twenty people a year, then a hundred and, eventually, three or four hundred a year. Slowly, but with gathering momentum, there began to be different understandings and the rejection of outmoded conceptions about each other.

Looking back on it, from the vantagepoint of the post-Soviet age, Sharon Tennison in fact played a major historic role in some aspects of *perestroika* in Russia. Not only were the Americans and Russians who had shared the experiences of her tours beginning to appreciate each other in totally different ways, but the Russians who came to the States were getting insights into American ways of doing things in economy, industry and so on. Eventually, over the space of very few years, Sharon was arranging visits by a thousand Soviet citizens each year: visits that included home hospitality and "internships" in American corporations and businesses. An essential rider to the internships was the concept that the American hosts would follow their guests to Russia, to help and advise them in setting up their own businesses.

Her experience and achievement was so unprecedented that, in 1993, acting on the American government's new initiatives to aid in the stabilization of Russia, the State Department called Sharon Tennison in to work out the details of a countrywide American program to help Russia.

But, in 1987, all that was in the future. In one of her early visits, Sharon brought to my home a group of leaders of American foundations, including the president of their roof organization. During the course of the evening, and after I had told my story, she said: "Lily, why don't you go to America to look for your family and tell your tale there? I have just invited a Soviet Peace Committee delegation, and I'll ask them to include you."

I dismissed the suggestion in the knowledge that people of my kind in USSR are not allowed to travel. I was not a member of the Communist Party. There were no wheels I could turn in the KGB. It wasn't possible, so why waste time discussing it? I underestimated the forcefulness of Sharon Tennison. She started a campaign with the Peace Committee. Thus far, in inviting upwards of four hundred Soviet citizens a year, at no cost to them, she had made a few uncompromising demands. Those chosen must be common people, not Party functionaries who could find other means for travel. There was to be an age limit, since travel around the United States could be exhausting for old people. They must know a few words of English to be able to speak with their hosts. (Soviets who traveled were compelled to stay only in hotels, where the KGB could watch them). Sharon was placing her guests in private homes; each group must contain one or two candidates that she would pick for herself, as she was doing in my case.

If that makes it sound easy, then it misrepresents the truth. Each time that a group was to go, Sharon had to fight to maintain the basic principles. Whatever Soviet organization was involved, there were inevitable attempts to replace the people that Sharon wanted with KGB agents and Party officials, some of whom were neither young nor conversant in the English language. Often Sharon would meet a plane at Kennedy Airport, take one look at the passengers and run to a phone. She would tell Mikhail Gorbachev or other high powered Soviets—directly, not through bureaucrats—that if she did not get the people she had selected on the next available plane, she would send the whole delegation home immediately. Mostly she succeeded. But the Peace Committee was a particularly hard nut to crack. Despite the pretentious name, the Committee was involved in arranging junkets for Party functionaries, their families and "significant others" to places where the peace that they supported may not have been the one that the world wanted. The organization was, in fact, strictly controlled by the Party and KGB and was carrying out precise instructions with no freedom to act by itself.

The first Peace Committee groups arrived in America obviously without me. Sharon's reaction was predictable. She informed the Committee that "if Lily Golden is not in the next delegation, there will be no more groups..." Eventually, months after that evening in my home with representatives from American foundations, it was announced in July 1987 that I would be going to the United States in September. Still I had to go through all the routine bureaucratic requirements for an exit visa. Whatever the old adage claims, I know from experience that there are far more than seven stations in hell. *Perestroika* apart, I needed to get, in the correct order, permissions from: the Communist Party committee in my department, the KGB representative in the Institute, the Party committee of the Institute, the regional committee of the Party and so on up the ladder.

Chapter Nine

Several years earlier, I would not have gotten higher than my department. But things really had begun to change. At last, after two months of the bureaucratic treadmill, I got a visa. Then I was invited to the Peace Committee to listen to a compulsory lecture on "how to behave abroad." I was informed that Sharon Tennison was an agent of the FBI, that I must never be alone with her, but always accompanied by someone from the group. I was told what I may say and what not to say. The lecturer looked me straight in the eyes and said: "One more thing... If you have an invitation to stay longer in the United States, you must refuse!"

At the end of September 1987, I finally boarded an Aeroflot plane that flew in the vague direction of America. However, as it happens often with Aeroflot, we landed not in the U.S.A., but in Canada—in Montreal. It didn't disappoint me. I was being given a chance to see another country not on my itinerary. Because the group included some famous and distinguished names, the Soviet Embassy gave us permission to go into town. We were collected by embassy limousines and taken on a tour of downtown Montreal. After a day of English and French contrasts in Montreal, we flew on to Chicago. I couldn't be aware of how important Chicago was going to become in my life.

At the airport we were met by a group of Americans, some of whom I was already acquainted with from their visits to Moscow. Indeed the head of the welcoming delegation was Barbara Rennan, an old friend from Sharon's missions to the USSR. I was lodged in the Oak Park home of the Tibenski family, Barbara's neighbors. I was very excited. I knew that Chicago had the largest Black population of any city in America. I couldn't wait to meet them. In fact I sat by the windows of the Tibenski home, looking for black faces on the street. Soon I began to understand that there were no black faces in Oak Park. It was my first step in understanding that Chicago is the most segregated city in the world.

A few hours after my arrival, Barbara's husband Bob, a most charming person, took me to the DuSable Museum in Hyde Park to renew my acquaintance with its founder, Margaret Burroughs. Coming off the expressway, I suddenly felt that I was in Africa. Black faces in the cars, on the steps of the houses, playing in the streets. For the first time in my life I was encountering a city that housed two entirely different and separate worlds.

Our Chicago visit was well organized by Barbara and her friends with a very tight and heavy schedule. I spoke to the Council on Foreign Relations and on several radio and television talk shows. We had an opportunity to visit the Board of Trade and walk the streets of the city. I remember standing on La Salle Street and looking up at the highest buildings, the thought came into my head. Could I live in such city? I doubted it. But I liked the idea. Knowledge of the city's outstanding architecture had travelled as far as the Soviet Union, and I was expecting to be impressed. But the reality of the tallest building in the world, and of towers operated completely by computers, far exceeded my expectations. Had I stayed much longer in Chicago, I would have had to adjust to a head permanently tilted 45 degrees upwards. In the Art Institute I saw for the first time the works of Russian artists of whom I had heard, but who could not be exhibited in the Soviet Union. But it was difficult to understand the curator's logic in dividing up the works of particular painters and sculptors by school, period and relationship with others, instead of the strictly artist-by-artist presentation.

In San Diego, Vira Williams hosted me. Her kindness was overwhelming. She took me everywhere, including to a lunch at the St. Vincent de Paul Center for the homeless. Here, the modern technology was amazing. Self-repairing carpets, computer keyed door locks, basketball hall, swimming pool and—pride and joy of the place—a central control room where a security man sat, scanning banks of closed circuit televisions. Despite all this, and despite the good food supplied by neighborhood churches, the center was empty. I asked why in a city literally crawling with homeless, none of them were here in this luxury, and was told that "they don't like the feeling of being watched and controlled." I mentioned this to the editor of the *Los Angeles Times,* who hosted me for dinner, and he told me about an aunt of his who lived on the street. Although the family persisted in inviting her to eat and to stay, she insisted that "being homeless is freedom."

My trip was interrupted by a call from Sharon Tennison, who said that I really should stay longer in the United States and look for my relatives. However, as she was aware, we would need the permission of the Soviet consulate, which we should visit together. My new hostess, Gretchen Bell in Los

Gatos, a beautiful woman with whom it was a joy to explore the world of California, drove me to San Francisco. Consul Kaminev was an unusual Soviet official. He was intelligent, educated, open, sensitive and understanding. But he knew, and I knew, that I was in trouble, even if Sharon did not know it. Both he and I knew that it could not be done, but neither of us was able to explain the finer points to her. He needed me to supply him a good reason since, as he told her, an application must be made to the Party Central Committee. I could not give him a reason because I was forbidden to make such a request. Sharon couldn't understand why I said nothing. Nevertheless, confronted by my silence, she fought bravely on by herself. Kaminev could not stand her pressure and, staring at me to arouse my sympathy for his predicament, capitulated and extended the period of my exit visa from the Soviet Union for three months.

In San Francisco I spent an evening with Louise Patterson. She visited my father in Tashkent in 1932 together with Langston Hughes. Louise returned to the Soviet Union in the 1970s and I escorted her to all the places that she had been forty years earlier with Langston Hughes. Now, though 83, she was blessed by a perfect memory, and we were both in stitches as we recalled our visit to Samarkand, one of the ancient cities in Central Asia.

Since Louise's husband was a very prominent American communist, we were the guests of the Tadjik Communist Party. One evening we were taken by car to watch a performance of *Swan Lake* at the City Theater, a theater of which our hosts were very proud. The entire audience consisted of our hosts, an interpreter, two soldiers and us. The ballet was so poor that the soldiers started to wander around the auditorium, banging seats. Louise turned to me and whispered: "Get me out of here before I start laughing!" I told our hosts that she was an elderly, infirm woman and needed to get back to the guesthouse urgently. They were in a dilemma because the car had been sent away, and would only return at the end of the performance, so I said: "Call an ambulance!" Once she was safely on a stretcher in the vehicle, Louise was no longer able to hold back her hysterical laughter. I had to reassure the doctor that this was a symptom of her sickness. That night, unable to sleep, she came to my room in her nightgown, and gave me a replay of the ballet. Now it was my turn. We laughed our way through the dawn.

Louise is working on her memoirs. Her husband wrote the definitive work on genocide of Black people for the United Nations. She had worked with Herbert Aptheker, the distinguished historian, who published many works on Black history and is the custodian of Dr. William DuBois' personal papers. I believe that she will produce a fascinating book.

The group left, on its way home to Moscow, and Sharon decided to send me to Sacramento, where Jesse Jackson had his Rainbow Coalition Conference. This was my first meeting with him. He invited me to attend the conference, where I saw for the first time a huge hall filled with thousands of Black people, including mayors, congressmen and industrialists.

Several days before the conference I had been interviewed on radio, and had mentioned my frustration at turning on the news to find out what was new in a world crisis, only to be treated to endless reporting on a gay march on Washington. On the plenum floor a man, looking as though he expected trouble, approached me. "You are Lily Golden?" When I admitted that I was, he started to harangue me, asking "how can you attack gays?" I asked if he was gay, and he replied, "No. I was sent to talk to you because I sympathize." After a long exposé on homosexuals back to pre-history, he gave me a stack of books and brochures with the strict admonition: "Take them to Russia! Distribute them there!" I asked him if he was crazy, "I will be arrested by Soviet Customs for smuggling pornography." In fact when I came back to Moscow I did try to talk about the gay movement to the Women's Club of the Union of Soviet Writers, but was met with whistles and catcalls. Russia hadn't changed that much.

Sharon thought that I should look for my relatives in the South. So I started in Memphis, then was taken to Delta University in Mississippi, where I was housed on campus. There I was treated to a gospel service in my honor. But my sights were set on Clarksdale in the north of the state. I had found an old army document stating that Oliver Golden had been drafted into the U.S. Army, in 1919, from that city. At the entrance to Clarksdale, Mayor Mayo and his colleagues from the council met me. I was invited to a reception with all the wealthy citizens of the town. Then I was asked to speak at the history class of Coahoma Junior College. Mr. Mayo gave me a guided tour that included cotton fields. Something was very strange there for me. In Uzbekistan at this time of year the entire population, especially women and children, would be out in the fields harvesting the cotton. Here there wasn't a soul in sight. The Mayor explained that the work was done by machine. I was struck by the irony that the Blacks of my generation in the United States no longer shared the experience that I had had as a child in Tashkent, of picking the bolls by hand.

Mayor Mayo had very kindly collected a number of elderly African Americans who might remember my father. But I still don't know whether they were too old to remember or too deaf to hear my questions.

After a short visit to New York and Washington where I lectured in the universities, I returned to Moscow. Sharon was not satisfied with my lack of success in the quest for family roots. She insisted that I join a delegation in the following year for another visit. This time she wanted me, first of all, to attend the World Women's Conference in Dallas, which would begin on 8 August 1988. The organizers, who included Vivian Castleberry—a famous journalist who had written at length in support of women's issues—wanted me to sit as co-chair of the conference, and to address a session as keynote speaker. Bureaucracy again reared its ugly head, and I arrived in Dallas some two days late. The delegates were meanwhile convinced that I had been arrested, and were preparing a demonstration to protest my ill treatment. My speech on behalf of peace and the diversion of vast sums spent on armaments into joint U.S.-USSR attacks on the ills that beset the planet would really have guaranteed my arrest a few years earlier. In 1988, I think it passed unnoticed, and perhaps even positively in Moscow.

I was whisked from Texas to Alaska, via Oregon. The McKenzie Valley had to be the most beautiful place in America, but Alaska was for me the most fascinating part of the country. The scenery was familiar yet different from that I had seen in Yakutia, Kamchatka and Chukotka on the other side of the Bering Straits. I visited that region on my lecture trips. Both sides are rich in natural resources. But Alaska also revealed to me its traces of a Russian culture and religion dating back to the days when the area belonged to Russia. Among my hosts were members of the Bahai faith. They, quite simply, phoned Anchorage Airport, asked for a Bahai pilot and said that they were entertaining a guest from the Soviet Union. He promptly offered to fly me in a helicopter around the Indian villages. I found myself back in a very familiar world. There were Russian built churches from the sixteenth and seventeenth centuries, complete with icons and even Russian language bibles. The settlement names were often Russian in origin. In fact, I began to subscribe to the theory that many of the Indians of North America had migrated north from the Baikal area of the Russian subcontinent. When they reached Alaska they had moved south leaving splinters of their tribes on the way. There were too many similarities between the native peoples in both countries for it to have been pure coincidence.

Again the delegation went home without me. This time, my main focus was on the South. In Mobile, I was hosted by a famous writer, Jay Higginbotham, and taken to speak in a number of places, including Alabama State University and the city library. But the highlight was my visit to Tuskegee University, where my hosts had declared "Lily Golden Day." (The same happened in Cleveland and Anchorage). Throughout the city were banners attesting to the fact. The University honored me with a performance of their renowned gospel singers. There, in the archives, my kind hosts showed me my father's correspondence with George Washington Carver. It was a highlight moment of all my life. Oliver Golden died when I was six, and I never had a chance to hear from him firsthand about the events surrounding his move to the USSR. Here I discovered that the Soviet Union had been willing to appoint Carver to the post of Minister of Agriculture, but he had declined, arguing that he was too old and ill. My father had pressed him on the grounds that it would enhance the prestige of African Americans.

In Atlanta, I visited Spellman College, Emory University and Georgia State University. At Lincoln University, in Connecticut, I met Niara Sudarkasa, the President of the University, who had made of Lincoln a center for African students. She impressed me with her knowledge and friendliness. Maybe I was most struck by the fact that the achievements and prestige were those of a Black woman.

On my third visit, in 1989, I came alone. Sharon had invited me without a delegation. It was a very successful tour of many states, full of speaking engagements, seeing beautiful places and meeting interesting people. But, though I could not know it, there were to be two high points at the end.

One year earlier, my daughter, Yelena, came to the United States on an exchange program. She was a journalist on the staff of *Moscow News*, which was arguably the first newspaper to support Gorbachev's reforms, and was sent to the *Christian Science Monitor*. This in itself was a sign of the changing times in the Soviet Union. She was unmarried, not a member of the Party and not even Russian—Black, Jewish and daughter of a Zanzibarian father. People like that simply do not exist. They never were allowed to travel: there were no strings to hold her to the USSR if she chose to marry and stay in the States. But the times changed already. She was assigned to cover Mikhail Gorbachev's state visit to the White House. While she was there, when Gorbachev and Reagan debated in the Oval Office, the bored reporters began to interview each other. And Yelena was a natural target. She was Black, Soviet and one of very few women covering the story. The interviews made front pages, together with reports about Gorbachev. This happened when I was traveling around the United States. It was so funny when I found out that because they saw in the papers the portrait of Gorbachev together with my daughter, they were asking me whether she was his daughter. One of my hostesses said one day, looking at the picture of the president and my daughter: "I understand this is your daughter. Right? And who is this white guy with her?"

One thing led to another. A crew from *20/20* came to interview our family in Moscow. ABC showed the program, which included me showing a photo of my father. A few days later I received an excited phone call from a woman who identified herself as my first cousin. She had recognized her uncle in my photo. I had scoured the south, but had not thought of looking in Chicago.

This time I toured America for three months, including another visit to Alaska at the invitation of black churches. After visiting several cities in Alabama, California, North Carolina and Washington D.C., I came to Chicago. I will never forget that day. As I emerged from the plane on to the concourse, a vast crowd of relatives besieged me, all carrying welcoming banners. At last I was meeting my father's family. There was no measuring my pleasure at the encounter.

As I wrote in the first chapter, my grandfather had ten children, who in turn produced many offspring of their own. So I had innumerable first cousins. But, by the time I arrived on the scene, there were only two survivors of my generationin our family: myself and Mamie, the woman who recognized me when *20/20* had documented our family's history and had phoned after the television interview. Though she was the oldest of the clan, born in different times, Mamie always dressed elegantly. She imbued in me a sense that she had lived so long solely because she was waiting to find me. Mamie, at 82, was the only member of the family that could still remember my father. Sadly, she died within a year, leaving me as the only surviving member of our generation in our family.

Because my father was the youngest of my grandfather's brood, some of the generation after me are in fact older than I am. But, being Americans, they all seem to my Russian eyes youthful and full of energy. Traveling around the United States with them, meeting countless other members of the tribe, has proven an unforgettable experience. I had lived most of my life with no relatives or close family other than my mother and daughter. Now, all of a sudden, I have a huge, warm and supportive family. I think this was one of the main reasons I chose to stay in the United States.

There are, at last count and including the children, perhaps one hundred members of the clan, and there is no way that I can write about all of them, much as I would like to. However, Ollie Morris occupies a special place. She invited me to stay with her in her apartment and taught me all I needed to know about everyday American life. I had to be taught everything that American people instinctively know from birth. I knew nothing about taxes and services, or even about shopping.

Dolores Harris became my public relations officer. I had difficulty in the beginning adjusting the sensitivity of my ears to American accents and dialects over the phone. She helped decipher the language and took over the arrangement of all my speaking engagements in churches, on radio and telvision.

Another cousin, Rosalyn Trevis, is a dentist. She looked at my gold-plated Russian mouth in a state of shock and bewilderment, then set to work to remodel me for America. Now I can smile like a local. Jay Green, the vice president of the American Heart Association, introduced me to San

Francisco. Melvin and Junior Chamberlis traveled with me across America. They took me to Mississippi among other places, while Jakie and Jerry drove me to Texas, where I spent several days with their wider family and attended the marriage of their daughter. They, together with Dolores Harris and Jay Green, visited me that same year in Moscow. Together, we flew to Tashkent to see the grave of my father, then continued to Leningrad to visit the apartment of Alexander Pushkin. Their trip was arranged by Barbara Rinnan, my old friend in Chicago.

There are many more who have shown me hospitality, given generously of their time and concern. And the acquaintance with all my cousins has brought friendship with all their friends including Adolph Slaughter and Marianne Heard, who invited me to all the jazz clubs and cultural events around Chicago.

I began to feel like a rock star traveling with my own fan club. Invited to speak at Jesse Jackson's Operation Push, I found thirty members of the family in the audience. They were there again when Malcolm X College President Brown declared "Lily Golden Day." He gathered black musicians and artists, adding to my insights into African American culture. Then, to my surprise, there was a naming cermony for two rooms in the College: the library was named for Betty Shabazz, the wife of Malcolm X, and the conference room became the Lily Golden Room.

It is with considerable pride that I am able at all these gatherings to introduce my "new old" family, especially when I am invited to speak about my long journey home to the United States.

That was 1991. In 1992, I was on a lecture tour in Los Angeles. The *Los Angeles Times* carried an interview in which I spoke about my mother, Bertha Bialik. It was read by one of my still unknown white relatives, Doris Goldstein, who remembered hearing the name in the family. She had telephoned all her cousins across the United States. In Chicago my first cousin Irv Bialik had arrived at his rendezvous with me armed with a thick notebook. He wanted to know everything about his aunt, my mother. It was all carefully recorded in his notebook.

I had not been looking for my mother's relatives when I initially arrived in America. Simply put, during all the hard years, including World

War II, no support had been given or offered to Bertha, the only girl in the family. But to my newfound white relatives were extremely kind to me and to my daughter. Irv often takes me to Jazz concerts and Jazz venues, where he has introduced me to the most famous of the black musicians. In Washington I met Irv's son, a senior attorney in the State Department. His legal advice has always been very helpful.

In New York, Irv's brother Al took me out to his Long Island estate, where I spent several days relaxing in his garden. Also in New York, I met the son of one of my mother's cousins, a world renowned violinist, Arnold Steinhart. Arnold, a highly educated and knowledgeable man, has traveled widely and won many international awards.

I returned to Los Angeles to meet the children of my mother's three brothers. My first cousin Doris told me that her brother had gone to Japan and married a Japanese woman. Consequently, I was now made aware that I had Japanese cousins. I was also to meet Eugene, the son of my mother's favorite brother Jack. Eugene, two of his sons and a daughter all work in the wine business.

Having collected a sizeable entourage of both African and Jewish American relatives, the time had come to put them together. In September 1992, we held a family "reunion" in the downtown Chicago Inn, attended by 130 black and white cousins from all over the United States. In advance, both sides were wary. A Jewish cousin asked, "Will they actually talk to me? A black cousin matched that with, "You'll probably spend the evening with your white family and ignore us." But, in the event, the sense of brotherhood was immediate and unreserved. My Jewish cousins danced the electric slide, and my black cousins learned the hassidic dances. Two orchestras played: the All Star Blues Band and a Jewish orchestra from Kishinev. At one stage they all lined up together to get copies of my daughter Yelena's book, *Soul to Soul,* which she had written while at the Rockefeller Foundation. Many of our friends had joined in the reunion, and were helpful in organizing the event.

When my daughter Yelena came on her exchange program between her Moscow paper and the *Christian Science Monitor,* Lee Young read about her in the newspaper and invited her to speak to the League of Black Businessmen in Los Angeles. Lee has three daughters, but he and Maureen his Irish wife readily accepted Yelena as the fourth. He became her business advisor and quickly took the place of the father figure that she had never enjoyed.

During my travels around the United States, I made a lot of friends, all of whom were trying to help me. It started with the followers of Sharon Tennison who were spread across all the states of the Union. They arranged my lectures and media interviews, on radio, television and in the newspapers. Many of them tried to assist me in the hunt for my relatives and for documents about my father and grandfather. William Smith, of Los Angeles, and Roy Kauffman from Cleveland were particularly helpful, as was the head of the municipal archives of the city of Mobile, J. Higginbotham, and Edwin Bridges, the director of the Department of Alabama History and Archives in Montgomery. But far and away the greatest gift was that bestowed by Daniel Williams in the archives of Tuskegee when he found the correspondence between George Washington Carver and my father. Altogether, I visited forty states, spoke in seventy five universities and met thousands of Americans. In the course of this odyssey, I made several hundred new friends.

Still I am not indifferent to events in Russia now, the situation there is very complicated. Over a decade has passed since Gorbachev began *perestroika*, but little has changed. True, there are things to be brought in the shops, but the prices are way out of reach. Russians are allowed to travel, but tickets are extremely expensive. Totalitarianism has gone, but democracy has spawned fascism and racism. On the positive side, intellectual and artistic censorship is a thing of the past, but the creative intelligentsia are no longer supported by the state.

In 1989, I brought a group of five black Soviet artists to take part in a festival, in San Diego. The trip was the inspiration of Angela Davis. The group included, apart from Yelena and myself, a black singer from the Moscow State Philharmonic, Eleanor Ross Johnson and Maggie Scott, a famous choreographer from Bolshoi. James and Tom Patterson were brothers, the one a poet and the other a television cameraman. This was the first time that a representative group of blacks had come from the Soviet Union. And every single one of the participants, apart from the professional success of the visit, found relatives in the United States.

CHAPTER TEN

America, America!

Though my education had been in American history and despite my visits to the United States and my many friends there, I was beginning to learn that there was much I did not know about America. Clearly, one needed to live in America and to share the African American experience in order to understand the hardships. Perhaps my first confrontation came when, critically ill with cancer, I arrived at a hospital in the United States hoping to see a doctor quickly. But first I had to answer questions that had never been relevant before: "What is your religion?" "What color is your complexion?" When I answered, truthfully, that my skin was brown, I was told that this color did not exist in America. I told the nurse that the problem was hers, and that I saw no reason why these questions had to be answered as preliminary to seeing a doctor.

I had lived most of my life among European and Asiatic people. I was living in a predominantly black area of Chicago and all the faces around me were black. Slowly the recognition dawned that there was more than one color, and there were societies where this mattered. Truthfully, I was also learning that there are degrees of black, from almost white to coal. I was also seeing that these well-nourished African Americans were beautiful people—especially the women. The standard of living of Black Americans is very high in comparison to the life of Black people around the world including Africa, South America or even Europe. In those countries Black people do not have houses, cars or even welfare. As a nation Black America economically is ranked sixth in the world after Japan and several European countries. They are spending more than 600 billion dollars a year. Some statistics say 800 billion dollars.

In parallel, I was shocked to find how uninformed they were about African history, despite their obvious attempts to adopt African culture and at the same time retain the benefits of American society. Though they crave recognition as Africans first and Americans second, their entire experience, education and mannerisms are American going back at least two or three generations. Some seek to dress in tribal garb, and often mix up the hair style and dress of women and men. If they attempt to describe themselves to people in Europe as "African Americans," the invariable response is: "What part of Africa? Which tribe? What country? Maybe you are from South America? Or, you are from North America? Is it Canada?" Very confusing.

Few among Americans, as I have discovered during my lectures in American universities, can comprehend that Africa is a complex phenomenon. The term Africa is often improperly used to define an entire continent. However, Africa has six races (and not all of them are black,) sixteen hundred nations and ethnic groups and more than fifty countries—each with its own history, culture, religions, languages and musical styles—occupying the vast expanses of a continent. Whenever I talk to classes about the ancient and continuing Arab slave trade which is almost the equal of the Atlantic slave trade, invariably I draw the response, "But they never told us." When I ask who are "they," the answer is "the white man." My standard retort is, "It's all there in the libraries and computers. Why do you sit and wait for white people to teach you the culture and history that you claim as your own?"

Alexander Pushkin, the great Black Russian poet, once said of the Russians that they are lazy and lacking in curiosity. I am sure that he would be willing to extend the definition to encompass others who don't learn their own origins. Interestingly, there are many among them who have never heard of Pushkin, a great thinker of the world of African origin. They are willing to swear, however, to their dying day that Beethoven was Black. Such apparently is the power of his picture with curly hair.

I understood the paradoxes even more when, in 1993, I went together with 800 African Americans to the second African-African American Summit in Gabon, Central Africa, a conference hosted by President Omar Bongo. My impressions of the trip were conflicting.

The first Summit had been held in Abidjan, in the Ivory Coast, in 1991, and hosted by President Felix Houphouet Boigny. The third and fourth were scheduled for Abuja, Nigeria in 1995 and Dakar, Senegal in 1997. The last was in Zimbabwe in 1998. The entire series has been conceptualized and convened by American Reverend Leon H. Sullivan as a tool to strengthen the links between Africans and African Americans. The United States delegation to Gabon consisted of political leaders, like Governor Douglas Wilder of Virginia, members of the Congressional Black Caucus, Rev. Jesse Jackson, Minister Louis Farrakhan, Dr. Ben Chavez and representatives of many other American organizations that deal with Africa. The leaders of 15 countries and senior government officials represented the host continent.

I personally believe that the reestablishment of links between Africans and African Americans, after as much as four centuries of physical and psychological separation, was a great idea. The promotion of the social and economic development of the countries of Sub-Saharan Africa is a worthy ideal. The Summit gave birth to a number of important subcommittees on business opportunities, the role of the woman, agriculture and food production, student support, information exchange and so on.

The very fact that 800 African Americans were prepared to spend upwards of $2,000 each for a one-week visit to Africa was something of an indication of how seriously the concept was accepted, and how much some of the American community wants to know and understand Africa. However, listening to the speeches I had the distinct feeling that much of the proceedings would remain in the domain of talk alone. I first noticed this when, on the way to Libreville, we stopped in Casablanca. The intention was to show as much as possible of Africa in a short time. So the government of Morocco sent many buses to the airport to take the delegation sightseeing. The moment that we descended from the planes, a meeting had begun on the tarmac. Throughout most of the day, while the buses waited, each of the American leaders had his say about "we have returned home!" Needless to say, the buses eventually departed empty, and we never saw Casablanca or anything else of Morocco–our first African country. The same kind of rhetoric, often bordering on the demagogic, was to dominate the sessions in Gabon. Though many of the participants dutifully applauded, cheered and echoed phrases, there were others who shared with me their deeper understanding and rejection of the demagoguery.

I will not mention all of the ideas with which I could not agree, and which left our African hosts on the sidelines in a state of bemused astonishment. It was clear very soon that our hosts were not interested in listening to the discussion among African American leaders about their relations. They wanted to hear how Black Americans are going to help Africa. But I must mention one speaker with whom I did agree. The famous comedian and activist, Dick Gregory, said his piece on the last evening, and succeeded in touching on the issue that troubled those among us who had been silent through the theatrics. He posed the question: "Do you not see where you are? Why do you speak of coming home? You came to a neo-colonial country where everything belongs to the French. Gabon is rich with oil, but the population is poverty stricken because the revenues go to Frenchmen and a very few families in local high society." His was the most sober presentation of the summit, and the nearest to true leadership. Perhaps his most scathing remark applied to "African American women who brought to sell to African women African dresses that they had bought from Hong Kong."

I spoke at the summit about African children in exile, but this did not interest the delegates. I had expected sincere discussion of African concerns, but nothing was said, or hinted, about the majority of countries on the continent, which had tyrannical dictatorships or about the Arabic slave trade and slavery that exist in our time in several African countries. There was no comment about the hundreds of Gabonese who were arrested just one day before the opening of the Summit, a happening that was repeated in Senegal when we arrived there from Libreville.

I believe that the time has come to stop blaming others for our own shortcomings. We Black people must bear some of the responsibility for the continuation of repressive regimes, supported by our silence. From the very beginnings of independence, many African leaders, such as Kwame Nkrumah of Ghana, Kenneth Kaunda of Zambia, Julius Nyerere of Tanzania (who helped to destroy my husband), and Hastings Banda of Malawi, declared their countries "one-party states" and themselves "president for life." The opposition was banned and dissent was not tolerated. Since 1957, there have been more than 160 African heads of state, but less than 15 in the history of post-colonial Africa have relinquished power voluntarily. Apart from two monarchies and eleven democracies, all the other forty African countries are brutal dictatorships maintained by a police state. Many of the dictators have become immensely rich men in worldwide terms. President Mobuto Sesse Sekou had a personal fortune of ten billion dollars, while

Zaire's entire foreign debt is seven billion. Each year some 15 billion dollars leave the continent to be deposited in the European accounts of the leaders. None of this appears to be of the least concern to African American leaders, and their constituencies, who worship at the altar of "African history and culture."

I sat, listened, watched and thought that we Black people need another leadership. To my mind, the time of former civil rights leaders has passed. What is needed are young, educated, professional men and women who are prepared to put aside the saccharine dogma of "we must go to Africa to help them"—the slogan of those who go to the "dark continent" to make money for themselves. Dr. DuBois once told me: "I always thought that we Black Americans will go to Africa to help them. I was mistaken. It is Africans who will help Black Americans to free themselves." He was reacting to his first encounter with African activists at the Fifth Pan-African Congress in Manchester, England in 1947.

In comparison to my Black American students I was astonished during a visit to the University of Libreville to discover that all African students spoke at least five languages. French—the language of the previous colonial power, English—now the second language in school, Arabic—because Gabon had been colonized by Arabs long before the Europeans arrived, and two or three African languages—the dialect of the father's ethnic group and of the mother's. As for geography, most were capable of drawing a reasonably accurate map of Africa with very precise borders for their own country. As a footnote, in a University in Arizona back in the United States students who came to listen to my lecture were unable to tell me where Mexico was—though the frontier was only 40 miles away. The Libreville students knew very well the world and African history, while the best response I got in Arizona to the question, "do you know about World War II?" was "that one in nineteenth century?" Another answer was "If you are speaking about the World War II it means there was also World War I?" In my own experience, Arizona State University is not unique among the other universities in the States.

That is why I considered myself lucky to be invited to come to Chicago State University as "Distinguished Scholar in Residence." I had received invitations from many other universities, both Black and White, around the United States. Chicago State University has a long history. It began almost one hundred and thirty years ago as teachers' college. In recent years it has evolved into the principal state university for minority students in Illinois. Now CSU is home to more than one-third of all African American students attending Illinois public universities and produces one-fourth of all the bachelors' degrees attained by that community.

The invitation to teach in this university came from Dr. Dolores Cross, a remarkable woman. From very modest beginnings in an underprivileged area of New Jersey, she pulled herself up to earn a doctorate in education from the University of Michigan. After some years teaching, she became president of the New York State Higher Education Services Corporation where she created the scholarship program that became state law. In 1990, she came to CSU as the first African American woman to head a public university in the state of Illinois. Perhaps typically, she began to run marathons in her early fifties, and started to acquire prizes for the best performance in her age group.

I have been able, with Dr. Cross' encouragement, to establish the Alexander Pushkin International Project. The goals of this foundation are to strengthen the links of students of Chicago State University with the outside world, to give them confidence in their own intellectual abilities, and to prepare them for their responsibilities in changing the world and improving the economic and social conditions of humankind.

With the support of Dr. Cross, the University now has a Department of African-American Studies. The head of this department is Bart McSwine, a man well versed in Black history with extensive experience in education. In 1999, we arranged the trip for 40 faculty and students to celebrate the 200th birthday of Alexander Pushkin. Later that year, I took students to South Africa where we participated in the 8th Congress of Black women.

The year I came to the United States, I was invited to participate in the work of several organizations. I am on the Board of Directors of the Center of Citizen Initiatives with Sharon Tennison. She is still very active and develops more and more initiatives. She has an agreement with the Russian government to bring to America thousands of Russians, place them in homes of American businessmen and give them the opportunity to see the way they work. Two times a year I go to San Francisco for the meetings of the Board. I always feel happy when I hear her deep analysis of the situation in Russia and discussion of other members of the board. All of them are very dedicated people.

I am also involved in the work of the organization called Pegas. They bring children from Russian orphanages to Chicago hospitals. After the treatments and a good rest for almost three months in the homes of Americans, we returned the orphans to Moscow. It was a sensation when we brought a Black orphan, Katya. Several Black families struggled to get her to stay with them. At last a family from the South side of Chicago won the struggle and took her in. Katya felt very happy with this family. Very quickly she began to speak English and even taught her new siblings some Russian. Everything was okay but Katya was missing her Russian girlfriends with whom she came from Moscow. They lived in the families in Barrington. It was very difficult to explain to her the problem of segregation in Chicago. Pegas is comprised of very dedicated people. The president, Peter Keeler, has four of his own children and has adopted two. He is a very charming person, and speaks Russian almost without an accent. He is very kind and very sensitive. There was a very funny story about how I went to Russia with him to spend the New Year celebration with two Moscow orphanages. We brought with us seven very big boxes with presents for children, but were delayed in the customs at Sheremetyevo airport in Moscow. One after another the different levels of custom people tried to make us pay several thousand dollars for our presents, money we did not have. And to each of them Peter explained in detail, in good Russian and very seriously, that he is a Grand Father Frost. Everybody was looking at us as if we were joking. At last came the biggest boss of the custom. He listened very carefully and then said, "Okay. You are a Grand Father Frost. I understand. But who is your Snow girl? I do not see her." Very seriously Peter pointed at me and said: "Don't you see? This is she." The boss smiled. "Why I did not think about this before?" He began laughing. "You are free to go." And now I call Peter only Grand Father Frost and he calls me the Snow girl.

Another organization I am working with is International Cross-cultural Black Women's Studies Institute. I am in the Council of Elders of this organization where we have thousands of Black women from all the Diaspora — Africa, the United States, South America, Europe and even Asia. The Council consists of Elders from the United States, Trinidad and Tobago, France, Australia, Virgin Islands, South Africa, Uganda, Hawaii. Information Headquarters is in Medgar Evers College of the City University of New York. Our International Coordinator is Dr. Andree Nicola McLaughlin. She invited me to participate in the work of the Institute in 1980 while I was still living in Russia. But then I was not permitted to travel out of the country. I met her in 1987 during my first travels around America. Later she found me and proposed that we to work together. The objectives of the Institute are: To develop international, cross-cultural cooperation to promote peace; human, national and democratic rights; and development by presenting an opportunity for women of diverse nations and cultures to exchange information, share experiences, identify resources and build links. It is committed to empowering women in our various struggles for self-determination and autonomy. The Institute also aims to develop women's leadership in international service. The meetings of the Institute include a one to three-week seminar, workshops, public forums, visitations, and cultural events. Our Congresses were held in London, England with a focus on Women's Conditions (1987). In New York – with focus on Women and Communications (1988). In Harare-Bulawayo-Zvishvane, Zimbabwe with focus on Women and politics of Food (1989). In Auckland, Aotearoa (New Zealand) with focus on Human Rights & Indigenous Peoples in the "Information Age" (1991). In Frankfrut- Bielefeld - Berlin, Germany with focus on Black People and The European Community (1991). In Caracas, Venezuela with focus on Black Women: Five Centuries of Resistance and Cultural Affirmation in the Americas (1993). In Honolulu, Hawaii with focus on Pacific Women: Culture, Identity and Self-Determination. The Congress was held in 1998 in Johannesburg, republic of South Africa with focus on African women and technology. Because we held our Congresses in different countries and continents I had an opportunity to see those countries. It helps to understand the problems of the population of those regions of the world and the problems of African women in those countries.

This was where my long journey home reached its conclusion. Chicago had become a focal point in my visits to the United States. I had passed through Chicago dozens of times, always on the way to somewhere else. I had never conceived the idea that I might find my family here, and that the city would become my home after a long journey around the world.

Precisely because it is in many respects a segregated city, Chicago's black cultures have become consolidated. Thus, the city's Black communities have provided fertile ground for jazz, blues and gospel music which I never heard before but now love very much. The African Americans, in general, develop their own culture as rich as any that they will find in Africa. That culture has much to contribute to the world civilization. If you speak of different nations you can shortly give the main role of their culture in the world. For example, Germany—great music and poetry. Russia—great music, writers, poetry, ballet. The United States—blues, gospel and jazz. This is what America has originated and contributed to the world and African Americans developed it along with many industrial inventions.

I am very happy to have had the opportunity to teach African American students. From my experience of teaching in different countries I have concluded that there is a big difference between teaching African Americans and students from other races. Teaching students of other races I appeal to their intellect. Teaching African American students I appeal not only to their intellect but also to their heart and soul because they consider the history of Africa as their own. I am happy to see their shining eyes when I tell them about countries I visited, people I met and worked with, about events in which I had a chance to participate. They are eager for knowledge which they are denied by education in American public schools.

And still, it was not because of America itself or the famous architecture of Chicago, or blues, gospel and jazz that I decided to stay in this country, although each of them are worth of it. The main reason was highly peronal. In Russia I was doing well. I had a good job, and could afford an ample-sized four bedroom apartment which I shared with my husband, my mother, and daughter. Time and circumstance have changed these conditions of my life.

My mother died in 1985. My daughter Yelena Khanga came with

Gorbachev to meet Reagan and was working for *Christian Science Monitor.* She became quite famous in the USA. She got a scholarship from the Rockefeller Foundation to write a book, *Soul to Soul,* which was published in 1992 by W. W. Norton publishers and was a great success. Her articles are published in the American press and always attract public attention. Then, she received a scholarship of Fullbright Foundation, which gave her the opportunity to attend Harvard University. In 1997 she became a hostess of a talk show on Russian TV. It can be seen in Paris, Germany and Israel. At the same time she became a hostess of the program *Just An Anecdote* on Russian TV in New York. In addition to her television show hosting duties, Yelena also tours as a member of a performing arts troupe she started with some humorist friends from Odessa. With such a demanding professional life, it is difficult for her to visit or meet with me; but we manage. When I travel to Europe or Africa I go through New York to meet her. When she goes to the Midwest or California we meet in Chicago at the airport. Also we meet together in other cities, like Moscow, San Francisco and so on, when we come there on business at the same time. When we miss each other badly, she will come to see me just for 2–3 days in Chicago, or I will fly to New York. Sometimes we go together to other cities. Once we went together to the Bahamas. She did not feel comfortable with me there because, as she explained, when a single woman travels with her mother everybody will think that she does not have a boyfriend to travel with. This became our private joke.

We have developed the kind of relationship that I've always wanted;—to be not just mother and daughter, but friends with the same interests in life. When she was three years old, I started bringing her to the symphony concerts I loved to attend. At nine she began to play tennis and was a finalist in the All-Soviet competitions to which I had taken her as a child. We like the same books, the same music, films and humor. She is my best friend. In 2001, she married and now I have a granddaughter, Liza, which means I'll be spending more time in Moscow.

All my life I lived alone. But then I came to America, suddenly I found out that I have more than 100 relatives. This is a very nice feeling, that I am not alone in this world. I have a very supportive family in America.

There is not enough room here to name each of my relatives; but I do want to extend my warmest thanks to all of them for all of their love and support.

I do not consider myself an emigrant because I was an American from the day of my birth. My long journey home brought me from Uzbekistan and Moscow through Africa across America to Chicago—All "home, sweet home." Each place, I left a part of my heart.

Newspaper clippings on the Scottsboro Sentence

Cotton Specialists Protest Scottsboro Sentence

Among those who joined in the world-wide protest against the conviction of the eight Negro boys in the Scottsboro case, is a group of Negro cotton specialists who are at present working in the cotton fields of Soviet Central Asia. The following is the text of a letter of protest sent by them to the Governor of Alabama, according to the Stalinabad local newspaper:

"We, American Negro Cotton Specialists, at present working in the USSR, protest vigorously against the death sentence passed on eight Negro working class youths in the Scottsboro case.

"Our protest is based upon our knowledge of the Scottsboro case and actual experience with the discrimination against Negroes by the white ruling class of the South. Therefore we look upon this condemnation as a legal lynching and a concession to white chauvinism.

"We, together with millions of workers throughout the world, know that these boys are not guilty of any crime and demand their immediate, unconditional release."

4-13-32

ТРЕБУЕМ НЕМЕДЛЕННОГО ОСВОБОЖДЕНИЯ УЗНИКОВ СКОТТСБОРО!

Американские негры-специалисты отправили губернатору штата Алабама—Б. Миллеру следующий телеграфный протест:

Губернатору Б. Миллеру.
Г. Монтгомери, Алабама, САСШ.

Мы, американские негры-специалисты по хлопку, работающие в СССР, решительно протестуем против смертного приговора семи негра-юношам рабочим по делу Скоттсборо.

Наш протест основывается на нашем знании дела Скоттсборо и на практическом знакомстве с тем отношением, которое проявляют к неграм белый правящий класс юга САСШ. Мы рассматриваем этот приговор

только как узаконенное линчевание и разжигание белого шовинизма.

Мы вместе с миллионами рабочих всего мира знаем, что эти юноши не виновны ни в каком преступлении и требуем их немедленного и полного освобождения.

МР И МРС О. ДЖ. ГОЛДЕН,
ИОСИФ ДЖ. РОАН,
ДЖ. В. СУТТОН,
МР И МРС. ФРАНК ФЭЙСОН,
В. С. КЮРРИ,
БЕРНАРД К. ПОУЭРС,
ДЖОРДЖ В. ТАЙНЕС,
ФРАНК ГОРДОН,
А. М. ОВЕРТОН,
МР И МРС Б. Л. ХОПКИНС,
МИСС ШАРЛОТ Б. ХОПКИНС.

Телеграмма протеста, отправленная американскими неграми — специалистами по хлопку губернатору штата АЛАБАМА.

Oliver Golden's Registration card

National Archives, Southeastern Branch and Records Service East Point, GA.

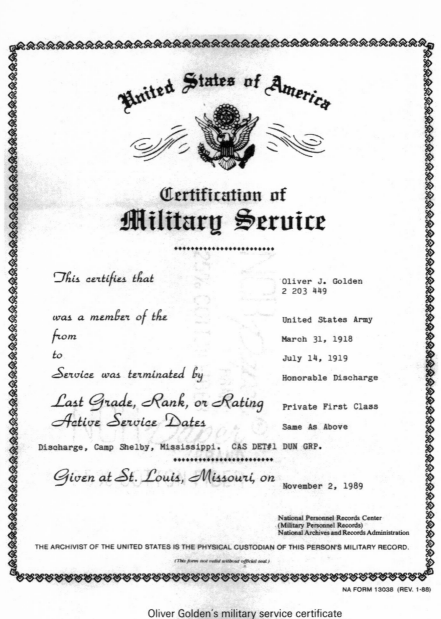

Oliver Golden's military service certificate

Letters to G.W. Carver from O.J. Golden

O.J. Golden
1800 - 7th Ave.
New York, N.Y.
December 12, 1930

Prof. Geo. W. Carver
Agricultural Dept.
Tuskegee Institute
Tuskegee, Ala.

Dear Sir:

Up to date about 50 of America's largest industrial
concerns have sent 2000 of their representatives to
Soviet Russia to help to develop the Russian industry.
So far we have not on record any Negro specialists in
Russia.

Soviet Russia is putting forth great efforts to
develop her cotton industry. I wonder if you would
consider the following proposition:

I have proposed to organize a group of Negro
specialists, who have had a theoretical and practical
training in the production of cotton, to be sent to the
Soviet Union. This group is to be indorsed by you or
your department.

If it meets with your approval, I shall also arrange
a tour for you to the Soviet Union to demonstrate your
findings in the field of agriculture. The expenses of
this tour will be taken care of.

If you are interested in the above proposition, you
will please let me know at once and I shall come down or
send a representative to discuss the final arrangements
with you.

Will you kindly send me some of your pamphlets or
any written matter you have on the production of cotton.

Very truly yours,

O.J. Golden

O.J. Golden

OJG:BB

O.J. Golden
136 West 28th St.
New York, N.Y.

January 15, 1931

Professor G. W. Carver
Research and Experiment Station
Tuskegee Institute
Tuskegee, Alabama

Dear Sir:

I regret very much my delay in replying to your letter of December 16.
It took quite a while to complete the plan of work. However, this plan has
been worked out in detail and sent to the Commissariat of Agriculture, U.S.S.R.,
for final indorsement. We expect to hear from them within three weeks.

The plan of work is as follows:

To select 25-30 of the most capable cotton experts to be sent to the
U.S.S.R. for a period of not less than two years. Such experts would be
assigned to certain regions in the U.S.S.R., presumably to the new regions
which are to be opened for cotton plantations, and would work there in the
capacity of supervisors and advisers in the work done by the population in
those regions.

The organization employing the specialists takes the obligation of
paying the transportation expenses to the U.S.S.R. and return to U.S.A. of
the employed man and his family.

In my first letter to you I proposed to arrange a tour for you to the
Soviet Union. I think it is important that you go on this tour, for at least
six months, for two reasons:

1. To demonstrate your findings in the field of agriculture.
2. To advise the proper circles on the best methods of cotton production
   which could be used there.

As to the work, I am sure it will not be strenuous, you will be given all
assistance necessary and the best of accomodations.

In the mean time, in order to expedite time, I suggest that you have some
preliminary selection made among the people whom you have in mind. And as soon
as I receive the indorsement from the Commissariat of Agriculture, I shall come
down for a conference and final arrangements.

Very truly yours,

O. J. Golden

OJG:BB

Response letter from G.W. Carver to O.J. Golden

January 24, 1931

Mr. O. J. Golden
136 W. 83° St.,
New York, N. Y.

My dear Mr. Golden:

Thank you for your splendid letter which has reached me, and I have looked it over quite carefully.

As soon as you hear from the Commissioner of Agriculture, U. S. S. R., I shall be interested in knowing the further plans.

I shall endeavor to select the twenty-five or thirty men you wish, although the number of rather large and I am not sure about them. The remuneration, naturally, would have much to do with their decision to go. As to myself I can give you no definite promise until I talk the matter over with you, as it will mean much for me to be away from the Institute six months, or naturally any length of time, but I shall endeavor to do the best I can in this important matter.

Yours very truly

G. W. Carver, Director
Agricultural Research and Experiment Station

Golden's proposal letter to G. W. Carver

C. J. Golden
130 W. 28th St.
New York, N.Y.

April 18, 1931

Professor G. W. Carver
Research and Experiment Station
Tuskegee Normal and Industrial Institute
Tuskegee Institute, Alabama

My dear Professor Carver:

At last we have an answer from Moscow. The reason for its delay was due to the thousands of applications coming in from various countries. Take for example in this country. We have from the New York Branch alone, on an average of a thousand applications a day, and it takes some time to choose those that are acceptable. When we view the situation as a whole, we can readily understand why it took so long to get the answer.

Now for our proposition. Instead of 25 or 30 cotton specialists, we want specialists of all branches of agriculture. Such as cotton, live stock, gardeners, poultry, rice raisers, etc., numbering 50 or more if possible. This does not mean only men, women specialists are accepted on the same basis as men.

As I have stated in my previous letter, the passage to and from the U.S.S.R., for the men and their families, will be paid by our office. The minimum salary will be between three and four hundred rubles a month. (Equivalent to one hundred fifty and two hundred dollars). This is the minimum. The maximum will be much more, but this will be determined according to your recommendation and their ability. But no one will receive less than the above figure.

The working conditions will be as follows:

Five day week; sick benefit insurance; free medical and hospital service and one month a year vacation with full pay and free transportation to the various summer resorts.

It is necessary that we know the names of the specialists that you have chosen, or will choose, whether they have families, if so, how many in each family, in order to prepare visas and make arrangements for their transportation. When I shall have received this information from you, I shall come down to Tuskegee to accompany the group to New York and thence to the Soviet Union.

Now Professor Carver, we think that it is absolutely necessary that you go on a tour to Russia for the following reasons:

1. Russia is inviting you to see her country, the largest agricultural country in the world, and to get your views.
2. It would be a pleasure, we think, for you to accompany your men into a new field of work.
3. Tuskegee is nationally and somewhat internationally known, but your going to the U.S.S.R., and the success of these men will give Tuskegee an international charater.

Letter continues on following page

4. You owe it to your race. Russia is the only country in the world today, tha
gives equall chances to black and white alike.

There are many more reasons, but we believe, that these will suffice to co
vince you of the importance and significance of your tour.

It is necessary to get these men stationed in leading positions, so when
other groups come, whether white or black, they will work under the supervision
of these specialists.

Our biggest task is over. Now is only left to select the men and give in
their names and my trip to Tuskegee. The sooner I get this information the
quicker we shall be on our way to the U.S.S.R.

Hoping to hear from you very soon, I remain

Very truly yours,

O. J. Golden

Carver's correspondance letter to O.J. Golden

May 7, 1931

Mr. O. J. Golden
136 West 28ᵀ Street
New York, N. Y.

My dear Mr. Golden:

Your splendid letter was here upon my return, along with a whole mail bag of mail, much of which remains unopened.

I have read your proposition over and studied it as much as I have had time.

Fifty specialists among my people who would be willing to go, I fear is impossible. I had nothing definite before to offer them. This may be attractive.

I regret to state that at the present I can be practically of no service to you, as my physician has prescribed complete rest in a very emphatic way. I am not able to travel any distance alone. Some one has to accompany me and look after every detail of the trip. Therefore, even if I were able to travel, I could not take on the responsibility of heading a group of any kind. You may not know that I am advanced in age.

I appreciate the invitation to study Russia. I hope I can do it, but not until I get stronger. I believe if you come down, we may be able to work our a plan that will work, but please consider some one else to head the group. My plan would be to put any applicants name in touch with your New York office so that all correspondence could be done from there, which would keep it regular and involve no additional dities upon me.

I suppose you would want each applicant to enter into a contract. All this can be settled, if you come down, along with some other minor details, which will arise, of course.

Mr. O. J. Golden   #2

I think it important that you come to Tuskegee now before any names are submitted.

It is important also that you talk with Dr. R. R. Moton, Principal of the Institute.

Very truly yours

G. W. Carver, Director
Agricultural Research and Experiment Station

O.J. Golden
136 West 28th St.
New York, N.Y.

May 14, 1931

Dr. G. W. Carver
Research and Experiment Station
Tuskegee Normal and Industrial Institute
Tuskegee Institute, Alabama

My dear Dr. Carver:

I am very sorry to hear of your poor health. I hope that you
will feel strong again and will be able to come on this trip. If
you do, we shall have some one to accompany you and look after every
detail. At any rate, we shall discuss this more thoroughly when I
shall see you, for I am leaving for Tuskegee in a few days. I shall
let you know the exact day by wire.

I shall be very glad to meet Dr. Moton to discuss this proposition and also other plans of work.

Very truly yours,

O. J. Golden

O. J. Golden

OJ:BB

32 Union Square
Room 505
New York, N.Y.

June 15, 1931

Dr. G. W. Carver
Tuskegee Institute
Tuskegee, Alabama

Dear Dr. Carver:

After my return from Tuskegee, I found it necessary to go on another short trip up New York State. Apart from that, during my absence work in my office had piled up tremendously, most of which had to be attended to immediately. Due to the unexpected trip and great amount of work, this letter to you was unwillingly delayed. However, permit me to thank you for the courtesy extended to me and the great interest you showed in my proposition.

I am very successful in the organization of the group. Each day brings many new enthusiastic applicants. I only wish that, your health permitting, you would join us as our adviser.

I shall keep you informed as to the further development of this group and the date of sailing. In the meantime, if you can find some men who you think capable of joining my group, I shall appreciate it very much if you would forward their names and addresses to me.

Again I want to thank you for the many suggestions pertaining to my work that you so wholeheartedly gave to me.

Very respectfully yours,

O. J. Golden

OJG:BB

32 Union Square
Room 505
New York, N. Y.

August 19, 1931

Dr. G. W. Carver
Tuskegee Institute
Tuskegee, Ala.

Dear Dr. Carver:

 I have succeeded in organizing a very
healthy, young and intelligent group of
agriculturists. I expected to be on the way
to Soviet Russia by this time, but due to the
delay in negotiations the trip has been postponed until the early part of October.

 Today I received a letter from Mr. Sutton
of Texas. He has filled out and returned his
questionnaire and a recommendation from you.
Although Mr. Sutton is an excellent agricultural
expert, a recommendation from you naturally adds
to his prestige.

 I shall appreciate very much a recommendation from you, it may be necessary. I was
born and reared on a cotton farm in Mississipi,
as you know. I had many years of practical
experience in agriculture and two years of theo-
ratical training at Tuskegee Institute.

 Thanking you for all you have done for me,
I am,

Very respectfully,

O. J. Golden

OJG:BB

A p p e n d i x   B

John Sutton's Western Union wire to Carver

WESTERN UNION

SIGNS

DL = Day Letter
NM = Night Message
NL = Night Letter
LCO = Deferred Cable
NLT = Cable Night Letter
WLT = Week-End Letter

NEWCOMB CARLTON, PRESIDENT   J. C. WILLEVER, FIRST VICE-PRESIDENT

filing time as shown in the date line on full-rate telegrams and day letters, and the time of receipt at destination as shown on all messages, is STANDARD TIME.

TIME IN TRANSIT

NEWYORK NY 1224A OCT 15 1931

PROF G W CARVER

TUSKEGEE INST ALA

AM TAKING SHIP FOR RUSSIA TONIGHT

JOHN T SUTTON

804A

THE QUICKEST, SUREST AND SAFEST WAY TO SEND MONEY IS BY TELEGRAPH OR CABLE.

Tashkent, Uzbek SSR.

September 16, 1956.

My dear Viola,

I received your letter last week yet, but the reason I didn't answer right away was that on the first of this month I underwent an operation on appendicitis. Thank God I am over it, and everything is allright. I am up and around again.

Dear Viola, what a shame the way we neglect our near relatives and don't write them for years. It's distressful. I have been writing to my people in the States all these years, and I can't forgive myself the fact that I never made Oliver write to his people. I am to blame for this; I should have taken a greater interest in my husband's near relatives. Now it is so hard for me to write you, to convey the sad, grievous news.

I married Oliver in New York, in January, 1928, about a year after he had returned from the Soviet Union, where his first wife had died. Three years later, in October, 1931, we left for the Soviet Union. We came here on contract, just for two years. In 1933, the contract was renewed for another two years, and we thought we'd return to the States after that.

In July, 1934, a baby girl was born, and by the time the second contract expired, Oliver and I decided to stay here for good, and we became Soviet citizens.

Oliver and I got along wonderfully well together. He was the best husband and father in the world. He was loved and respected by everybody who knew him.

In 1939, he started ailing. Notwithstanding the efforts of the best doctors and specialists here, nothing could be done to save him. He suffered from a kind of kidney disease, uremia, and on July the 31st, 1940, my beloved husband, and your dear brother, Oliver, passed away, at the age of 48, in the flower of his life. I was 35 then, and Lily, our daughter, 6 years old. I won't even attempt to describe to you my state then. His sickness and death was so sudden, so unexpected. During the 12 years we were married, he was never sick. A big, strong, healthy man, and suddenly such a serious, fatal disease. Oliver thought that his kidney had been injured in New York during a demonstration, when a policeman hit him hard on the hip with his club. I remember him complaining about it in N.Y.

Sixteen years have passed since his death. I devoted all my love and life to bringing up Lily, our only child. She took after her daddy in looks and character. She was my only consolation. In 1952, she finished highschool here in Tashkent. I wanted her to go on with her education in the best school available -- the Moscow University. I took her to Moscow, where she passed the exams for admittance to the University. She is now in her last year at the University, at the History Department.

In January of this year, she married. I went down to Moscow to get acquainted with my future son-in-law, and to celebrate the wedding. Her husband is a young fellow of her own age, a Russian, also a student. He studies at the Moscow conservatory, a pianist talented; a youth of great promise.

Viola's letter to Bertha page 1
Page 2 on the following page

His parents are Muscovites. The father is an architect, the
a music teacher. Very pleasant, cultured people, and all lo
dearly. They've taken her nto the family and are treating
royally.

How Oliver loved her! What joy it would have given him
her married happily!

I am enclosing a couple of pictures of Lily, so you can
what she looks like. They are not very recent photos, but tha
all I have right now.

I have been living in 'ashkent all these years. I teac
English, and I've been getting a substantial pension from th
Government since Oliver died, to help me bring Lily up. It'
a great help. This pension will continue till she finishes
studies. Besides that, she also gets a State Scholarship.
my dearest dream that she should go on with her education af
finishing the University and enter a post-graduate school.
is capable and takes her studies seriously. Well, we'll see
that.

Now, when I found this old letter of yours addressed to
I became conscious of a strong feeling of guilt towards you,
near ones, and decided to write you all about us. I'll be h
to hear from you again. Please write. I shall answer your
more promptly in the future. Describe your life to me, as v
the life of the other members of the family.

I haven't written Lily yet that I have contacted you.
can imagine how happy she'll be to know that I've written t
daddy's relatives.

Much love to you all.

Most affectionately, your sister

Bertha

Bertha.

P.S. Dear Viola! I beg sister Biddie to excuse me if I do
write her right now. I will after a while. I can't 1
you how hard it was for me to write this letter, but 1
considered it my duty to tell you everything. Forward
letter to Biddie, and I'll write her some time later.

With kindest regards to all,

Bertha.

Alex Haley

NORRIS, TENNESSEE 37828

October 23, 1989

Ms. Lilia Golden-Khanga
c/o Mr. Walter Anderson
PARADE MAGAZINE
750 3rd Avenue
New York, New York 10017

Dear Ms. Golden-Khanga:

How very much I wish I could be present at the dinner to meet you!

I have tried and tried all of the airline schedules. It is simply impossible to insert a flight to New York in between two fixed lecturing appointments that I have, one in Vicksburg, Mississippi, then the next in Atlanta, Georgia.

So as I have told my dear friend Walter Anderson, the best thing I can do is to send you a copy of my book ROOTS, as a token of my pleasure that you are visiting in the United States, even as I surely do hope that I will have a chance to travel much the same in your native USSR.

With warmest of wishes to you, I am

Sincerely,

Alex Haley

Encl: cc ROOTS

FIND THE GOOD—AND PRAISE IT

A letter from Alex Haley to Ms. Golden-Khanga

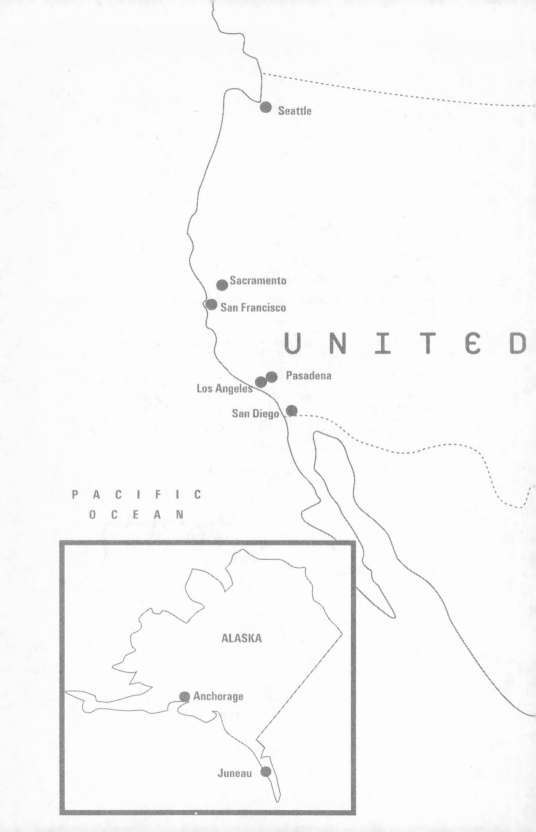

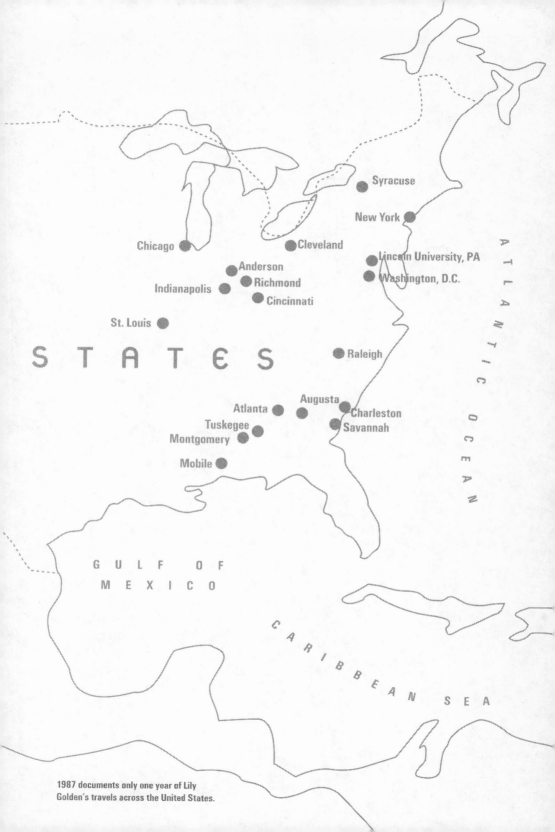

Syracuse

New York

Chicago

Cleveland

Anderson

Richmond

Indianapolis

Cincinnati

Lincoln University, PA

Washington, D.C.

St. Louis

S T A T E S

Raleigh

Augusta

Atlanta

Charleston

Tuskegee

Savannah

Montgomery

Mobile

A T L A N T I C   O C E A N

G U L F   O F   M E X I C O

C A R I B B E A N   S E A

1987 documents only one year of Lily
Golden's travels across the United States.

L ily O. Golden, professor of history and art, has taught both in the United States and in Russia. For over three decades, Professor Golden served as Senior Researcher in the Institute of African Studies in Moscow. Most recently, she served as the Distinguished Scholar-in-Residence at the Chicago State University where she was able to continue research in African Studies. She received a bachelor's degree in History from Moscow State University and her doctorate from the Academy of Science in the Soviet Union. Lily Golden has lectured across the Russia and the former Soviet Union, Europe, Africa, and the United States and is a prominent voice in many international organizations including the American Citizens Initiative and the International Cross-cultural Black Women's Studies Institute where she serves on the Council of Elders.